SANE ADVICE FOR CRAZED PARENTS

"LeShan has much insight and...applies her skills in a most sensitive manner."

—Dr. Lee Salk

"LeShan comes closer than ever to the essence of understanding the complex relationship between children and their grown-ups. She has done us all a great favor by allowing us to read her truth."

—Fred Rogers of
"Mister Rogers' Neighborhood"

For over forty years, Dr. LeShan has worked helping parents and children to understand each other better. A frequent radio talk-show guest and columnist, she was co-creator and host of the acclaimed PBS-TV series "How Do Your Children Grow?" and a daily CBS Radio Network commentator. Among her nineteen books are:

The Wonderful Crisis of Middle Age
The Conspiracy Against Childhood
Oh! To Be Fifty Again
How To Survive Parenthood

Also by Eda LeShan

IN SEARCH OF MYSELF-AND OTHER CHILDREN

When Your Child Drives You Crazy

EDA LeSHAN

ST. MARTIN'S PAPERBACKS

WHEN YOUR CHILD DRIVES YOU CRAZY

ISBN: 0-312-92930-7

Printed in the United States of America

St. Martin's Press hardcover edition published 1985
St. Martin's Paperbacks edition/May 1986

10   9   8   7   6

*For Wendy—the mother
I love the most—my daughter*

Contents

PART III
THE CRUCIAL YEARS

PART IV
READING BEHAVIOR

PART V
THERE ARE NO
GOOD AND BAD HABITS

PART VI
DISCIPLINE

PART VII
SIBLINGS AND SOCIABILITY

PART VIII
CREATING GOOD CITIZENS

PART IX
SPECIAL PEOPLE, SPECIAL TIMES

PART X
SUMMERTIME

CONCLUSIONS

Acknowledgments

I would like to express my gratitude to the magazine editors who gave me my beginnings as a writer: Dorothy Barclay Thompson *(The New York Times Sunday Magazine)*, Eva Grant *(National Parent-Teacher Magazine)*, the late Mary E. Buchanan and Genevieve Landau *(Parents' Magazine)*, and Geraldine Rhoades, Rebecca Greer, and Ellen Levine *(Woman's Day)*. The encouragement as well as the good editing they brought into my life was invaluable, and remains so in my long and profoundly satisfying relationship with *Woman's Day*.

I would also like to thank editor Lisa Wager for her enthusiasm about this book, my agent Phyllis Wender for tender loving care at all times, Jo-Ann Straat for the orderliness of my manuscripts, Milagros Ortega for the orderliness of my home, and Larry LeShan for making it all matter.

✱

Our thanks to *Parents' Magazine, Woman's Day, The Money-Paper,* and *The Journal of the National Education Association,* in which most of the articles in this book first appeared in print, for their cooperation.

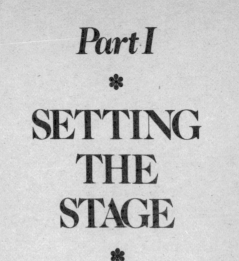

Part I

❋

SETTING THE STAGE

❋

Why I Wrote This Book

❋ The young woman on the telephone was urging me to attend a conference on training leaders for child-study discussion groups. The meeting was in a distant city and I was busy trying to finish a book. I said I was afraid I just couldn't make it. "But you must!" she pleaded. "After all, you're the grand old lady of parent education!"

That was several years ago, and the shock has not worn off yet. I never expected to be a "grand old" anything. But I guess I am, and this book is a reminder of the impossible fact that I have been studying and working with parents and children for over forty years. The only thing that makes that rapid passage of time endurable is that I think I have been able to sift through all the child development theories that have come and gone in my lifetime, and through the direct experiences I've had with children as a teacher, a therapist, and a mother, and come at last to a distillation of what seem to be the most fundamental principles necessary to the most important task ever set before us—raising children who will, we hope, be better human beings than we are.

I think I know why children sometimes (often!) "drive us crazy," and if there is any value in becoming old, I like to believe, it is that I now know a good deal about how to handle this special kind of craziness. There are really only a handful of important attitudes and skills essential to successful parenting. The catch is that these comprise some of the most profound and courageous challenges we can ever give ourselves; they have to do with our ability and our willingness to grow and change all the days of our lives. Still, it seems more sensible and practical to learn to deal with a few fundamental ideas than to feel you must wander, often confused and alone, in that sea of expert advice in which too many parents have found themselves drowning.

We all have a tendency to go in search of simple answers to very complicated problems. Nothing in nature is more complex, more mysterious, than human beings, yet we search endlessly for an easy way to solve the problems we face: some guru who will give us a formula by which we can deal with temper tantrums; a page in a book that promises to show us how to stop nail-biting, stuttering, bed-wetting, and fifty other issues that drive us crazy. Or when faced with older children who seem genuinely unhappy and self-destructive, we may hungrily swallow an outrageous—but beautifully simple—idea that throwing them out of the house will solve our problems. In fear and despair we begin to think that maybe the people who say that what's wrong with today's children is that they don't get spanked often enough are right. In this age of super-technology and with our fascination for the world of computers it is extremely difficult to face the fact that when we deal with children there are simply no absolutes, no easy answers, no fool-proof techniques—and no magic.

However, there *are* attitudes and skills that can and do make a difference; there are children growing up today who may sometimes irritate and often exhaust their parents but do not drive them crazy. One of my main goals in life is to increase the number of such families!

We need, first of all, to examine those times when our children drive us crazy. This often occurs when children do things that we were not allowed to do when we were children. When our daughter was about 2½ years old and my husband told her to get her pajamas while we were still sitting at the dinner table, she said, "I will not, you old dope!" Larry was a psychologist with a Ph.D; he had studied developmental psychology and knew he was dealing with a normal 2-year-old phenomenon. Yet in spite of that, his hand was shaking as he reached for his coffee cup. He turned a pale shade of chartreuse and said, "I feel like throwing up." As we discussed this reaction, he added, "Of course I know that if I had *ever* spoken that way to my parents, I would have been struck dead by lightning."

The parents I've met and worked with over these forty years are the bravest people I've known. Because of rapid changes in general life-styles and a better understanding of children's needs, we have for the most part become parents who are trying to raise our children differently from the way we ourselves were raised. We are trying not to repeat those experiences that affected us so profoundly. Because I was toilet trained at 6 months, changing diapers when my daughter was almost 3 sent me into a panic. If, when you were a child, you were never allowed to express any jealousy or rivalry with a brother or sister, it can be quite terrifying to allow your own children to express any hostility toward each other, even though you have been assured by a dozen experts that this is normal. *First of all, then, we can be driven crazy by children who are not as repressed as we were.*

The second kind of behavior that drives us crazy occurs when our children won't do things we were forced to do when we were children. They refuse to kiss Great-Aunt Hattie with the wart on her nose, who used to scare us, but we did what we were told. They refuse to eat the vegetables that we gagged on but ate when we were children. They ask us why a bath is necessary every night— something we would never have dared to ask. They want to know about birth control at an age when we had not yet been told, in so many words, that there were special reasons for there being two sexes. *Sometimes when they drive us crazy it's because we are green with envy!*

The most important cause of our frequent distress is that our children seem to be behaving irrationally: We can't figure out why they do what they do. The truth is that we *do* know, but in the course of trying to grow up and please our parents we have repressed our understanding of how a child feels. That fact is the source of most of our irritation, frustration, exhaustion, and ultimately our anger at our children. *When they behave in ways that really upset us, they are forcing us to remember, at least on an unconscious level, how we once felt, and the memories are just too painful to endure.*

Linda, at 4, becomes terrified of the dark; she wants not only a night-light but a light on in the hall as well as in the bathroom. Even then she cries unless someone sits with her until she falls asleep. Her father, John, is furious that his wife wants to give in to all these demands. His daughter's fears drive him crazy—he can barely control himself—and he wants to spank her and let her scream. His feeling of rage conflicts with the equally strong feeling that he doesn't know why he's so upset. Chances are that Linda's normal 4-year-old anxieties have awakened something John cannot bear to remember: that in order to get the love and approval he so desperately wanted from his own father, thirty years earlier, he had repressed his terror of the night. His father had said, "Boys don't cry and boys aren't afraid of silly things," so he lay in his bed, in secret terror, because a pat on the head from his father was more important than screaming his fear.

Now this 4-year-old daughter has the nerve to unsettle something long buried; his craziness at her expression of her fears is that he just does not want to remember. We don't want to be reminded that once upon a time we were naughty. We don't want to remember being so tired we felt like we were going crazy! We don't want to remember hitting a little kid; we don't want to remember the time we played with matches; we don't want to remember stealing seven pennies from Mother's pocketbook. What we don't want to remember is a parent saying, "Why do you do such things? I can't understand you at all."

The problem is that most parents have never been able to make a particular distinction that children need to hear. Parents have rarely said to a child, "You're not bad, you're just young." Children have no way of knowing that the reason they do things that are not allowed or that nobody seems to understand is that they can't help themselves; what they are doing and feeling is just part of being a child. But if nobody tells them this, they assume—and this is the source of most of the world's problems in my estimation—that they are bad children. Normal feelings get buried, and a lifetime of guilt feelings, or repressed anxieties and hostilities, are in the making.

What children need more than anything is love, and no price is too high to pay for love. The first step in solving your crazy times is to begin to ask yourself how you sold out as a child. What did you give up for love? Did you give up wanting to play baseball because your parents said nice little girls didn't want to play rough and tough? Did you bury the secret longing to take ballet lessons because your father said only sissies danced? Did you act as if you were crazy about the new baby in order to get whatever attention and approval you could get? Were you relieved when you got spanked for throwing a toy out the window because you were sure you were bad and needed to be punished? Can you dare to remember the time your grandmother washed your mouth out with soap for saying a dirty word?

Most of the neuroses we bring with us into adulthood are the direct result of repressing normal feelings in order to gain approval and love. Deep inside we view ourselves as badly flawed human beings, not really worthy of being loved—even, or most of all, by ourselves. *Whenever our children behave in ways that are exactly like the way we ourselves once felt as children, it drives us crazy.*

Finally, our children drive us crazy when they want to be nurtured in ways in which we were never nurtured when we were children. This is the kind of craziness that is most serious. It often results in child abuse. A parent who has never been able to get the love he or she needed even after trying desperately to be good can become almost insane with anger when a child pleads for love. It is almost impossible to be a nurturing person if one has never experienced nurturance as a child.

There is a court in the state of Washington where the judge "sentences" abusive parents to go to a special nursery school with their children for a specified period of time. What happens is that the parents are able to observe good role models (the teachers) and the way they treat children. They are helped to understand their children's needs and are taught wise ways of disciplining a child. But far more important, the parents themselves are given the loving attention they have never received before; they are treated with tender concern and compassion, often for the first time in their lives. *It makes a person crazy with anxiety and anger to try to give love if he or she was not greatly loved as a child.*

If these are the causes of most of the discomforts of parenthood, what can we do to change the picture? The very first task, and probably the most important skill any parent can develop, is *remembering*, finding ways to remember his or her own childhood. If we can face the pain of our own anxieties, angers, confusions, the sometimes costly bargains we made for love, we will be far less likely to feel so anxious when our children behave like children.

You have probably heard the expression "You have to get in touch with the inner child in yourself." That's what remembering is. The child we were doesn't disappear when we grow up. Every-thing we experienced as children is still inside us—somewhere—and the more we can bring memories into consciousness, the less we will be controlled by them. It's not just good for our kids—it's terrific for us as well. What we need to do is try to find out about the wrong messages we got—the messages that we were bad, that we didn't measure up to expectations, that we had disappointed our parents. These messages come to represent self-destructive freight that we carry around with us because it is too painful to remember or we feel too guilty to think we deserve to remember.

There are many ways to remember our own childhood feelings and experiences. Of course this is one of the goals of counseling and psychotherapy, and if we not only are concerned about our feelings toward our children but feel emotionally crippled by many aspects of our life, this may be the choice we need to make. But there are many other ways of remembering: talking to siblings, to parents, to aunts and uncles, for example; asking about events you only vaguely remember, seeking corroboration of memories that seem bizarre, disturbing.

I chose the route of psychotherapy for both personal and profes-sional reasons, but there were some strange images I couldn't seem to deal with. Having lived in a house with my grandparents, aunts, and uncles when I was young, I asked my aunt about my "fanta-sies." One was the recurring image of a man lying in a pool of blood on a cement floor, covered by an overcoat. The other was a fearful image of someone in a black cloak leaping at me. My aunt said,

"First of all, there was a man who came to fix our furnace who was an epileptic. He had several seizures on the basement floor and we would cover him with his coat. Sometimes he lost control and urinated during the attack. And as for the other, Uncle Edward used to scare us by jumping out of the dumbwaiter wearing a black cape and pretending to be Dracula." Because I was too young to know any better, I had interpreted the sick man on the floor as somehow being my fault—maybe my angry feelings had killed him! As for my uncle's teasing, I suppose I felt it was something *I* deserved for not always being a good girl.

Sometimes the only way to unscramble a wrong message, originally misconstrued because little children think irrationally, is through a therapeutic examination of the past. The most extreme example I know of was a young woman who could never allow herself to fall in love because she was so afraid of rejection and loss. She finally uncovered the memory of herself as a 3-year-old waiting in a long line in her mother's arms. Suddenly her mother had passed her back to the woman standing behind her, saying, "Here! Take your kid. I can't be bothered carrying her anymore!" That was the last time she ever saw her mother. The line happened to be in a concentration camp; her mother realized that every other person was being sent to the gas chamber and saved her child's life by her action. But the only message her 3-year-old daughter got was that she was being deserted.

Unless parents are very much aware of the way in which children can misinterpret events, they are unable to avoid serious misconceptions. My grandmother died when my mother was 4 years old. In an effort to protect my mother, her father and grandparents told her that her mother had gone on a trip; she learned of her mother's death a year later from a neighbor's child. By that time she was certain that her mother had gone away because she was a bad child and her mother didn't love her. In spite of her later understanding that young children always blame themselves for any disaster that occurs (death, divorce, illness, etc.), she never fully recovered from the view of herself as a bad child. Children frequently get a message of having been bad and unlovable when nothing could have been farther from the truth.

During my childhood I wrote a great many letters to my parents and they to me, and I wrote compositions and diaries. Fortunately I kept some of these. Attics and trunks, garages, old files, can often prove to be a source of useful information in the process of remembering. My father gave me a letter I had written to him and my mother when I was about 12 and had refused to go with them to a family party. I promised to try to stop being such a rotten person. Years later, when my mother died, I found a letter she had written at about the same age to her father and stepmother, promising to try to do better and not be such a bad person and never to get angry again. Two generations apologizing for being human! We both learned as adults that teenagers quite naturally go through a period of trying to separate themselves from the family and that there is surely nothing abnormal about losing one's temper on occasion, but in some ways the knowledge came too late. These and other reinforcing events had left us both feeling unworthy.

Looking at old albums of snapshots and rereading old school report cards may help to bring back memories. I remember reading a report card that said, "Eda needs to do 50 percent better in math and French." I was flooded with that long-ago sense of failure, of hopelessness—that my lack of talent in those two areas would surely ruin my entire life. (It didn't.)

Because our parents were caught in many of the same traps that snare us, asking them questions about their upbringing can be very revealing. The more my daughter learned about my childhood, the better she was able to understand and forgive some of the times when she was the victim of my limitations. Understanding that awful episode in my mother's life certainly helped me to understand some of the ways in which she communicated her feelings of unworthiness to me.

Sometimes a chance comment on the part of a relative can also be revealing. A friend once told me that her aunt had said, "I really hated your mother when we were kids. She was always so smart, so good, so pretty; she seemed perfect. I was the klutz!" My friend said, "Suddenly I made a connection; my mother had made me feel that I could never be as wonderful as she was. My aunt's memories opened up doors for me."

Remembering isn't something we do all at once. It's a skill we work at forever if we understand how valuable insights about our childhood can be in our own growth and development.

The second skill that is essential to becoming less crazy with our children is also a lifetime task: *learning how to read behavior.* This follows naturally from remembering but also depends on our learning as much as we can about the inner world of childhood. We need to get as much information as possible about childhood fears, normal development problems, the irrational ways in which children think. We need to become sensitized to their feelings of guilt, their frustrations, even their fatigue.

The hardest part of reading behavior occurs when children behave badly. One mother told me that she was standing in the kitchen when her 7-year-old hit her 3-year-old. She said, "He stood in the middle of the kitchen with a weird smile on his face. My first reaction was, he's really a rotten kid to hit and then smile. Then I saw the shock and panic in his eyes. He'd hit impulsively, without thinking, and I heard myself saying to him, 'You don't know what to do, do you?' His eyes filled with tears and I said, 'What you can do is tell Sarah you're sorry, and you'll try to be more thoughtful in the future.' He looked so relieved!" This was an acutely sensitive reading of behavior. Young children do react to sudden impulses and then immediately feel guilty but haven't any idea what to do. As a result they may actually smile or even laugh out of nervousness and embarrassment. By instinctively taking the right measure of the situation, this mother did not accept her son's behavior at face value but recognized that he felt guilty and needed a way to make amends.

Jonathan, aged 5, had gotten very overstimulated at a family Thanksgiving dinner. Racing around the room, showing off, he knocked over one of his grandmother's vases. His father scooped Jonathan up in his arms, sat down in a rocking chair, and said, "I know you must feel awful about what just happened. You're very tired and too excited, and it's been a long day. Let's tell Grandma that we'll try to find another vase just like the one that was broken."

Does that sound like wishy-washy discipline? Not to me. Jonathan's father was teaching his son how to read his own behavior, to begin to understand why he did the things he did. Jonathan was a decent, nice kid who loved his grandmother. His father was teaching him what it means to be a civilized person—to accept one's human frailties and take responsibility for any way in which we may hurt another person.

Whenever I see a young child being dragged along, or sitting down and refusing to walk, or screaming in a store at lunchtime, I can immediately read the behavior as a special kind of fatigue. I can read the behavior because I remember experiencing a kind of exhaustion that left me feeling out of control. Having regained contact with that feeling, I can even acknowledge it myself. When I begin to fall apart at the end of a long, hard day, my husband says, "You're whimper tired," and I feel comforted at once. I only wish I'd had this insight when my own child was "whimper tired," but fortunately I developed this essential skill in time for my granddaughter!

Parents have sometimes commented to me, "But can't an interpretation be wrong? Suppose you think you're reading behavior, and you're really way off base?" It doesn't really matter! When children behave in irrational ways, they feel terribly lonely. They think nobody ever felt that way before. They *never* think a parent *ever* felt that way! Even if an interpretation is wrong, a child recognizes the human kindness of someone who is trying to understand, rather than simply taking it as a sign of a child's being bad.

One day when my granddaughter was visiting me, she suddenly began to cry at a neighbor's house. We all thought this was because she saw a father playing with a baby and felt sad because her own father was away overnight at a conference. So we offered comfort and "insight"—it was okay to cry when you miss your Daddy, we could all understand. She seemed comforted, but when she went home she began to have nightmares, and what finally emerged after initiating a lot of dramatic play, was that she'd been terrified by some geese on our lawn!

Dramatic play is an excellent tool for helping us to read behavior. You have, I'm sure, discovered that the most useless question to ask a child is "*What* is the matter with you?" If *we* can't figure out what's gone wrong, how in the world can an inexperienced, immature child know? Dramatic play is making up imaginary games together, because play is the language of childhood. A psychiatrist once commented, "Compared to child's play, the atom bomb is child's play." The value of play in the lives of young children is so great that I rage against those who would like to replace it by earlier and earlier reading, writing, and arithmetic, cutting too soon into a child's natural way of learning about himself and the world around him. In the case of my grandchild, my daughter invented afternoons of doll play about a doll going to bed and being scared, and was eventually informed that "Sarah doll is scared of the geese."

Feeling all alone with emotions that seem unacceptable to an adult is one of the great burdens of childhood. Unless we can try to remember how we felt about going to doctors and dentists when we were children, we may be likely to say, "Don't be silly. There's nothing to be afraid of, it's not going to hurt." The truth is that things can be scary just because they are unknown or uncertain. To a child, being told not to be silly means "I guess there is something wrong with me. Grown-ups are smarter than kids, so they must be right." Feelings of isolation and self-disapproval soon follow. On the other hand, a parent can say, "I know just how you feel. It's scary, and even though you know an injection only stings for one second, you're frightened. You can sit on my lap, or you can cry. That's what crying is for—when you're afraid. I'll hold you tight and we'll get out of here as soon as we can." The child feels that she is neither depraved nor alone; somebody understands.

As we learn to read behavior, the distinction between being bad and being little becomes clearer. A 2-year-old bites another child; instead of saying, "Bad! bad!" we could say, "You're too little not to bite. You forget. I'm here to help you remember you can't do that. We have to sit on the bench for a while so you can think about remembering not to bite. In a little while you'll be old enough to remember by yourself."

Or when Justin is discovered lighting matches in his room, instead of telling him he's a terrible child, his mother might say, "Lots of kids your age get an urge to play with matches, but of course it's too dangerous and we can't let you do it in your room.

If you want to light matches, you can do it in the bathtub while I stay with you, or we can take a pail of water outside and you can drop matches into it while I watch." The behavior is accepted as normal, but it is not permitted for a perfectly legitimate reason that a child can understand and accept, especially if he doesn't feel like a bad child.

Patricia came home from kindergarten one day with a box of crayons. She told her father, "The teacher told me I could have them because I was such a good girl." Instead of assuming that Patricia had embarked on a life of crime and communicating this to her, her father said, "Lots of five-year-old girls can't stop themselves when they want something. Tomorrow morning we'll take the crayons back and explain that you are too little not to take things that don't belong to you." The same behavior often reappears in early adolescence—an overwhelming impulse to take a piece of clothing from a friend or relative, for example. If we behave as if this is the first sign of juvenile delinquency, we may be encouraging such a prophecy to come true; adolescents steal things that they think will make them more handsome, more beautiful, more popular, or more courageous. They do it because of feelings of inferiority. A reaction that increases their sense of self-hatred can bring about more of the same behavior. Instead a parent might say, "I used to have overwhelming impulses to take something that I felt could make me feel better about myself. But of course we can't behave that way toward other people, so it must be returned. It's all right to say it happened by accident or you just forgot, but privately, we need to talk about why you felt you needed that jacket so much."

The more you learn to remember and to read behavior, the more certain other things seem to fall into place. For example, I consider pushing children to perform certain tasks before they are ready one of the most serious problems in the lives of today's children. We all feel pressured, life is full of stress, we are too crowded together in an environment that is becoming increasingly dehumanizing. We feel, quite accurately, that a great many people are more fascinated by machinery than by human beings, and feel impelled to turn people into computers as soon and as often and as much as possible. The fact that they are doomed to failure is beside the point; the effect of all this is very serious. If I have ever learned anything about children, it is that children who are pushed too hard and encouraged to skip any normal phase of growth will become emotionally crippled adults.

If I told you, for example, that you should put splints on your 7-month-old child's legs in order to teach him to walk sooner than nature would do the job, you'd tell me I'm crazy. But every day parents try to teach 2-year-olds to read and 3-year-olds to tie shoelaces and 5-year-olds to dive off the high board. I see scared and screaming babies being forced into the ocean or a swimming pool. I see 6-year-olds who are too immature to focus their eyes correctly being forced to do homework in workbooks appropriate for 10-year-olds. We seem to have become impatient with nature, frustrated by childishness; we want to get childhood over with as fast as possible because children have an annoying way of reminding us of our own human vulnerabilities. The technological age has made us value the good product—the machinery that can make a better car, the machinery that creates something as wonderfully useful as a CAT scan or antibiotics. We are fascinated by the technology that can land a man on the moon. All of these new miracles and wonders entice us, seduce us, into the false notion that we, too, can produce a miracle product: good children who won't be such a nuisance.

Children learn so wonderfully well! Nature provides them with such a sense of adventure, such curiosity. There is an inner impulse of enormous force that creates physical and mental growth as long as we provide an atmosphere in which a child can expand his or her limits. If you keep a 10-year-old in a tiny crib, his growth might be stunted; if he moves into larger and larger beds, his body grows. If we fill the world with toys and books and adventures and a chance to talk about ideas and feelings—a safe place to ask any question—the mind expands. There is a ready moment for everything. You can teach a 2-year-old to tie her shoelaces, but you will have to work at it seven days a week, and when you stop she will forget it. If you wait until she is 5 and say, "Hey, how would you like to learn to tie your shoelaces?" you can teach her in about half an hour and she'll never forget. In one study, twins were taught to read on different schedules. Lessons for one twin were started at age three, while the other twin didn't begin reading and writing until age six. At the age of eight they were on the same level. If we can recall our own pain when we failed, our panic if other kids seemed smarter earlier, our shame when we weren't equally good at all subjects, we may be able to help our children feel confident and optimistic about their own future by assuring them that there is plenty of time to learn what they need to know. Perhaps it is primarily those psychiatrists and psychologists who see psychologically crippled teenagers and young adults—those suffering from anorexia nervosa, suicidal thoughts, migraines, colitis, severe anxiety and depression—who are fully aware of the price children pay for trying desperately to measure up to parental dreams and impossible expectations.

Remembering and trying to read behavior also provide us with another important insight: The reason that no theory, no expert's advice, "works" all the time for all children is that no two children are any more alike in temperament, talents, growth rates, than their fingerprints. An early group of psychologists (behaviorists), led by Dr. John B. Watson in the 1920s, thought that children could best be raised by conditioning, which worked so well with Pavlov's dogs. Some of the children raised by rigid rules did very well. They were probably the kind of children who had a lot of inner chaos, both physical and emotional, and having order imposed from the outside was helpful. On the other hand, in the 1940s, Dr. Spock reacted *against* many rigidities in childraising because so many children were miserable. In his first book he suggested that children needed to develop their own patterns: Demand feeding and toilet training were born. This was wonderful for children who had some inner sense of order—those who knew when they were hungry and when they needed to go to the bathroom—but created havoc for those children who needed external order in their lives.

What Dr. Spock and every other caring, sensible expert has come to understand in the intervening years is that no pattern of childraising is sound for all children, and methods must be adapted to individual needs. If we have been trying to remember successfully, we know that one painful aspect of our growing years was the feeling that we were out of step, we were too different, we didn't fit in. We now have the opportunity to help our children enjoy their differences and take pride in the ways in which they are unique.

In my experience the people who have been most helpful in increasing our understanding of individual differences are Dr. Stella Chess, Dr. Thomas Alexander, and Dr. Herbert Birch, who have written about their research in the book *Your Child Is a Person* (the book is now a Paralaz paperback). They began to study a group of babies at birth and continued until the same children were adolescents. They proved that children have different styles of coping with the world and we are far less likely to "get crazy" if we can fathom, understand, and respond to these differences.

If newborn babies are put on an examining table, they will react differently to certain stimuli. If a bell rings or a light goes on, Caroline goes on sleeping, while Matthew screams, gets red, flails his arms and legs. When it is time for the same two children to adjust to a feeding schedule, Caroline seems to get hungry every three hours while Matthew cries, doesn't seem to have any idea when he's hungry or too full, and wants to eat every three hours one day, every four hours the next. Toilet training may be relatively easy for Caroline, while a long struggle ensues with Matthew. When they get to nursery school, Caroline is very quiet, sucks her thumb, sits on her mother's lap for several days—and then moves happily into the group. Matthew runs in, pulls all the toys in sight off the shelves, can't seem to settle down to any activity for more than two minutes—and by the second week has accepted the routines and become a natural leader.

By studying the coping styles of individual children, we can learn to meet different needs in different ways. A very sensitive child may cry if you reprimand her in a whisper; another child hardly pays any attention to a spanking or any other kind of punishment. One needs many more controls than the other. I remember one mother who told me about the differences between her twin daughters. She said, "From the moment of birth there was no problem telling them apart! One took to nursing easily, the other had such trouble figuring it out we eventually had to use a bottle. One was calm and good-natured, the other seemed always to be in a state of turmoil. The other day we went to a birthday party and the children were given boxes of crayons. Unfortunately, a lot of them were broken. One twin said, 'Look, I have twice as many!' and the other screamed bloody murder about having broken crayons."

As I studied the new research and listened to parents, it seemed to me that there were two extremes of coping styles with many variations in between. At one end of the scale are what I call the "wave riders." These are the children who, if put into an ocean during a hurricane, would ride out the waves. At the opposite end are the "wave fighters," children who, if put into a calm lake where there isn't as much as a ripple, would churn the water up so violently, they might drown.

The advantage in trying to examine a child's unique style is that then you don't go crazy half as often. Jill, at 9, had said all winter that she was dying to go to camp with her best friend, so her parents paid the full amount for the sleep-away camp. A week before going, Jill got hysterical; she'd be too homesick, she wouldn't like the food, her friend would desert her, she'd get poison ivy! That sort of thing could easily drive a mother crazy, but Jill's mother remained calm and collected. She told Jill, "When we moved from an apartment to this house when you were two years old, you cried for two weeks. When you went to nursery school, you cried every morning and I had to stay with you for a week. The first week you went to elementary school, you threw up every morning. Now you love this house, you loved nursery school, and you were crazy about your first-grade teacher. You're just the kind of person who worries a lot in advance. After a while, you have a fine time."

Children find it comforting to know that their differences are understood and accepted. It's another bulwark against feeling lonely or bad.

What I have tried to do is outline a basic philosophy that requires the development of certain skills. I know I haven't offered any panacea or "quick fix," but I hope the rest of this book will clarify and reinforce my point of view. It's not easy to reconnect with your inner child, and it's very hard to nurture that inner self. Especially now, when so many parents are raising children alone, so many mothers have outside jobs, and the society we live in causes so much stress. I should add that nobody can do the job of getting over craziness with children all alone. We need support groups— relatives, neighbors, friends, other parents, specialists such as the pediatrician, teachers, and recreation workers. We need information; we need a chance to share our feelings with others like ourselves; we need sympathy. We need time away from our children, other interests, other love relationships that can nourish us. Nobody can ever be a perfect parent, and it is absurd to try. None of us will raise perfect children. That is the human condition. But we can enjoy ourselves and our children more fully if we make the effort to develop self-understanding, the first skill necessary to understanding children. Fred Rogers (of "Mister Rogers' Neighborhood") wrote, "When you become a parent it is your biggest chance to grow again. You have another crack at yourself."

When Your Child
Drives You Crazy

❋ I was huddled in a chair trembling, crying, praying that my husband would get home soon. In the next room my 2-month-old daughter was screaming in her crib and I couldn't do anything about it. I was terrified that if I went near her I might shake, beat, or maybe even kill her.

This happened more than thirty years ago, but it is not an experience one forgets. My daughter was a colicky baby, and at times she cried almost all day and all night. I was certain I was a failure as a mother; otherwise how could I possibly be so furious with a tiny, helpless baby? I felt utterly miserable. The sound of that endless wailing made me feel I'd made a terrible mistake in becoming a mother; I would be in chains forever. What further exacerbated my shock was the fact that I'd been a wonderful nursery school teacher and had a master's degree in child psychology. *I was a fraud in every department.*

In the years since I was a young mother, a lot of attention has been given—as well it should be—to parents who actually hit and hurt their children. What warrants equal attention, I think, are those of us who *feel* like hitting and hurting but have managed to control ourselves. We often feel as frightened and guilty as parents who act out their rage.

As I look back, I find there are many steps parents can take in that twilight zone between *feeling* and *doing* that can provide more satisfactory solutions. We need to understand and relieve the causes of our angry feelings.

We are more likely to experience rage and fear with very young infants than with older children. This is due partly to a baby's obvious defenselessness, but I think there is something deeper at work. The wailing of an infant evokes memories of our own infancy. In the most remote parts of our subconscious a crying baby reawakens the terror *we* felt at being lost and alone in a frightening world in which we had no sense of time and space, no language, no way of knowing whether our needs would be met. If we recognize these primitive feelings, we can then identify with a child's cries instead of being frightened by them.

Beyond that faint echo of our own infantile past, we feel powerless; there is no way to explain the realities of life to a baby. Feeling so helpless infuriates us. Later on, when a child begins to develop clear images of the world around him, it gets easier. And of course the greatest antidote to a parent's feeling of incompetence is language—a child's ability to say, "I hurt, I want, I need."

"The thing to do," I heard one young mother advise another, "is to have a good cry *with* the baby! If you pick her up and rock *together*, you can give *each other* comfort!" That seemed like good advice to me.

We know babies need to be cuddled and loved and cared for, but we sometimes overlook the fact that Mommy and Daddy do, too. Few parents, no matter how much they've tried to prepare in advance, are really prepared for the total helplessness of an infant. A baby's need for nurturance is all but limitless, and that's a terrifying responsibility.

The urge to hurt a child can be controlled only if you have a reservoir of loving feelings yourself. Knowing that grandparents or neighbors are sympathetic and will help, that a kindly baby-sitter is available, that your wife or husband understands and is going to give you all of Saturday to do whatever you please—these are essential for nurturance. But more important, we must nurture ourselves—and not feel guilty.

Each of us needs to figure out what will give us the comfort and support we need—from others and from ourselves—in order to give love and attention to our children. "What I kept saying those first months," one mother told me, "was 'I haven't got it, I just haven't got it!' My husband kept asking me what 'it' was and I couldn't tell him. Then my mother decided to come for a visit. When I saw her walk through the gate at the airport I began crying. When she hugged and kissed me, I turned to my husband and said, 'This is what *it* was!' I needed some mothering myself. A week later I was able to give *it* to the baby!"

A father told me about a day he had when his young son was teething. "No matter what I did," he said, "Seth kept screaming until I thought I'd go nuts. I felt like shoving him down the incinerator, and that really scared me. In desperation I put Seth in the canvas sling my wife uses when she takes him shopping. I wrapped it around us and busied myself doing things around the apartment. I put up the shower curtain and hung a few pictures. As I moved around, doing things, I felt better. Seth soon stopped crying, and that was great. Then I suddenly realized that having that warm little body nestled against mine was making *me* feel better!"

How I envied that young father! When I was a young mother we had no such contraptions for carrying babies on our backs or chests. We also thought it was important for babies to "get used to" being alone in a crib or carriage. That was utter nonsense. If I had a chance to do it all over, I'd carry my baby around during the day and take her to bed with me at night until the colic was over. I'm sure my anger would have decreased in direct proportion to my capacity to make my daughter more comfortable. And by providing the physical contact that comforted her, I would have allowed myself the same pleasure.

New parents need to examine their fantasies to make sure they're not expecting things no baby could possibly provide. For example, an 18-year-old mother who had beaten her infant son severely admitted to a counselor that she'd expected the child to make up to her for his father's desertion. "I needed a lot of loving," she said, "and I thought I'd get it from the baby. When I realized that I'd have to do most of the loving for a while, I just went nuts—I couldn't take it."

Children do love their parents—madly, passionately, unconditionally. But the fantasy that a child can give unlimited love and gratification is dangerous. A father who sought counseling because he feared he would hurt his infant son told me, "I began to realize that deep inside me I wanted a child who would make me feel that I was a wonderful person. What I had to learn was that the only person who could do that was me. It was laying a heavy trip on a little kid to expect him to give me the confidence and approval I couldn't give myself."

We need to remember that we all have our own idiosyncrasies. Things that don't bother some people drive others up the wall, and vice versa. Once my daughter was over the colic, she and I got along beautifully. She was adorable, curious, adventurous. Then, at about 18 months, she went through a phase when she couldn't bear to let me out of her sight. I knew perfectly well that it was a normal phase all children go through—but that didn't help. I was an absolute nut about privacy. I simply could not stand being unable to close the bathroom door without leaving a screaming child outside.

A father I know almost had a heart attack the day his son rolled around in a mud puddle. When he told me about it, I laughed; that wouldn't have bothered me at all. In fact, I liked making messes with my daughter, in mud and paints and clay. But when I told this father about my problem with privacy in the bathroom, he said, "You're crazy! Who'd bother to lock a poor little kid out of the bathroom?"

If we would accept the fact that we have a right to our peculiarities, we'll enjoy our children much more. In my case, I tried to compromise; I locked the bathroom door, but I sang and talked to my daughter so she'd know I was still there! When I met my needs, I no longer got so angry at hers.

Sometimes our anger reflects ways in which we and our children are very alike or very different. "I see all my own traits in Jerry," a father reflected. "When I was a kid my father called me a sissy. I was afraid of the dark, of loud noises, of animals—you name it. I hated being that way, but the more my father pushed and challenged me, the worse I got. I swore I'd never be that kind of father, but Jerry is just the way I was—and I feel like beating the hell out of him! I tell him he can't have a night-light the rest of his life and he cries. I leave the room shaking, horrified by feelings of really hating him. I guess I really hate myself."

On the other hand, a mother who had been a sweet, quiet little girl has a daughter who's a little brat. "Louise hits me, she calls me names. I could kill her because I never dared behave that way!" she said. It may be that this mother would like to have been less "perfect" herself. Children often sense such things and live out our needs for us. Or it may be that raising a child who's totally different is very upsetting.

As a child gets old enough to understand, it often helps to talk openly about such feelings so that neither child nor parent gets caught up in a misunderstanding. Jerry needs to hear how his father felt when he was little. Louise needs to know that although she doesn't have to be *like* her mother, it's not easy to have a child with such a different temperament.

Sometimes anger springs from a stage of development about which we are sensitive. One mother doesn't understand people who lose their tempers with infants. "I *loved* that period," she said. "What I can't stand is when they get old enough to talk back. When Suzie says something fresh, I know I have to leave the room or I'll beat her." Another mother feels just the opposite: "Taking care of a helpless baby just about did me in," she said. "But later, when my son wanted to explore and was into everything, I had a ball!"

It is often comforting to know that however difficult it is to be a parent at one stage of a child's development, we may well do brilliantly at another. Each child has his or her own rough times, too. A child with a lot of energy and curiosity may drive everyone crazy when she learns to walk; a shy, hesitant child may suffer when it is time to play with other children; a very physical child may have a hard time sitting still in a classroom. A sense of perspective can help us to avoid becoming tense and anxious about a particularly difficult period.

Most feelings of rage reflect our attitude toward ourselves rather than the child. When nothing seems to be going right, we're sure we're incompetent. Taking action—*doing something*—is an important antidote; it gives us a sense of autonomy.

If a parent is actually hurting a child, it's essential to get professional help. Fortunately, such help is now available in almost every community. A local hospital, mental health clinic, minister, or pediatrician can supply details. No one should try to solve the problem alone.

When a parent is only *thinking* about hitting a child, other types of action may be helpful. In my case, for example, I visited my parents for a few weeks, knowing that both my daughter and I would get the tender, loving care we needed. I went back to work part-time so I could afford an excellent baby-sitter. I discussed my problem with a wise and sensitive pediatrician who assured me that my child would never have an easygoing bone in her body no matter *what* I did. (He was absolutely right!)

Learning as much as we can—by talking to pediatricians and experienced parents, by reading books and magazines about child-raising—is always helpful. It's important to understand, however, that each situation, each parent and child, is too different for any absolute answers. Knowledge gives us more choices, but it will not make us perfect parents. And getting over the notion that there is such a thing is probably the single most important step toward having more fun with our children.

Another thing I found helpful was making a plan. My husband and I sat down and wrote out a child-care schedule. I hardly ever followed it, but knowing I had a support system made me feel better. One mother wrote notes in a diary every night before going to sleep. "I poured out my poor little heart, had a nice cry, and felt better," she said. "When I read over what I'd written—even a week later—I realized it was out of proportion, and that was helpful. I gave my diary to my daughter when she had her first child!"

Ambivalent feelings are inevitable, but if we're aware of them and make a conscious effort to grow and change, we can cope. As I look back on my daughter's infancy, I see many images other than the one of me huddled, shaking, in that chair. I see myself bathing a baby and giggling; I remember squeals of delighted laughter when I kissed her stomach; I see myself rocking a sleeping baby and feeling waves of love and happiness. I wasn't a monster at all, just a frightened young woman aware of a tremendous responsibility. If only I'd been able to see that more balanced image of myself then!

Most of all, I've learned that the less I felt like hitting *myself* (for being stupid, incompetent, imperfect), the less I felt like hitting my child. The desire to hit a young child is an expression of anger against ourselves, one that can be cured by giving ourselves a loving pat on the head.

My daughter didn't do badly either. Despite my fumblings and failings, she survived very nicely! The demands of young children are great and cannot always be met—and shouldn't be even if they could. Part of growing up is learning to deal with frustration, discomfort, and life's inevitable limitations.

The period of a child's total dependency is really very short. By age 3, my daughter was in nursery school all morning; at 6 she was more thrilled about sleeping at a friend's house than staying home; by 14 she found it difficult to live with us at all—and at 18 she was gone. It's been many years since I was "not free," and I often think about how much I miss being around little children!

Why Every Child
Needs a Fortune-Teller

❈ I was walking through Central Park on my way to the dentist.
It was warm and sunny—Indian summer—with the muted colors
of fall just beginning. I was feeling wonderful. It was a special kind
of exultancy that comes to me from time to time when I have
solved some old problems and feel on the crest of new creativity,
new adventures. I was thinking about a new book I was about to
begin—letting my mind wander, soaking in the beauty around me,
letting it fill my soul, getting ready for another beginning of another stage of working and learning. It was good to be walking fast
and breathing deeply; for a change the New York sky was blue and
clear. It was a pleasure to be in my own company.

Without any conscious plan I wandered toward a place in the
park where I had played as a child. The elementary school I at-
tended was on Central Park West, and every day we were taken
to the park for "recreation." Suddenly I realized where I was; there
were the big rocks where we had climbed and played "Tarzan"
endlessly, day after day for more than a year. I must have been 9
or 10. I stood and looked at the rocks. Nothing was changed. *Over
fifty years ago!* Suddenly my mood changed. I was no longer a
62-year-old woman—happy, fulfilled, sure of myself. I was a 10-
year-old girl who was frequently scared to death: sure I would never,
ever, learn long division; failing every test in grammar; seeing
myself as fat and ugly and clumsy; seeing myself as someone who

was always last to be chosen for a relay race; a shy little kid afraid that the other children wouldn't like me; deeply wounded by every rebuff, terrified of being teased. Actually, I went to a better than average school and had very loving parents. There was nothing seriously the matter with me except that I was a child.

I could almost see that child Eda sitting on the rocks. I wanted to embrace her, to shout *"Here I am! Look at me! It all came out all right!"* Suddenly I was weeping—for the little girl who could not imagine the woman, who needed so desperately to know that when she was a grown-up lady she would find herself talented and loved, admired and respected, and sure of who she was. If only I could reverse time, go back and take that little girl in my arms, hold her tightly, and say, "Eda, Eda, you are lovable and full of wondrous possibilities. Don't be so scared; the others who you think are so sure of themselves are *just as scared as you are!*" I wanted so terribly to go back to that time, fifty years ago, with a crystal ball containing the image of the woman I would be.

None of us can do that for the child we once were. *All* of us felt those uncertainties, and each of us had some special private terror: hair that was either too curly or too straight; legs that were too short or too long. We were either freckled or fat, had an impossible nose, worries about ever learning how to read, anguish about being ostracized, of not being popular, were terrified of the angry or sarcastic teacher, wanting so desperately to be loved for *being*, not for *doing*.

Did anybody ever tell us that we all felt the same way? Did anybody ever help us to look into that crystal ball and see the adult we would become? Perhaps there were a few lucky ones among us, but not many. Somewhere, deep inside, if we can return for a moment to a time and a place of being young and vulnerable, there was a little child hurting. If only we could confront that child, with the comfort of what we know was going to happen! Of all the "might-have-beens" this may well be the saddest one of all.

We can't go back. After a few minutes I forced myself to turn away from those rocks in the park, pushed away the memory of the child I saw there, and continued my walk through the park, letting go of memory, and finally, allowing myself to feel a sense of thanksgiving for the person I had become. As I walked away, I knew I would never really lose the memory of that child and that I wouldn't want to if I could, for there are other children to be comforted.

And that, of course, is the happy ending and the new beginning of such moments of reflection and memory. We can take that crystal ball into the lives of the children who are around us right now. It seems to me to be one of the greatest gifts we can bring to today's children—to become their fortune-tellers.

If I have learned anything at all about children in these intervening years, it is that they always blame themselves for whatever is wrong and never believe that anyone else is as scared and unsure as they are. If they are failing in school, it is never interpreted by them as the result of poor teaching or inadequate schools; it is because they are stupid. If they feel lonely or rejected, it is never because adults may have their own problems and limitations; it is that they, the children, are unlovable. Children also do not have enough experience in living to have any perspective on time. Whatever is happening at any given moment is going to go on forever. Whether they feel shy, clumsy, dumb, scared, rejected, or ridiculed by others, that's the way it's going to be *forever*.

Let us mobilize our forces against such misery! On with the kerchief and the gypsy skirt; out with the tarot cards or tea leaves! It is time to become our children's fortune-tellers. It's a heck of a game for a rainy day! It may be a game, but it is not a fraud; each of these self-conscious, insecure children will someday be an adult who can make decisions, feel successful, find a special place for himself. Children need to hear that it is all going to come out all right. They may not appear to believe us, but I am convinced they will be comforted. No, Janet, you will not always feel like a wallflower; no, John, you will not always feel like a klutz on a baseball field—maybe you'll be terrific at tennis; no, Kim, you won't always feel mortified because you are developing breasts; no, David, you won't always be three inches taller than everyone else you know.

If I had the magic power to go back, even for a moment, to be with the child I was, what would I tell her? I think I would say, "I am a gypsy fortune-teller and I want to tell you what I see in your future. You think you are dumb in school, but when you are a grown-up lady and can study the subjects that really interest you, you are going to be very, very smart. Nobody will care at all whether or not you can remember the multiplication table (in fact, when you are sixty-two, you still won't remember how much seven times eight is, or nine times seven, but you manage to survive.) The wonderful imagination you have right now—all the lovely stories and poems you write—are going to make you a successful writer someday. And your shyness and tenderness will give you a greater capacity to understand other people and to love them a lot—and they are going to love you back. There will be unhappy and painful times, but you will survive them and learn from them. When you feel afraid, you will be able to talk about it—you won't think you have to keep it a secret. You will know then that everyone feels afraid at one time or another, and you will actually be able to help other people with their fears. By the time you get to be sixty-two, you will know that you are one of the luckiest people who ever lived, because you will have a wonderful family and good friends and work that you love. And most of all, what I see in my crystal ball is a woman who is *so glad to be Eda!*"

Few of us have the special gift of seeing into our children's future. If we tried to do it too literally, it could be dangerous. There are some kinds of power games that can be disastrous. It is easy for me to play the game with myself because I know how it all turned out. What I have in mind for today's children is not a blueprint of events but a kind of communication that makes it clear that the way a child feels about him or herself is totally different from the way adults feel. That we do become more confident; that we do figure out, at least to an important degree, who we are, what our talents are, and how to use our strengths. That it is only little children who are expected to succeed at a lot of things they are no good at and don't enjoy, while adults specialize in and eventually get to focus on what they do well and delight in doing. That the process of growing up gives us greater self-confidence and many more options about what we want to be and do. That we learn how universal doubts and misgivings are and stop being ashamed and secretive about our inevitable failures. That we certainly go on feeling pain and confusion, but that we learn to deal with our problems and we know there are many other people who can help us. And that most of all, most grown-up people can and do learn to like being who they are.

None of us can guarantee a child that adulthood will be easy, but of one thing I am absolutely sure: *Being an adult is better than being a child.* Come to think of it, there was one beloved fortune-teller in *my* childhood. He was our music teacher and something of a philosopher. In between teaching us songs, he talked to us about life. One day, in the fifth grade, he said, "Listen, if anyone tells you this is the happiest time of your life and that childhood is wonderful, don't you believe it! I'm here to tell you that no matter what happens, you will never be as miserable when you are grown up as you sometimes feel now!" How comforting! There *was* someone, after all, who couldn't give me the details, of course, but surely released a hope in me—and maybe played some part in forming the person I became who now wants to comfort other children.

What Do the Experts Know About Your Child?

❋ Some time ago I appeared on a television program with a noted expert. Although we are in agreement on most aspects of childraising, we disagreed on the issue of spanking. His feeling was that if one ever spanked at all, it should never be in the heat of anger, and my attitude was that anger would be the *only possible* excuse. Because we are human, it is likely to happen occasionally, and there is no point in wallowing in guilt about it. What makes more sense to me is for a parent to apologize and admit that this is not a helpful way to solve problems, but sometimes parents reach the end of their rope. The show's other guest seemed to be saying that if you think a little slap is called for, do it calmly.

There was an audience in the studio and one mother asked, "What are we supposed to do, when experts like you two don't agree?" I replied that some confusion is part of learning; that nobody has final answers, but searching for understanding is the important point. In the final analysis each of us has to decide what our own children need and then adapt those ideas and theories that coincide with our own philosophy of life.

Parents are badgered from all sides with all kinds of specific or general, scientifically rigid or vaguely sentimental theories, instructions, and warnings, from quite a collection of child development experts. We have come to look upon parenthood as a profession rather than a natural and instinctive human function.

Many of the insights we have acquired have been sensationally helpful in the raising of children. I don't feel at all discouraged because parents are confused! Doubts and misgivings, trial and error, are necessary in any learning process—as are risk and failure. Of course one wants to minimize serious mistakes in such a crucial area as parent-child relations, but we must go on examining and changing if we want to improve our knowledge and understanding.

The more one examines any area of life, the more mysteries unfold. That is exactly what has happened in the field of child development research—and I fervently hope it will continue so that we can learn more and more, discarding misconceptions along the way. But though this is a nice philosophical approach, it is not very helpful to parents who are caught in the middle of this search for new and better answers! How are we to make reasonable judgments and adjustments while all this experimenting and exploring are going on? First, I think, by simply understanding that such a process *is* going on, and that because it is dynamic and changing, each of us must accept or reject what we hear or read according to what seems reasonable to us. This is what we mean when we advise parents to use their "common sense." If you live with a child and observe his or her reactions carefully, you learn what works—and what doesn't. If you remain flexible and open-minded, you will be willing to admit failures and try other approaches.

Just as important as observing children directly is the need to really think through one's own philosophy of life. What are your goals? What values do you want to communicate to your child? If an "expert" says that he has discovered, after much research, that beating a kid every Friday night is a good way to raise a child, are you going to listen? Or does that go against your grain—does it grate against something you happen to believe about human relations in general? A few months ago I read a book by a very famous and respected expert who feels that parents have failed so abysmally in raising children that it is time to let the children take over. They should be free to run away, live with whom they choose, vote, decide not to go to school, etc. How does that strike you? Will you accept this theory because the author is really "somebody" in the field of child development? Or will you decide that maybe he's gone around the bend a bit?

Of course it's easier to "use your own judgment" when advice tends to be extreme—or even ridiculous. What about advice that sounds interesting and attractive? How can you tell whether it's right for you and your children? Here is a list of criteria that might be helpful in making your own decisions:

1. The One-Theory, One-Answer Approach

When Dr. Spock and most of the rest of us rediscovered "demand feeding" during the 1940s, it seemed such a compassionate and sensible idea. I'm sure that feeding babies when they're hungry, letting them sleep when they're tired, and allowing them to use a toilet when they're ready had been part of childraising for much of human history, but during the 1920s and early '30s many parents were under the influence of a psychologist by the name of Dr. John B. Watson, a behaviorist who believed in very regimented child-care procedures.

What Dr. Spock suggested was a more flexible, humane, natural approach, and for a while most of us thought we had discovered The Answer to some of the childhood traumas we had related to the earlier, rigid handling of infants. Demand feeding worked wonderfully for lots of children but was an abysmal failure with others. Disillusion set in. The theory was rotten. "Permissiveness" became an epithet almost equal to "communism"!

What we have learned since the 1940s and '50s (always understood by perceptive parents but now proven by very careful research) is that children are born with very different internal, physiological, and psychological systems and child-care procedures need to be adapted to these differences. Some babies are apparently born with an internal rhythm; they know when they are hungry or tired, and when they have to urinate or defecate. All one has to do is follow the child's lead. Demand feeding, for example, works just fine with such children. There are others, however, who do not seem to have such a clear mechanism for self-adjustment. The permissive approach drives them up the wall. They have no idea when they will be hungry or tired, and by the time they are, they're hysterical about it; they seem to have no internal signals to alert them to the need to go to the toilet. These children *need* an external schedule in order to experience some sense of order in their world. The same variations occur when it comes to discipline. One child hardly ever needs external controls, while another seems unable to control impulses that constantly get him into trouble unless there are very clear rules and regulations.

Beware of experts bearing A Gift! When I was in college and graduate school, I was absolutely certain that we had discovered the Ultimate Answer to all childraising problems—psychoanalysis. As a nursery school teacher I could find "phallic symbols" in every child's drawing, "oedipus complexes" in every parent interview! It seemed to me then that since we had discovered unconscious, repressed needs, all we had to do was give people insight and we would raise a generation of perfectly adjusted human beings.

What an oversimplification that was! We learned a tremendous number of profoundly significant clues to the human personality from Freud and his followers, but life is far too mysterious and growth much too complex for all-encompassing answers. Each new theory has some contribution to make to our understanding, but none of them will ever provide us with a solution to all the challenges of parenthood. There are still plenty of people around who want to become your personal guru, want to tell you exactly what to do to solve all your problems. For such people there is only one answer: "Don't call me, I'll call you."

2. The Promise of Quick Relief

It is a great temptation to listen to people who promise quick relief from the anxieties, mistakes, and heartaches of raising children. There are literally hundreds of books on the market that would have us believe that all we need do is follow their instructions and all of our problems will be solved. There are very popular and successful courses that promise that in a few weekly meetings you can completely change your relationship with your child.

Beware of such gifts. There are no simple solutions to complex problems. Growing up is a struggle for every living creature. Birth is a struggle; being mortal is full of pain; life presents inevitable frustrations and crises; each human being is different and special and faces unique challenges both from within and without. Interpersonal relationships are the most complex and mysterious and the most difficult to categorize. Each of us brings a whole life history to marriage and parenthood. But along the way, as we struggle, we *do* learn, we *do* become wiser and more sensitive, and each little gain adds to our growth. All we can do is try to grow along with our children—not suddenly or quickly but all through our lives. Studying, listening, reading, and discussing are wonderful; this is the *pursuit* of knowledge and understanding, and it is a neverending process.

3. ONE Approach to ALL Children

I mentioned earlier that if we have learned anything about childraising, it is that no two children can be handled in exactly the same way. Many of the articles and books you read seem to fly in the face of this fact. For example, you will read such statements as:

"You must never, ever deceive your child about anything."

"It is never necessary or desirable to speak severely or in a loud voice to any child."

"No child is going to understand what you expect, unless you are completely consistent in your punishments."

"Never allow your child to eat between meals."

"Unless you can trust your 6-year-old child to make his or her own decisions about being able to walk to school alone, the child will never be able to trust his or her own judgment."

Any of these statements might well be true at some point in some child's life; they are all untrue if applied to every child. While being truthful with children is certainly a worthy goal, some children, at certain ages, may not be able to handle too much information too suddenly. We don't have to lie, for example, but with a sensitive, anxious youngster, it would be foolish to say, "The truth is, six months from now you are going to have your tonsils out." That's telling the truth—but it's slightly premature!

With some children, the quietest and most gentle reproof will send them into a tailspin of guilt and sorrow for the smallest misdemeanor. And then there are those tough-skinned hombres who look at you as if you are cuckoo when you make a gentle, polite suggestion that they shape up. As all of us discover sooner or later, some children only get the message if we shout it out!

Some children with small appetites seem to get along much more happily with six to eight snack times a day rather than three full meals. This may last only for a few months or a year at the most. But a rigid adherence to regularly scheduled mealtimes merely creates an unnecessary war, much discomfort, and an eating problem that could have been avoided. And while some children are quite mature, sensible, and responsible at an early age, others couldn't possibly handle traffic lights and ambushing bullies on the way to or from school.

4. The Scolding-the-Parents Approach

Nothing is easier than making parents feel guilty! We seem more than willing to blame ourselves for every problem, and there are experts who exploit our fears and self-doubts all too readily. Guilt is an immobilizing force; instead of freeing us to experiment with new approaches, it tends to paralyze us because no one is helping to build up our self-confidence.

The antidote to this approach—and one that I think can be of tremendous help to parents—is participating in some kind of child-study discussion group in which parents are encouraged to share their experiences and feelings and to see themselves as people with potential strengths for personal growth and increased understanding of their children. A professional leader in such a group uses the resources within the group for self-discovery. He or she capitalizes on the universality of some problems and creates a climate of mutual respect and shared compassion and understanding.

It is important to remember that sometimes the person with the most credentials may be the most punitive, or the most authoritarian. Not always, of course, but sometimes we tend to be so impressed by advanced degrees that we don't seek out the wisest or most human leader, who may be a school nurse or a nursery school teacher or a volunteer working in a mental-health clinic who has been in training workshops. Parents need to choose such leaders with care and to discontinue a relationship with a leader who makes them feel like failures.

5. Training Parents to Be Experts

In their zeal, some parent educators (especially those who are child therapists) try to teach parents to speak to their children in ways that are appropriate in a psychiatric clinic but not in a family. This is what I have come to think of as the Parent-with-the-Couch-on-His-Back Syndrome. Junior "accidentally" knocks over a lamp and you are supposed to say, "That's all right, darling—I understand. You really wanted to hit your baby sister, so you hit the lamp instead." Or to a 10-year-old who presents you with an abstract painting all in red and black for your birthday, "Thank you, darling —but I didn't know you were feeling so hostile. Tell me about it."

None of these statements is entirely wrong, but the approach is far too clinical. Children need some privacy; not all their thoughts and feelings need to be discussed unless they are exceedingly unhappy and under the care of a trained psychotherapist. Rather than practicing without a license, parents can take a chance with some of their more perceptive insights (although each of us needs to find his or her own style). For example, you might say, "I'm really upset about that vase being broken, but lots of people have accidents like that when they feel upset." Or, "Hey, listen here, young lady, yelling for Daddy isn't going to help; we *both* think it's time for you to go to bed!" As for the painting, it is best received with pleasure and praise. If you feel strongly that there is a message in the medium, talk it over with a friend, your minister, your pediatrician, the teacher, or a guidance counselor before making your own diagnosis!

6. Beware of Statisticians!

One of the problems that has beset the field of psychology since its beginning is the fact that it appeared on the scene when we thought we had discovered the Holy Grail—the scientific method. This involved research procedures that for a time seemed to prove very successful in the development of new insights in chemistry, physics, and various branches of medical research. The early psychologists wanted to be part of the new wave of scientists; they found such descriptions as "artist" or "philosopher" insulting in the age of technology. And so, over the past fifty or so years, we have been stuck with research procedures that work very well with laboratory rats but that I feel have, in most cases, been almost useless in the study of human beings.

Attitudes are changing slowly. For one thing, scientists now admit that the scientific method is not all that wonderful even in research in the "hard sciences." Telling parents that a percentage of all second children behave thus and so, or that this or that number of children can be predicted to have difficulty learning, is really quite useless because there are too many variables where human beings are concerned. One can get *suggested trends,* perhaps, from a statistical approach to research, but human observation by experienced specialists is far more valid in understanding what we are all about. *No important insight into human behavior was ever discovered by analyzing statistics.*

7. On Being Discouraged From Thinking for Yourself or Listening to Friends

As a young mother I found that while my "book learning" was often very helpful, some of the best guidance I ever got came from talking to a close friend who knew me and my child well and loved us both. Even our parents and relatives may be worth *listening* to, at least. Sometimes even a mother-in-law can see things you are blind to and can bring a healthy perspective to a problem. We should not be afraid of following every avenue, using every resource —and then, finally, *making up our own minds.* Whatever we hear or read, whoever we listen to, ultimately we must make our own decisions. We live with the child.

Parental observations and conclusions certainly can be wrong, especially if there are problems we're not ready to face. On the other hand, to be completely swayed by a "professional opinion" from someone who professes to know more about your child after a three-hour session than you do after five or ten years is just plain silly. Most of us tend to be very impressed by authority figures— too much so. We have every right to be questioning and critical; to ask for and get other opinions; to explore a problem carefully and slowly, never underestimating the value and importance of our gut feelings.

We are very lucky to have so many people spending so much time studying childhood. But we need to understand that no matter how much we learn, there will never be simple panaceas for anything as important, complex, exciting, and mysterious as raising children.

You now have an accurate and definitive set of standards for examining all theories—or have you learned enough from this article to have stopped reading this sentence as soon as you saw the words "accurate," "definitive," and "all"? Don't let anybody lead you down the garden path—not even me!

Part II

*

BASIC PHILOSOPHY OF PARENTING

*

When Parent Love
Goes Too Far

❋ "All through my childhood," Peter told me, "I had a recurring dream that I was a baby eagle learning to fly. But just as I'd get the hang of it and really begin to enjoy it, I'd get confused and bash my head against a cliff."

Peter is a charming man who gets along well with everyone. He rarely complains about anything, but he suffers from severe chronic headaches. He's also deeply depressed. "I never seem to make a good decision about my life," he told me. "I just take the easiest or most familiar path—and then I regret it."

Many people have similar life patterns. They seem to know they are marrying the wrong person, studying for the wrong vocation, making the wrong decisions about where to live and when to have children. They feel caught in the trap of their own passivity and indecision. What makes people like Peter continue to behave in self-destructive ways that only increase their unhappiness? There are many possible explanations, of course, but most of us would assume that somewhere along the way such a person was neglected or rejected or treated in a cruel and insensitive manner by his parents. And that may well be the answer in many cases. But in other cases, it's not lack of love but *too much love* that's the problem.

"My mother *adored* me," Peter explained. "She never let me out of my sight. Nothing was too good for me. I can't remember ever being scolded, but then I never did anything to be scolded for." Peter's mother was a bright, ambitious woman who was greatly disappointed by her husband. Peter's father lost many jobs and was never able to earn enough money. He was so quiet and submissive that everyone pushed him around. "My mother used to scream at him, 'Nobody respects you! You're a *nothing!*' " Peter recalled. "My mother was lonely and frustrated; I was her only interest in life. She was terrified of losing me—and she made sure she didn't."

Peter was never allowed to skate or play baseball because he might get hurt. His mother took him everywhere with her. "I was her date, her playmate, her only companion throughout my childhood," he reported. "Whenever I felt the urge to move away I was overwhelmed with guilt. She was so good to me; how could I hurt her?"

Peter is certainly an extreme example, but after I met him I became more aware of the ways in which parents can, without realizing it, suffocate a child and thwart the desperate need to try his or her own wings. Often this is done in the name of loving.

A mother tells a child, for example, that the jungle gym in the playground is "too high for you." A new friend's house is off limits because "he plays too roughly." A weekend trip with the seventh-grade class is refused because "there won't be enough supervision." A summer camp where a friend is going "is too competitive," and a bicycle trip with a youth group is "much too long and you'll get sick." Under such circumstances, eventual college and career choices tend to be made to please parents. It also takes a good deal of stamina for a son or a daughter to locate an acceptable spouse —and the ultimate choice is likely to be a parent's.

It is, of course, the parents' responsibility to protect a child from dangers, to assess whether or not a child is ready for experiences that have built-in hazards. Some situations are dangerous and undesirable, and children must be protected from them. But sometimes parents seem unduly alarmed and overcautious. Their behavior suggests that they were comfortable only when the child was a totally dependent infant. They are terrified to let go even in the most necessary and appropriate ways.

There are usually two principal reasons for extreme overprotectiveness—this smothering of a child's need to grow, to experiment, to become increasingly independent and autonomous. The first is that the parent is using the child to fulfill his or her own needs. The child becomes a substitute for all the other normal avenues of adult fulfillment, especially marriage and work. The second reason for smothering devotion seems to be quite different, but it has the same roots. Overprotection often conceals a great deal of hostility toward the child. Since such feelings are totally unacceptable and guilt-producing, they quickly become buried in the unconscious. Some discontented and frustrated parents are really afraid that their hostile or rejecting feelings might cause something terrible to happen to the child. Their guilt makes them overly concerned about real and imagined dangers.

Peter, in an effort to examine the source of his headaches and depression, speculated that his mother must have hated her life. "She was bright and capable," he said, "but not trained for any job. She was totally dependent on a man she neither respected nor loved. Maybe she'd have left him if it hadn't been for me! She probably thought something terrible might happen to me because she unconsciously wished I'd never been born. No wonder she was so terrified to let me out of the house! What a burden we were to each other; we both wanted to be 'eagles' and fly away, but instead we kept each other in chains."

Parents who live such unfulfilling lives and harbor such deep resentments may be the exception, but all of us have moments when such feelings surface. One recently divorced mother told me, "When Amy and I moved into the new apartment alone, I behaved like an idiot. I'd never been an anxious mother before, but suddenly I couldn't let her out of my sight. She was perfectly capable of walking to school alone, but I insisted on going with her. She wanted to go to a friend's summer place for two weeks and I wouldn't let her; it made me feel too anxious. Fortunately, Amy is a gutsy kid and she fought me—hard. I asked a psychotherapist, 'Why is my child so rebellious?' and discovered, instead, that I felt guilty because I sometimes wished I could be totally free, without a child to care for.

"My divorce was really a new beginning," she continued, "and part of me didn't want any 'fetters.' When I began to face that and to realize that my feelings are normal, I also realized that Amy was more than ready to start moving away from me—which, after all, was what we both needed!"

A father who had been unemployed for almost a year told me he'd had a normal, balanced relationship with his wife and two sons before he lost his job. "But" he said, "the shock of losing my job was incredible; I turned into a zombie. If Jess or Ernie turned me down when I wanted to play with them, I felt terribly hurt and rejected. They began to feel guilty and eventually gave up most of their extracurricular activities and friends in order to spend more time with me. I was clinging to them like a drowning man. One day my wife told me very quietly, 'You can't use your children to fill the emptiness you're feeling.' It was a shock and I was good and mad at first. But then, looking back, I realized I *was* using my kids to fill the void in my life—cutting them off from growing up. For the next few months, until I found another job, I became a hospital volunteer. I felt useful again—and my boys felt free to live their own lives." *

One thing we all know is that it's difficult for parents to strike a balance in any area of childraising. A young mother told me, "It's so hard not to go to extremes. I was the only child of older parents. They treated me like a Dresden china doll and I felt stifled and resentful. I swore I'd never be an overprotective mother and I bent over backward not to be. I encouraged Jennifer to try everything; I insisted she make her own decisions and kept saying, 'Be adventurous, don't be such a sissy!' By the time she was eight or nine she was a nervous wreck—afraid to do anything!

"I finally realized," she continued, "that by going to the opposite extreme, I was creating a fearful child who was just as hampered as I had been. She wasn't ready to make all those decisions, try all those activities. One day I said, 'Jennifer, I have come to a decision; you are *not* old enough to ride your bike on the main road and I do *not* want you to choose your own day camp. You're too young; that's my decision.' She was so relieved! It's hard to find that balance between overprotection and underattention.!"

Some time later I shared Jennifer's story with a nursery school teacher who said, "You know, that challenge is becoming more and more crucial as people have fewer children. In our school at least half the parents do not plan to have more than one child. Striking that delicate balance between being oversolicitous and encouraging a child to move along too fast calls for even more careful thought in single-child families."

Whatever the size of our families, all of us sometimes feel frightened, dissatisfied, bored, frustrated, unfulfilled. "Life can't be cured!" a friend said to me recently—and that says it all. Each of us has periods when it would be easy to turn to our children for too much comfort, or when we are so angry and resentful that we become smotheringly affectionate. For me, that image created in Peter's dream will never be forgotten; it is an important theme for all of us to keep in mind. We all want to give our children good roots for growing, but we must also encourage them to fly—to become brave and soaring eagles, not broken birds.

Some Don't Want
to Be Hugged

❉ My friend Millie has a 14-year-old daughter and a 17-year-old son. She called me one afternoon recently in a state of euphoria; she was baby-sitting for a young married niece and was sitting at the telephone holding a 2-month-old baby. With an ecstatic purr she informed me, "She's so tiny and adorable, and I can *hold* her!" As the mother of a tall, rangy, squiggly 10-year-old, I knew just what she meant!

There must literally be hordes of frustrated parents roaming the land who like to hug cute little children and who find that the objects of their affection are less than enthusiastic about this adult weakness. As expectant parents, most of us looked forward to having an adorable baby to lavish our love on; we mothers especially probably had an erroneous fantasy that this baby would be just like the dolls we played with as children—indestructible, consistently receptive, and willing to be cuddled indefinitely. What a rude awakening it often was to discover that sometimes even the tiniest and cutest babies are squirmy and look upon being hugged as a form of imprisonment. Even if we are lucky enough to have a child who likes to sit on our laps, be kissed and hugged, it is a short-lived privilege. One day when our backs are turned that huggable infant gets to be a *person;* he wants to be hugged when he is sleepy or sick or when we are reading a story, but it is he who decides when and where and how often, leaving us feeling deprived and rejected.

Some of the feelings that parents have about expressing overt affection to children stem from the advice we hear on all sides that young children need and want to be held, to feel close, that the first learning about love comes from bodily contact with loving parents. As a matter of fact, with newborn infants this is quite true. Our difficulties arise only if we interpret this kind of affection as the only kind that counts with children, as something static that remains the same at all ages. When we discover that our children don't remain infants and that they want other kinds of demonstrations of love, we sometimes feel baffled and uncertain.

If we are astute and willing to learn, our children often educate us very successfully about the broader view of love. When 2-year-old Billy throws his arms around his mother because she has let him go down the slide alone, his mother, who hasn't been able to cuddle him for months, begins to get the message; letting an active, adventurous child test his growing prowess is often a clearer sign of love than all the hugging and kissing in the world. When 4-year-old Susie nestles in her daddy's arms while he tells her a story, her parents see that children are different at different times. That same little girl didn't want to be hugged or kissed before she went off to nursery school in the morning, and she finds it a real chore to sit in anyone's lap during the day, when she wants to run and play. But it's different in the evening, after a warm bath and a good supper, when she feels drowsy and ready for sleep.

We learn that children are different at different times of the day, as well as at different stages in their growth. If we have more than one child, we learn something else, that no two children are alike. Johnny was the type of child who lapped up physical affection like a sponge; his younger sister is a climber, a goer, a whirling dervish. She just hasn't got time in her busy explorations of the fascinating world to be cuddled.

Yet even the most unhuggable children need love. They often want our time more than our kisses; they want us to play with them, to take trips with them; they want to be read to; they want us to be interested in their adventures and ideas. All children want the kind of love that is represented by permission to grow—the genuine encouragement to try their wings, to test their skills, to explore the unknown. They want the love that says "We don't want to hold you too tight. You are a wonderful person and you can do many things; we will let you go a little bit more all the time."

There is nothing wrong with the child who outgrows some of his need for being hugged and kissed. There is nothing wrong with the child who just isn't always "in the mood." There is nothing wrong with his feelings for his parents. We needn't feel rejected—in fact, we'd better not! If our darling bundle of joy doesn't want to bundle, the only problem will be if we view this as abnormal on the child's part or as a judgment of the child's feelings for us. For if we feel that love can be expressed *only* by hugging, we are in trouble with ourselves as well as with our children. They will sometimes "give in" just to reassure us. They will also tend to lose their own good judgment that demonstrations of affection are a small part of a loving relationship.

Nor are all parents equally adept at or natural with physical expressions of love. Many a father, especially, feels uncomfortable about a lot of hugging and is still able to transmit the message of love with great effectiveness in ways better suited to his personality; he may like to take his 2-year-old son for a Sunday walk in the park, or he may feel close and happy telling stories to his 3-year-old daughter.

When it comes to expressing affection, none of us—adults or children—respond to what we think we are *supposed* to do. Pretense has no place in the deepest of human relationships. When children feel squirmy and smothered by physical demonstrations of love, there are other ways to express loving feelings. Children can tell when their parents are tired, busy, or tense. They can accept that having moods—different needs at different times—is a normal and natural part of being human, especially if we have respected them in this matter. They need not feel rejected if we say, "Not right now, Mommy's very busy. Later we'll be together." These are the ups and downs of natural feelings, and if we and our children are not afraid of them, if we can communicate openly and freely about how we feel, we can make room for the anti-huggers as well as the huggers. We can be ourselves, secure in the knowledge that love is many things and is strong enough to survive all kinds of individual differences and variations in mood.

The Need for Privacy

❀ A mother recently told me that she had read a notebook she found in her 12-year-old daughter's drawer. She was appalled. "I thought Peggy was a shy, innocent little girl and here was this diary full of dirty jokes, comments on which boys wanted to fondle her breasts and which girls were no longer *virgins!* I couldn't believe it. I got completely hysterical, called my husband at the office, and that night we both confronted Peggy with the diary. She flew into a rage, screamed about having no privacy, went into her room, and locked the door. Ever since she's been sullen and secretive, and I'm sick with worry and shock. What do I do now?"

What, indeed? The implications of this common parent-child dilemma are extraordinarily subtle and complex, and seem to me to go far beyond the matter of parental discipline. The question of personal privacy is one that affects us all at every age. Is Peggy's sense of outrage any different from that of the husband who finds his wife reading his personal mail or the newspaper columnist who discovers that her telephone is being tapped? Privacy, whether for adult or child, has profound importance in our lives and is worthy of some careful examination.

We can learn a good deal about it from our relationships with our children. The issue is especially dramatic and often confusing because we are responsible for our children's welfare, and that often makes us feel that we need to know a great deal about what they are thinking, feeling, and doing. Yet a child's anger at having her privacy violated seems to go far beyond being caught or the fear of punishment. It seems to have to do with the respect of others for one's human rights as a person.

It seems to me that we can find a clue to the special meaning of privacy if we think about when it begins to play a part in a child's life. It seems to emerge sometime around the age of 2 or 3—at the same time that a child is developing an acute sense of his own identity. A child's first "secrets" really represent the idea, "There is a me that is unique and separate." Privacy appears as a demand for selfhood, an essential aspect of growing and maturing. This explains why the child who is deprived of his privacy tends to become increasingly secretive while the child who feels he is trusted and respected as a person has less need to accentuate his demand for privacy.

When we violate someone's privacy, we are announcing a lack of trust and respect, making the victim of our assault a non-person. We are far more likely to influence our children's ethical standards if they know that we respect them as individuals. Peggy's outrage clearly alienated her and her parents rather than bringing them closer together. It would seem to me that the best expression of genuine caring by a parent is allowing a child to find his special identity, and that can happen only in a climate of trust and respect. Peggy cannot be kept in cotton batting; there is no way for a parent to have constant surveillance over a child, and even if one could, that would interfere with the necessary processes of growing. Chances are that much of Peggy's diary is fantasy; we know this from the reports of other adolescents and adults who have acknowledged this later on. The private diaries of some teenagers are so lurid, they couldn't possibly be personal experiences! Fantasizing is a normal and necessary part of exploring ideas and feelings about one's sexuality, and the more written in private notes, the less likelihood of dangerous acting-out behavior.

The concept of trust is a hard one to achieve. When I suggest this approach to parents, a great many of them react by saying, "Suppose a child is doing something that is really dangerous?" A father told me of his growing suspicion that his 15-year-old son was selling marijuana at the local high school. Steve had a whole new group of friends, seemed to be preoccupied, had a great deal of spending money, and was out of the house most of the time. His father said, "If I search his room or listen in on his telephone conversations or follow him, I feel like a member of the Gestapo —despicable, in other words. Such behavior is contrary to my whole sense of right and wrong. And yet if I do nothing and hide my head in the sand, my son may end up in prison."

If you have a basically trusting relationship with your child, you should be able to get necessary information without resorting to snooping; simply say what's on your mind. Quietly and directly, Steve's father should say, "Steve, I'm frightened. I have the feeling you're leaving yourself wide open for real trouble. I'm concerned that you don't respect yourself enough to value your future. Could we talk about it?" It is possible that Steve won't respond, but it seems to me that no parent can act as a permanent buffer for a child and that the best you can do as your children reach maturity is offer them your love and concern and go on trusting them. If a child goes on to make a serious mistake, you can be there to help him live through it and learn from it. When we snoop and acuse, we do such serious damage to the relationship that it cannot help in the long run, and frequently we don't even get the desired results in the short run.

I know of a mother who manipulated the lives of her two children by never allowing them an unaccounted-for moment. She went through their belongings constantly on the pretext of cleaning their rooms. I never knew more secretive and devious children than hers.

On the other hand, I knew a family of three small children and two adults who were forced to live in two rooms due to the acute housing shortage after World War II. The mother told me, "We were going out of our minds with all the bickering and jealousy and rivalry. One day Henry said he thought it was at least partly because the children didn't have any place or thing that was exclusively their own. He went out and bought three metal boxes with keys and gave one to each of the boys, explaining that because we were very crowded it was hard for anyone to have any privacy, but each boy could now have special treasures that were just his alone and no one else could touch or see. We were astounded at how much this helped. It was as if we had somehow reinforced the idea that each child was a person in his own right and that we respected his autonomy."

The problem of privacy increases with the degree of intimacy in a relationship. Children grow up and move into lives of their own eventually; husbands and wives may live together for fifty or sixty years. Nowhere does the question of finding a balance between individual privacy and shared intimacy become more sensitive and complex than in marriage. Here the problem is not so much responsibility for the partner's safety and well-being, but rather how to allow for the necessary autonomy of separate persons without deceit and subterfuge, which can so seriously damage an equally valued and important sharing and trust.

There seem to be some couples who say that the secret of their marital longevity and happiness is that they have practiced total disclosure with each other—no secrets. My impression is that these people tend to have similar personalities, both showing a "low voltage" in activity, interests, and aspirations. I have never met any world-shakers in this group. This is not a judgment; it is simply true that for people of high energy and creativity, with adventurous natures and a strong innate drive for change, this kind of absolute intimacy does not work. Instead of leading to closeness, it leads to feelings of strangulation.

My model for the perfect marriage was a couple who were almost never separated during fifty-two years of marriage. I assumed, since they loved each other so much, that this was a good model for me to follow. To my surprise and terror I discovered that I had married a man who needed to be alone, who did not want to tell me everything he was thinking, feeling, or doing. The more I clung and probed, the more he struggled to be free, and the more he succeeded, the more threatened and outraged I became.

When he finally had the integrity and courage to tell me that he was going off on a separate vacation to walk through Greece—that he needed time for private growing—I behaved terribly. I cried for six weeks and wrote whining, childish letters to destroy his peace of mind. A wise friend, listening to me carry on, said, "Eda, when you grow up yourself, you will understand that if you allow a butterfly to sit in the palm of your hand, and if you tell it to fly free, it will always come back; if you tighten a fist around a butterfly, you will crush it and have nothing."

It took me many years of growing (and good psychotherapy!) to learn that total dependence and total intimacy are not the best climate in which a marriage can flourish. If each partner is to go on growing and changing, there must be spaces between their togetherness. When I began to value myself more, being alone, being private, became precious commodities. And the more I respected my need for privacy, the less threatened I felt by my husband's need for equal autonomy and separateness. Now when we go our separate ways we share ambivalent feelings; instead of my being the clinger and he the deserter, we both feel bereft and sad as well as eager and alive to adventure. And when we come back together again, it is with joy and no sense of entrapment.

A significant influence in all our lives is the psychological revolution that started with Sigmund Freud. We discovered new ways of probing into the secret places in the mind and this has greatly diminished our privacy. Before Freud, you could have a cold without snide remarks about repressed hostility! Anger, jealousy, fears, might interfere with growth and cause serious problems, but neither you nor anybody else knew about your unconscious thoughts. Although I think the motives have been compassionate and these insights helpful, a price has been paid.

A friend of mine, a psychologist, was wise enough to pick up on his daughter's clues. He was operating on the theory that she would be a happier person if they probed and analyzed her feelings all the time. She really had a resident therapist rather than a father. One day when she was about 10 years old, she reported a dream in which her father was a jeweler and had a jeweler's magnifying glass in his eye all the time—it wouldn't come off. "It occurred to me," said the father, "that I was probably overdoing a good thing. I decided I'd better let Martha keep some of her thoughts to herself!"

The most recent expressions of the therapeutic effects of disclosure are manifested in family therapy and group encounters, where the method involves families or other kinds of groups revealing their "authentic feelings" to each other. A certain amount of self-revelation can be helpful; we begin to see that we all share common human feelings and are lovable and worthy. But too much exposure makes us feel violated by an intimacy that is not really so authentic after all.

Lewis Mumford, historian, social scientist, and author, recently observed that the more dehumanized we feel, the more frenzied we become in trying to reveal everything. The less we experience genuine love, the more we talk about sex; the less alive we feel, the more we spill our private thoughts to anyone who will listen. The more apathetic and hopeless we feel about control over our destinies, the more we seem to be willing to allow others to rob us of the right to privacy. When we take a good hard look at the issue of privacy we discover that the less we respect the privacy of others, the more we demean ourselves and all human relationships. The privacy of the individual person, which means respect and trust by others, seems to be so basic to mental health that it must be guarded with at least as much concern as the ways in which we share our lives with each other. Privacy and personal dignity seem irrevocably bound up with each other.

To return to Peggy, outraged at having her diary read by her mother, the road to re-establishing a close family relationship lies first of all in her mother apologizing for having invaded Peggy's privacy and promising not to do it again. Then Peggy and her parents need to have a quiet, honest discussion about the anxieties parents naturally feel about some of the hazards of adolescence, and Peggy needs a chance to talk about her need for increasing autonomy. Profound respect for each other's feelings makes trust —and privacy—not only possible but essential.

A Four-Letter Word
for Parents: Wait!

❊ When my daughter was supposed to make the transition from strained to chopped foods according to my timetable, she had another point of view that she made very clear by spitting in my face! By the end of the second day of struggle, I was convinced that she would *never* eat solid foods and would have to be cared for in a nursing home when she grew up. When she was not fully toilet trained by the age of 2½, I knew that my enlightened Spockian methods had failed abysmally and that she would never be able to go to school because she'd still be wearing diapers. My pediatrician assured me, "When Wendy gets married she'll eat regular food and be toilet trained." I was not at all sure I believed him and saw nothing the least bit funny about the situation. But I'm here to tell you he was really a very smart doctor; he turned out to be absolutely right!

Looking back, I cannot recall any crisis that wasn't 75 percent "age-appropriate behavior." There is no doubt that it helped if I behaved with sensitivity and compassion and that it hindered growth when I behaved hysterically and stupidly—but really and truly, a lot of it was just a matter of *learning to wait*, having faith in my daughter's innate capacity for growing and changing.

When I was a young mother, Dr. Arnold Gesell and his Child Study Institute at Yale had a great impact. Certain kinds of behavior were to be expected at each stage of growth and Dr. Gesell offered parents very specific developmental charts for each age level. For many anxious parents this was not as reassuring as Dr. Gesell hoped it would be. Whenever our children deviated by one month's difference from "the norm," we were ready to kill ourselves. And if by some lucky break our child was ahead of the Gesell "ages and stages," we were so insufferable in our superiority that we alienated all of our friends.

In general I am uncomfortable with rigid ideas about what to expect of children at a certain moment in their development. When we become preoccupied with that approach, children get locked into inflexible expectations that don't allow room for the wide range of normal differences in development. One has to keep one's sense of humor and take all the labels with a grain of salt. But having said that, I must also add, in all honesty, that while there may be broad differences in the timing of events, sooner or later most children do have similar growth experiences that tend to fall into a natural sequence and occur within an approximate range of months or years.

A mother came up to speak to me at the end of a lecture. Looking very agitated and unhappy she said, "I'm sure you're tired and I hate to bother you, but I'm desperate. . . ." Before she could go any further I said half jokingly, "You don't have to say another word; I can tell by your face that you have a thirteen-year-old daughter!" She looked at me as if I were a witch; I had hit it exactly. I wasn't using any psychic powers. My reaction was part instinct, part experience. I knew that look! I had seen it in the mirror and on the faces of hundreds of parents. Just recalling my own experience right now, I can feel my daughter's eyes—that death ray look she gave me. I begin to shrivel inside—and then feel a wave of relief when I remind myself that she only hated me for three or four years and that now she is a woman and my very best friend!

I assured the poor woman that I knew exactly how she felt. "*Wait, wait,*" I told her, "it gets better again." Of course it isn't quite that simple. We also spent some time discussing the agonies of adolescence and a child's need to express some hostility toward his parents as he moves toward the independence and autonomy of adulthood. I reassured her that a child who has the courage to rebel must feel loved a lot or he couldn't take such a risk. It helps a great deal to bring insight and sensitivity to any situation with children—but patience is still an essential ingredient in parenthood.

One thing is certain: No child can have perspective about growth. His past is too short, the future too dim—all he can cope with is the moment at hand. It is natural for a child to become panic stricken about his behavior. He can't understand it in the context of his total development and needs our help in gaining some perspective, not our confirmation that all is lost.

When a 2-year-old bites, he needs to be stopped—but also assured that he is little and will soon stop doing this because he is learning better ways to solve problems. When a 6-year-old steals some crayons from school he needs help in returning them, but he also needs to be assured that he is not heading for a life of crime —he just isn't old enough to control some impulses without adult help. And when a teenager cuts us to the quick by saying that if we show up at the PTA meeting, she will *never* be able to show her face again in that school—and we see remorse and guilt on her face for what she has said—we need to be reassuring. We will not faint dead away at this blow to our ego if we see it as an expression of adolescent anxiety—the awful need to be like everyone else and not encumbered in that goal by a mother who is not a size eight and dressed by Yves St. Laurent.

Not only do we need to learn the value of the word *wait*, we also have to help our children understand it. The world will not come to an end because there is no date for this year's prom; one does usually outgrow painful shyness; life may be worth living even if one has failed a math test; every grown-up once had a closest friend who betrayed a confidence. Most especially children need to understand that what they do is not "bad" or "dumb" but mostly just being "young," part of a perfectly appropriate stage to be growing through.

Waiting does not necessarily imply being inactive or passive. It is not in any sense a withdrawal from participating in a child's growth. What I mean by waiting is a philosophical awareness of the necessary and natural processes of growth; the capacity not to get hysterical worrying that a child will get stuck in some stage of development and never move on. It has been my experience that when a child does seem to remain at a particular level of development for an abnormally long time, or regresses to an earlier stage left behind, sooner or later we find some anxious and pushing parents in the woodpile.

Looking back, these are some examples of common "moments of truth" when I and legions of other parents seem to get most panicky. (And for those of you who are there right now, I am here to tell you, we all survived!)

Whenever my daughter screamed—and sometimes she did so for hours on end—I knew beyond a shadow of doubt that for the rest of my natural life I would never get a night's sleep; that although it was invisible to the naked eye, my child was attached to me by an iron chain from which I would never escape. I tried, sometimes, to let her cry it out on the very dumb principle that I didn't want her to "develop the habit of crying." That was sheer nonsense, and I have periodic waves of guilt because *wait* was not yet in my vocabulary. Babies stop that kind of incessant crying when they are old enough to figure out that the dark room in which they lie is not lost in space; that there are other rooms in the house and that people do not disappear, never to return; that if you are hungry and wet—or even just lonesome—someone *will* come— this misery is not forever. It takes about a year and a half for even the smartest kid to figure that out. He will figure it out whether you comfort him or ignore him; the only difference is whether or not he reaches this knowledge feeling loved and understood or rejected and terrified.

Just as we begin to recover from those feelings of being forever imprisoned by a howling infant who can't tell us what's wrong, all sorts of new challenges arise. For example, the baby who guzzled his bottles as if gluttony was going out of style, turns into a little boy who hates everything except the things he can't have, like hot dogs and soda. He picks at his food, and if you insist, he puts it in his mouth and leaves it there, like a wad of tobacco—for days at a time! "My child barely eats a thing," mothers will tell me, as I look into my crystal ball and tell them, "And at seven that means he'll eat you out of house and home." My predictions tend to be accurate simply because I've known so many children! The growth spurt of the first two years slows down almost to a halt for a while; somewhere around 3 to 5 years of age, appetite seems naturally to decrease. If we allow it and don't decide that food is a good grounds for warfare, it all comes out all right. Letting a child eat small amounts of food many times a day, not at three large meals; letting a child serve himself small portions; letting a child help prepare what he likes; being ingenious enough to figure out that some nuts and raisins and half a banana consumed while watching television may be just as nutritious as a long drawn-out meal with adults before a child can enjoy eating at the table; not keeping junk foods in the house; and not getting excited and worried, all lead to a happy ending. Suddenly that 6- or 7-year-old seems to develop a hollow leg and is hungry all the time.

When I reassured other parents, I was usually sensible and dispassionate. I could not always carry this out at home, and what frightened me most during the pre-school years was the development of fears and phobias that brought a new version of sleepless nights. When my daughter was about 4, having learned nothing, apparently from other earlier phases, I was sure once again that I would never sleep a whole night through. I was mortified; she was scared of everything; she was having nightmares; I was a failure.

As I have grown older and wiser, I have realized that never in all my experience in working with parents and children have I ever heard of a child who *didn't* develop some fears during these years. Fear of loud noises, fear of wild animals, fear of the vacuum cleaner, fear of thunder are some of the popular varieties. What they all represent to some degree at least are the ways in which the unconscious mind helps a child work through his or her feelings about discovering what it means to be a human being; to be both angelic and devilish; to feel love and hate; to accommodate to anger, rivalry, shyness, frustration, etc. Everybody thinks it's wonderful when a child is sweet and lovable, gentle and charming. But grown-ups can turn on you with a vengeance when you are sassy, impatient, mean, or mad. What shall you do with all those mixed-up feelings inside? When you are very young there seems to be only one answer: Get them on the *outside*—push them away. It isn't Daddy's yelling that scares you—it's the thunder. It isn't your own murderous impulses toward the baby—it's a tiger loose from the zoo and invading your dreams. You aren't the one who is so shy that your mother is ashamed of you—it's that shadow on the ceiling that scares you.

With a little bit of luck and a lot of help, children learn to accept all human feelings. They learn which feelings can be expressed (like hugging and kissing) and which ones may be *experienced* inside— not repressed—but not acted out (like wanting to drown the baby). All children will learn about feelings. Some *will* repress their anxiety and guilt because parents get so frightened and angry that they tell children they are bad, and punish them severely. Such repression may lead to later difficulties. Some will find ways to express their feelings that are not dangerous to others and to control those that are dangerous—but without being paralyzed by guilt. *How we wait* certainly makes a difference. But even when we are trying to be most understanding—and even succeeding some of the time— there is still that gnawing feeling that this will never end. It does.

Even as I write the words "school-age," a vision dances in my head and it certainly isn't sugar plums! It is my daughter's room, reminding me of the London Blitz. In the top drawer of her dresser there is a collection of rocks in among her clean underwear. Under the sweaters in the next drawer I know I will find one desiccated frog, one pack of contraband cigarettes, and three of my most expensive lipsticks. And finally, in the third drawer will be whole plates of left-over food—sometimes left for as long as two weeks before the stench gets to me.

I recall with discomforting vividness that I was absolutely sure that my child would grow up to be a Bowery bum. Also a pyromaniac because she secretly fooled around with matches, a robber because she occasionally took money from my desk drawer, and a pathological liar because she always denied everything. When she grew up and I visited her, she wanted to wash the coffee cup before I'd even finished, she yelled at anyone who messed up her kitchen, she knows how to build a fire in a wood stove to keep warm, she hardly ever spends money on herself, and I trust her veracity completely. Seventy-five percent of this is due to growing up. I like to think her father and I contributed 25 percent to this metamorphosis, but I can't swear to it.

At the point a child reaches adolescence, I think I began to believe that a child really does grow up; what bothered me was whether or not *I* would ever recover. I was convinced that I was the worst mother on the planet earth; I understood nothing; my demands were only surpassed (maybe) in viciousness by Adolf Hitler; furthermore, I wore terrible clothes and looked so awful that it would cause panic in the streets if I were to appear in public. I was prehistoric in my attitudes about dating, and my interest in such matters as learning to read and passing from one grade to another marked me as the reincarnation of Cotton Mather. My self-image was not what you might call at an optimum level.

As for my poor daughter, I was sure she was permanently suicidal, psychopathic, manic, catatonic, hostile, lazy, and rude. Fortunately most of her closest friends were even worse. If anybody had told me (I told myself but didn't really believe it) that those shaggy, mute characters who crossed my threshhold would someday be witty, kind, articulate, sensitive, supportive, and loving, I would have assumed that they were in even worse shape than I was. Looking back, I know that crazy, mixed-up hormones had a lot to do with what was going on with those young people—to say nothing of the storm and stress of having to work at the agonizing task of moving from childhood to adulthood in a few short years, in a social climate of change, instability, uncertainty, and unrest. But that's what it really was all about. It was important that I kept trying to understand, to grow in awareness and compassion, to keep up the struggle for better communication—but also, I just had to *wait.*

These days my sleep is untroubled by a crying infant or a frightened child. My days are spent in the calm serenity of a well-ordered home. The dirt is gone, so is the yelling and the calls to come see the school guidance counselor—with the accompanying terror that I was doing everything wrong. The quiet is palpable—and unsettling. And do you know whom I enjoy now? My daughter, who is living through it all with my grandchild! I think I have matured considerably and I now have a profound respect for nature's timetable. I hope I'll be able to pass some of this wisdom on to my daughter, but I know perfectly well that she will experience some of the same feelings of anxiety and impatience. It is hard to have faith in the miracle of growth when so much is at stake. I know I will repeat that four-letter word many times—the magical *"Wait!"*

Secrets: How Much to Tell a Child

❋ The staff at the nursery school had been quite worried about Laurie for several weeks. She seemed pale, withdrawn, and uncharacteristically touchy, so we asked her mother to come in for a conference. We discovered that Laurie's parents were in the midst of a bitter and frightening divorce. Laurie's father had deserted his wife and daughter, but his parents were trying to get custody of Laurie. When I asked what Laurie had been told, her mother looked at me blankly. "I haven't told her anything," she said. "She's much too young to understand." It was perfectly clear to us, however, that Laurie did understand that *something terrible* was going on—and because she was 4 years old and had been given no other information, she probably thought it was her fault.

At the other extreme is a young woman whose mother had marital difficulties that she told her daughter about as she was growing up. "There are things about my father," she told me, "that I wish I hadn't known—that I have to live with all my life. It wasn't fair of my mother to burden me with his infidelities!"

Deciding how much to tell a child about the painful realities of life is one of the hardest decisions parents must make. Too much truth too early may, indeed, be overwhelming. On the other hand, a known reality may be less frightening and painful than what a child may imagine.

Although it's impossible to make hard and fast rules, certain guidelines can be helpful in deciding what to tell or not tell a child about those difficult subjects that are bound to arise.

A child's hospitalization is apt to be his first experience with a serious and frightening reality, but if he's given some reassuring information, he can usually mobilize his own resources to meet the challenge. If you tell a child nothing about a tonsillectomy, for instance, his natural pain and discomfort will be increased by shock and a sense of utter betrayal by the people he needs and loves most. If, on the other hand, he has visited the hospital and been told just where he'll be, who will be with him, and why the operation is necessary, he'll be able to get through the experience without severe emotional wounds.

Children need to know what is going to happen to them so they won't imagine something much worse. I once heard a 4-year-old dash onto a playground three weeks after a hernia operation, and shout gleefully to his playmates, "I had an operation—but I'm still a boy!" By telling him too little about a frightening procedure, his parents let him tell himself too much.

Play is a young child's best preparation for an upsetting event. A mother whose 6-year-old daughter had to have an emergency appendectomy told me how they played on the way to the hospital in the ambulance. Mother pretended to be a little girl alone at night in the hospital, feeling awful and missing her mommy. Her daughter played the part of a nurse. "I felt sure Karen would be all right," she explained, "when she patted my face and said, 'It's all right; don't worry. Your mommy will be back in the morning. Soon your stomach won't hurt anymore.' By playing the part of the nurse, she provided her own reassurance."

You might tell a 10-year-old two weeks ahead of time, and a 5-year-old only a few days before the event. If the child becomes frightened and protests, you can say, "Of course you're scared. I know how you feel, but it must be done—and it will be all over in a couple of days." The child who cries and protests is responding normally. This is far better, in the long run, than skipping happily down the hospital halls with a balloon in each hand only to emerge two days later trusting no one, too weak to cry, and burdened with nightmares for the next three months.

Above all, it's important to let a child experience his real feelings. Don't tell a young child, "You're too big to be such a baby," or "Only babies cry." It just isn't true! If you are scared or hurting, you *do* need to cry and protest. Some years ago my daughter needed stitches in a badly cut hand. When the nurse said, "Now, there's nothing to cry about—you're a big girl," our pediatrician interrupted sharply. "Don't tell Wendy that," he said. "She's scared and can cry all she wants to." When I expressed my appreciation, he told me, "I learned my lesson when I was an intern. I told a little boy not to cry and he threw up all over me! I realized that nature is wiser than I—that tears do serve a purpose."

Do children need to know if a brother has leukemia or a grandfather is about to die of heart disease? Each family has to make its own decisions, but children ought to feel that their questions will be answered. Even if they are not told all the facts, they should understand why everyone is so sad and worried. Children need to feel that everything possible is being done to help and that there is always hope. Most of all, they need to be assured that they are not responsible for what is happening.

One mother described her young son's reaction when his sister had to have open-heart surgery. "Jerry began failing at school and crying over the slightest thing," she said. "One day I just blurted out, 'Darling, all brothers and sisters fight and get mad at each other. That had nothing to do with what happened to Annie. She was born with a damaged heart.' I've never seen such a look of relief on anyone's face!"

When a parent is seriously ill, children are likely to see it as a desertion; it arouses fears that they might be left alone. They need reassurance that they are deeply loved, that the illness is not a rejection, and that they will always be cared for by the many, many people who cherish them.

We are the only creatures who ever reflect on our own mortality, and it's terribly hard for us to allow this knowledge into the lives of our children when they are so young and vulnerable. Perhaps the thing that is most comforting to us as parents is the fact that not being told can be far more devastating to a child.

My own mother's mother died when she was four and for a full year every time she asked for her mother, she was told, "Mommy's away on a visit." She finally heard the truth from children on the street. "I know I have been maimed and scarred by that all my life," she said. "All I knew was that the person I loved most in the world had just left me, and I was sure it was because I had been a naughty girl and she'd stopped loving me."

The mother of a 6-year-old gave birth to a premature baby who lived for only two days and was cremated. She told her son that the baby was not strong enough to live, but when Steve asked where the baby was now, she was evasive. "I'll tell you more about it when you're bigger," she said. Steve became very apprehensive; he would not go into a room alone or open a closet or a dresser drawer. He began to cry before school, and when his parents insisted he had to go, he threw up.

When the mother asked me for help, I suggested telling Steve what happened to the baby. She was horrified. "How can you tell a child a baby was *burned up?* He'd never get over it!" But when Steve began to have nightmares and refused to leave the house, she relented. Passing by a cemetery in the car one day, Steve's father explained, as gently as possible, what happens when a person dies. "Sometimes the body is buried in the ground," he said, "and sometimes it's cremated, which means burned in a fire."

Very casually, Steve asked, "Where's the baby?" When he was told it had been cremated, a look of tremendous relief spread across his face. "You mean it's *not* in the *house?*" he asked. Because everyone was so reluctant to tell him anything, Steve had decided that the baby was hidden in the house and that he might find it by accident. Cremation was a far less terrifying idea.

When talking to young children about death, it is important to remember that they think very concretely. Abstract ideas are just too difficult. For a young child, memories of the person who died are likely to give the deepest sense of ongoingness. "Grandma can't come back, but we will never forget how she loved to hold you, and those wonderful cookies she baked." Or, "We can't ever see Rover again, but we have pictures to remind us of how much we loved him. Remember the one of him as a puppy riding in your carriage?"

It is natural to want to protect children from suffering, but it is also impossible. Suffering is a part of life, and what children need most is help in dealing with tragedy. They learn from us. If we hide our tears, they cannot cry; if we put on a brave front, there is no place for them to take their sadness. I know one mother who tried to protect her two little girls from her grief when her husband died. To keep them from seeing her suffering, she left them with an aunt and went away for a month. When she came home and held her arms out, they both ran away. She had deserted them when they needed her most—when they needed her help to live through their own mourning.

It's important to be honest with children about your grief, to draw them close so you can comfort each other. Children also have the right to mourn in their own way. A father told me about the overwhelming grief he felt at the age of eight when his own father died. "On the day of the funeral," he said, "I wanted to do something that would have pleased my father. I was very clumsy with tools, and he was impatient and disappointed in me because he loved to work in the shop he'd built in the basement. I decided that to please him I would build something—and do it very well. My mother heard me hammering and came to the head of the basement stairs with a look of shock and horror on her face. I will never forget what she said: 'What kind of monster are you to play on a day like this? Have you no feelings for your father?'"

When my daughter was about 4, my grandmother died and I took Wendy to the funeral. An aunt was horrified that I'd expose such a young child to death. She had left her two little boys at home. I wept during the service, and Wendy climbed into my lap and hugged and kissed me. When she questioned her great-grandmother's whereabouts, I answered truthfully. "I'm terribly sad," I said. "I loved her very much, and I'm missing her." Wendy was somber, but when we got home she ate her supper and went to bed peacefully.

My aunt called the next morning. "I apologize for all the awful things I was thinking about you," she said. "I've been up all night with Ben and Jim—they had terrible nightmares. At three o'clock in the morning, we gave them cookies and milk and told them exactly what had happened at the funeral. We all had a good long cry for Grandma, and then they went to sleep."

A child's natural tendency to feel responsible for the bad things that happen comes into full bloom when his parents fight or separate. From Sarah's vantage point it seems obvious that if she hadn't lied about taking the money, her parents wouldn't have had that fight. Jim is convinced that if had only been less talkative, his father couldn't have left him or his mother. These, of course, are irrelevant and need to be clarified as such to the child. Parental arguments can be endured by most children, but shrieking and yelling between parents in cruel and crude language is not helpful in any way. Sometimes you may have to say to a child, "I know you're worried because I was crying this morning. Daddy and I had an argument and I was feeling angry and sad. That happens sometimes when you're married, but it has nothing to do with you."

When the rift is serious and parents decide to separate, it's essential for a child to know that his parents have tried hard, still love him, and will make sure he's always cared for. Unfortunately some parents, caught up in their own unhappiness and bitterness, provide too much truth, forcing the child into the position of arbitrator or judge. It is one thing to say, "Daddy is a sick person. I'm sorry for him, but I just can't help him," and quite another to say, "Your father is a liar and a cheat."

At one time alcoholic aunts and mentally ill uncles were never talked about. Today's children see and hear just about everything that's going on, however, and can probably tell you the best place for treatment of these ills. How much to tell depends partly on the child's capacity to refrain from discussing the matter with everyone on the block; on his ability to understand that it's a sad and private family matter. Children, who experience so many complicated feelings and fantasies themselves, can understand that grown-ups sometimes become mentally disturbed. They need to know that nobody else is responsible, that the sick person needs love and understanding, and that a cure is possible.

Almost every family experiences some anxious weeks when a parent is out of a job or a serious financial crisis arises for some other reason. And whether the children are 3 or 13, you can assume they know that *something* is making Dad so withdrawn and causing Mom to lose her temper every five minutes. The facts will probably come as a relief. They don't need all the facts about the perilously low bank balance, but they should be told that it's a difficult time and you *are* worried. Reassure them that with friends and relatives to help you'll always have what you need . . . and things will improve.

Children feel better about almost any situation if they can *do* something. In times of crisis we all need to reaffirm our competence—to know that we have the strength to surmount the problem. If Daddy's out of work, the children can take over the chores that used to be done by the once-a-week cleaning lady; they can take a cut in their allowance, or, if they are old enough, earn their own spending money. "It may sound crazy," one mother told me, "but in a way an unemployed parent can be good for a family! You're all pulling together and you realize how much you care about each other."

Obviously some facts ought to be withheld, if possible, because they are confusing or needlessly painful. If Mother has an abortion, it is enough to explain that it's a minor operation. If Grandpa dies leaving all of his money to an unknown paramour, it is enough to say that he left it to charity. It is always wise to be protective of a child's feelings, but it's important to tell him at least enough to keep him from manufacturing serious distortions that are more painful than the truth.

At times it is quite appropriate to say to a child, "I've really told you as much as I think you can understand right now; as you get older, we'll talk about it some more." This comes up especially in relation to information about sex; the facts may have little meaning or be utterly confusing to a child who is too young to understand what it's all about. I was once practice-teaching in the kindergarten class of an elderly teacher who was determined to prove how modern she was. She had just explained to the class that Mama and Papa Rabbit had become an expectant family—and how they got that way—when I overheard one child say to another, "I know *what* they do, and I know *when* they do it, but I don't know *why* they do it."

One way to avoid confusion is to be sure you know what the child is asking before you offer more information than he wants. When one youngster asked how babies live in the womb, his mother told him to ask his father, a doctor. "He knows too much," the child replied. "Just tell me what *you* know."

When a child asks a question, it never hurts to say, "Tell me a little more about what you mean." One mother was going out of her mind because her 6-year-old daughter kept asking, "But where were the egg and the sperm before?" Finally, the mother asked, "Can you tell me why you want to know?" and her daughter replied, "Because I want to know where I was before I was me!" This is a philosophical question that could never be satisfied by a biological explanation!

It's important to interpret the facts in the context of larger ideas and feelings. You're trying to teach family and human relations, not a course in gynecology. Along with the facts, you should communicate the idea that this whole subject is involved with the way people love each other—that it is, at its best, a private matter between people who care very deeply for each other.

Few situations confuse parents more than telling a child he is adopted. For a long time now, adoptive parents have been told by the most authoritative social agencies that a child's feelings about adoption depend on how his parents feel about him and on the manner in which he is told. When a child feels loved and wanted, they say, and when the adoption has been accepted by his parents, his attitudes will, ipso facto, be healthy and happy.

I think this is a great oversimplification. The excessive number of adopted children being seen at child guidance clinics does not suggest to me that adoptive parents are more neurotic and destructive than natural parents but that the fact of adoption itself can have painful consequences—no matter how good the climate of the home. Children *must* be told that they are adopted since they will almost certainly find out anyway. But I think it would be wiser and more realistic to assume that it will be a painful and difficult reality for most children.

The crucial problem, it seems to me, is that no matter what you say about the biological parents, a young child simply cannot imagine any circumstances under which a parent could give a baby away —unless there was something terribly wrong with it. One mother told me that her adopted son had been a beautiful, sweet, nearly perfect baby. "He was adored by all his relatives," she said, "and had been told that over and over again. Yet suddenly, at the age of seven, he turned with a sad look and said, 'What was the matter with me that they gave me away?' "

Adopted children are delighted with the first stories of being found; that's the wonderful part of it. But by the age of 5 or 6 or 7, the anxieties begin to surface. Before being found they were abandoned, and no explanation makes sense to most children under the age of 12 or 13. As a matter of fact, the happier the adoptive home, the more impossible it seems that anybody could give a baby away.

The relief felt by many adopted adolescents when they find out about unwed mothers is testament to earlier doubts and worries. Many teenagers with complex hangups about being adopted become far more comfortable when they discover that a couple of kids, just like those they know, got into trouble and had to give the baby up because they couldn't take care of it. Thank God, it was something as simple and understandable as *that!*

Although a clear explanation of adoption, given with love, is far better than letting a child find out from a mean cousin or snoopy neighbor, I believe you should go easy on such information when the child is younger than 5 or 6. Questions should be answered briefly—nothing hidden, nothing stressed. This gives a child the chance to establish himself as a worthy and lovable human being before he tries to handle the idea of abandonment.

In giving more information when the child is of school age, it seems to me that parents have to accept the fact that this is likely to cause some emotional disturbance—especially in those who tend to be more volatile and sensitive—and that there is little they can do about it except to reassure their child that he is thoroughly loved and lovable. You might say, "Right now you can't think of any reason why anybody could give up a darling baby; nobody you know could do it. But when you are older you will understand that even grown-ups get into very serious trouble and have problems that make such things necessary. I just want you to believe one thing: It had nothing to do with you; you were a wonderful baby in every way."

As with so many other truths, this may cause a child to suffer somewhat. But our job as parents is to help our children live with all that it means to be human, not to avoid it or escape from it.

The powerful impact of the mass media makes it impossible to keep children from hearing about war, poverty, hunger, racial hatred, and the ever-present danger of an atomic holocaust. In fact, one recent study indicated that grade-school children may be more preoccupied than their parents with the dangers of water and air pollution (a sad commentary, indeed). These issues are so complicated and controversial that some experts suggest you avoid discussing them with children as much as possible, especially if you hold a minority position. It seems to me that this is a serious mistake.

By the time a child is 4 or 5, he is well aware of human imperfection. He experiences it every day of his life. He needs help in living with this fact of life—accepting it and doing what he can about it along with the rest of us. Children need to develop a strong sense of values, and we are obligated to pass ours along as a frame of reference—keeping in mind, of course, that children have the right to go beyond us just as we have gone beyond what our parents believed to be right and wrong. Children need not be devastated by hearing about seemingly endless and meaningless wars, and starvation of children in many parts of the world if—and this is a profoundly important—they feel we and they can do something to make things better.

I cannot imagine anything more beneficial to mental health than having all children, from 3 on up, feel that they play some part in improving the lives of others. This doesn't mean burdening little children with impossible problems or making them feel responsible for the suffering of others. Rather, it means that a 3-year-old can help you bake a cake for the sale that will raise money for African children; that a 6-year-old can have a lemonade stand to raise money to send city children to summer camps; that a 10-year-old can be encouraged to write to the President about something that bothers him with the understanding that this is a serious part of citizenship. It also means recognizing the hunger for peace and decency among high school and college students, and working with them to bring about the changes that are necessary.

What shall we tell the children? The truth as we see it, acknowledging that most truths have many facets. The truth in limited doses, protecting them only from what they cannot understand or have no right to know.

We must allow our children to suffer, to feel pain—and to exult in their strength in overcoming it. Whatever is tragic in life has a counterpart that is poignantly beautiful. To mourn the dead is also to affirm life; to accept defeat is also to hope for a new beginning; to face the terrors of the human experience is also to stand in awe of its wonders. When we share this with our children, we prepare them for life.

Do Kids Whose Mothers Work Get Shortchanged?

❋ Andy's mother came to the nursery school conference ready to turn in her attaché case because Andy was having nightmares. It was with considerable relief that she found the *real* reason for the nightmares: Andy was 4 years old! The children in his class whose mothers stayed home *also* had nightmares.

Most of the problems encountered by working mothers are more related to guilt than reality. In spite of all the dramatic social changes that have taken place during this past century, some things remain the same. There have always been working mothers and they have always felt guilty.

Children are never adversely affected by any one factor in their daily lives. Not by being the middle child (or the oldest or the youngest), not by being tall or short (or fat or thin), and not by having a working mother. What adversely affects children is a lack of unconditional love and the pressure of impossible expectations.

Mothers who stay at home and hate it; mothers who are so busy cleaning they never have time to play; mothers who hover too much—these can adversely affect a child's development. Most of all, mothers—at the desk or at the sink—who wish they'd never had kids are the ones who make a mess of parenting. Guilt is appropriate when we deliberately set out to hurt someone, not when we try to accommodate the needs of everyone in a family.

Because stay-home mothers go shopping, play tennis, work hard as volunteers for community services, meet friends for lunch, they are seldom available at the moment their children need them. Working mothers are often easier to reach in an emergency.

Honesty with children is the best policy under all circumstances. There are usually several reasons why mothers work: economic necessity; a wish for extra comforts; dislike of housework; the desire to use one's talents and training; and, most important of all, personal fulfillment and pleasure. There is no reason to withhold any of these reasons from a child. It's all in the way you tell it. Financial necessity doesn't call for such comments as "We'll starve to death if Mother doesn't work." Something more positive would be better: "Mothers want to take care of their children."

There is nothing wrong with admitting that a job is pleasurable. This frees children to set worthy goals for themselves and encourages them to find their own fulfillment, to sing their special song in the world. The best role model is a mother who is glad to be alive. Working mothers don't have to do any more to make their children proud of them than mothers who stay at home. Children become proud entirely on their own if Mom happens to be an interesting, lovable, compassionate person who brings meaning to her life by caring about others as well as herself.

Mothers who make a big deal out of the special luxuries bestowed by the job, such as camp, private school, or piano lessons, are assuaging their guilt, not helping their children to accept their work. The main point is that there is no need to be apologetic.

Some mothers hate their jobs. Children can understand and sympathize with the fact that some realities are unpleasant—they know all about that! Like giving up the bottle or having to sit at a desk when they'd rather be out playing. Sharing frustrations is fine. It just should not be overdone.

It's wonderful if a kind and understanding boss lets you go home to feed a sick kid some chicken soup; it's wonderful if your hours can be flexible to match a school schedule. It's wonderful to have a great support system. But reality isn't always like that, and it doesn't really matter so long as children feel reassured; that's a feeling, not an action.

Women who work solely for the pleasure of using their talents and fulfilling their deepest needs have always experienced the most conflict, not because they are any different from other mothers who work but because they can weigh the benefits of their work against any possible damage to themselves or their families.

Some young women growing up in the shadow of the women's movement have developed a seething ambition—a kind of hysterical compulsion—to be successful, to "make it." Whereas their mothers and grandmothers might have felt like second-class citizens if they couldn't sew or cook, many of today's young women feel second-class if they don't have fantastic careers. Ellen is a young woman who took to the women's movement like a duck to water. Her mother fit the stereotype of the trapped homemaker. Always very bright and ambitious, Ellen is now a senior partner in a law firm that represents the underdogs of the world: Third World countries, poor people, and political rebels. When she talks about her clients, she radiates excitement and total dedication. She hardly ever mentions the children she had along the way.

We have come to a time, in this new age of women's rights, when each woman must accept the need to make difficult choices. This takes enormous maturity and responsibility. It also takes a profound sense of perspective and the recognition that there are different stages in life and some things may be more important at one time than at another. A case in point is the woman judge who commented, "I went to law school when Jenny was barely two. I thought I was too intellectual to sit in a sandbox or finger paint. Now that she's grown, I deeply regret missing that childhood I might have shared with her. I wonder why I was in such a rush and wish I had waited until she was older to go back to school."

Another mother, a buyer in a very prestigious department store, took a brief leave of absence when her daughter was born, then hired a governess. When her daughter was 4 years old, she was called in for a conference at the nursery school and told that her child had feelings of unworthiness, that she couldn't imagine that she was lovable when her mother spent hardly any time with her. "I knew all about feelings of rejection. That's probably what made me so ambitious—the need to prove I was somebody," the mother explained. "I gave up working full-time, and I don't feel sorry; I feel relieved. It took a smart little kid to remind me that love is most important. There will be plenty of time for me to work at a more demanding job when my daughter is older."

Another mother, the principal of a grade school, expected to take a short sabbatical when her daughter was born. The child was born with a serious birth defect, and this mother gave up her job entirely. Although she won't deny that she is miserable, she is convinced that for her there was no other course. "When life hands you a terrible blow, you either act like a grown-up or you fall apart," she said. "I hate giving up my work, but I also want to be able to live with myself."

What we need to do is analyze the meaning of the word *self-fulfillment*. It is *not* being selfish or thoughtless or unconcerned about other people's needs. It is the right to be the best human being we can possibly be, using our talents as fully as possible, in the context of our relationships with others. This means spending a good deal of time weighing values, judging the needs of a particular phase of our lives, and including those we love in our planning. If we think the women's movement means that we can have everything, we're dead wrong. What it does mean is that we can choose.

Part III

✽

THE
CRUCIAL
YEARS

✽

Stuffed Animals and Special Blankets Are No Laughing Matter

✻ I slept with a stuffed animal. Nothing very remarkable about that. But the time I'm talking about happened to be when I was 50 years old!

It happened many years ago while I was taping segments of a television program, "How Do Your Children Grow?" in San Francisco. In the midst of a busy schedule, I got word that my mother had died suddenly in New York. I flew home for the funeral but could only stay with my family for three days before returning to California. I was extraordinarily close to my mother, and the shock of her death, coupled with the agony of having to leave my family at a time of mourning, left me profoundly shaken. But there seemed to be no choice. My mother had been terribly proud of my television program, and I knew she would have had a fit if someone else had shown up on the screen for four of the segments.

During the three weeks I had to stay in California, I lived in a state of limbo—wanting desperately to be home, feeling unable to deal with my grief 3,000 miles away from my family. I had led a lucky and protected life, so the irreversibility of death was new to me—and a staggering shock. I wanted so much to see my mother —at least once more—to say good-bye. I wanted to hug her and tell her how I'd loved her, how deeply I had understood her pain, her terror of dying; how much I admired her zest for life. The idea that she could never hold or comfort me again was unbearable.

One day, in an effort to find distractions, I went shopping. Seeing a toy store, I decided to buy a gift for a grand-niece I would soon be meeting for the first time. Nothing suited me until I spotted a stuffed gray baby seal with large brown eyes. It was love at first sight. When my daughter was 3 or 4 years old, my husband made up a story about Furry, a seal who didn't want to learn to swim until he was good and ready. The character my husband had created was adorable—and there he was, just as I'd imagined him.

When I got back to the hotel I unwrapped Furry and put him on the twin bed next to mine. That night I called my father, as I did every night. We could hear the pain in each other's voice, but we both felt helpless and unable to comfort each other at such a distance. When I hung up I burst into uncontrollable sobbing. Although emotionally and physically exhausted, I was unable to sleep. At about three o'clock in the morning I turned on the light, thinking I'd read for a while—and there was Furry looking at me with sad, mournful eyes. I burst into tears again—overcome with a feeling of isolation, I was a lost and motherless child with no one to comfort me in my pain. I picked up Furry and, holding him in my arms, began to sing a lullaby my mother used to sing to me when I was sick as a child. Fifty years old, married, with a grown daughter, I cried for my lost mother as if my heart would break.

Some minutes later, when I realized what I was doing, I was shocked and ashamed. But the need was so great that I turned off the light and held on to Furry for dear life. It was wonderful. I felt comforted and slept the rest of the night with Furry in my arms. He was my close companion for several nights until my husband was able to join me and I could have the human comfort I so desperately needed.

This experience has stayed with me. In some profound way it was a turning point in my understanding of childhood and the child always present within myself. One of my first reactions was a feeling of remorse for having failed to understand what stuffed animals meant to my daughter when she was little. Oh, I'd always tolerated them, but I saw them as a crutch—something I had hoped she'd soon outgrow so I could get rid of the dirty, tattered things.

Holding that toy in what I came to think of as my moment of truth, I began to understand what such things mean to our children. Stuffed animals and special blankets are substitutes for human love and warmth. What I learned was that I could not bear to float alone in the universe. I needed bodily contact—touching —when I hurt the most. And it suddenly seemed intolerable and inhuman that we expect and demand that our children sleep alone, with no one to cuddle until they grow up and marry.

I find it shocking to realize how much childrearing practices have changed. Until about seventy-five years ago, most children were nursed for a year or two, then kept physically close to their mothers or other adults until they were 6 or 7 years old. Human nature hasn't changed since then, but social customs have. Studies show that the number of breast-fed babies leaving the hospital dropped from 38 percent in 1946 to about 22 percent in 1970. (Now, fortunately, the figures are beginning to reverse.) However, in the large majority of hospitals, babies still spend their first days of life in a nursery crib, with limited human contact. The cuddling that helps us survive as human beings often seems to be at a premium.

Some months after the episode with Furry, I went with my husband to see a new baby gorilla in the zoo. It was three months old and surprisingly tiny. Mama and Papa were enormous, but the baby looked like a premature human infant. A friendly guard explained that this was nature's way of enabling the baby to cling to its mother's body almost continually for the first year or so. After that, it would grow very rapidly. The baby was so deeply embedded in its mother's body that it wasn't always possible to tell where one began and the other left off. Once in a while it would let go and venture forth for a few minutes with its mother watching every move, but she would soon scoop it up in one palm and place it against her abdomen again.

I watched this symbiotic relationship with a new awareness. It seemed to me that nature had planned a pretty close parallel for human babies, but modern life tends to limit this early closeness between mother and child. In the name of progress, many women are still drugged when their babies are born, separated from them for most of the first few days of life, and expected to continue this isolation by means of cribs and carriages at home.

In recent years, however, there has been an awakening to the dehumanizing aspects of our child-care procedures. More and more couples are seeking natural childbirth as well as prolonged nursing. What has pleased me most—and made me terribly jealous for having missed it—are the wonderful new snugglies that allow a baby to nestle warmly against his mother's or father's body while they shop or travel. Perhaps we are returning to less "civilized" and more natural baby care.

It is significant that so many adults who were handled in the more antiseptic and sophisticated ways when they were babies are turning to new ways of touching, of being close. Whatever misgivings I may sometimes have about some of the flakier or more far-out examples of group encounters, they do reflect a genuine need that has not been met in childhood. I see these as a symptom of our times, a yearning to redress the wrongs of childhood in which we were not held and rocked enough.

Since the demands of modern life may well make it impossible to give young children as much cuddling and closeness as they need, it is surely legitimate to provide soft toys and special blankets as a substitute. But we also need to do some careful thinking about the ways in which we have robbed ourselves and our children of the deep gratification of holding each other. Independence and achievement have become the American way—far too much so and too soon.

What we have called progress and civilization has required us to give up what is instinctive and deeply human in us. Affluence, with its bigger houses and more bedrooms, its focus on getting ahead and acquiring more and more material possessions, has tended to negate the importance of physical mothering and fathering as the most fundamental need of our young.

In the early years of counseling parents of preschool children, I took the basically Freudian view that when children of 3 or 4 cry at night, we ought to go to them in their own rooms and *never* allow them to get into bed with us. I began to question this theory some time ago, as I observed that some young couples seemed quite unselfconscious and relaxed about sharing their bed with a baby. I think we may discover that these children will have no trouble tolerating the necessary separations from their parents when they are older.

Another attitude that kept my generation from doing what came naturally was the fear that our children would develop bad habits. If we "gave in" some of the time, wouldn't the child expect to be picked up, cuddled and held all the time? I now think that this was a needless anxiety. A habit continues only so long as it meets a need. When I no longer needed Furry, I didn't continue to sleep with him out of habit.

If I were a young mother right now, I would try to be a great deal more flexible about allowing my daughter to sleep with me. When she needed it most I would welcome her, at the same time making it clear that there were times when I would want to be alone or with my husband. When she was little and had a night-mare or was afraid of the dark, my husband or I sat in her room until she went to sleep. We were afraid we would encourage too much dependency if we let her sleep with us. What nonsense that seems to me now—and how sorry I am that I didn't get into her bed with her and hold her tight.

We have tried much too hard to think rationally about irrational subjects. We have searched for formulas for raising children in-stead of trusting our animal instincts. It cannot be wrong for us to hold each other when we need it so badly.

Many years ago a friend came to visit me in New York with her 4-year-old son. It had been a long trip and he was tired and cranky. She took a square of faded cloth from her pocketbook and said, "Here's your special blanket to comfort you." As he clung to this small treasure, she rocked him on her lap. As he began to fall asleep, he asked, "Mommy, did I have my special blanket when I was in your uterus?"

Special blankets and stuffed animals somehow make that funda-mental separation between mother and child endurable. They are no substitute for hugging and holding, but they do help provide additional comfort. Before I left San Francisco I went back to the toy store and bought two more Furries, one for my daughter and one for me. My Furry still sits in my bedroom in case I come upon a time again when I feel bereft and alone.

Why Children
Must Pretend

❋ I had the same teacher in both first and second grades. At the beginning of the second year she told us she'd changed her name from Miss Blackburn to Mrs. Finn. She was beautiful and kind and merry, and I adored her. The addition of romance to her life was almost more than I could bear. A few weeks after reporting this exciting news, I told my parents that Mr. Finn had visited us at school. "He's tall and has black hair and a large mustache, and he admired a boat I'm making out of wood," I announced.

I was delirious with joy when my parents invited Mr. and Mrs. Finn for dinner. At one point my mother said, "Eda told us how excited and happy the class was the day you visited, Mr. Finn." He and his wife looked blank, and the subject was quickly dropped. Later, when I was in bed, Mrs. Finn told my parents that she had shown the class a picture of Mr. Finn but he had never visited the school.

I heard that story many times when I was growing up. I knew Mrs. Finn would never lie, yet I can see Mr. Finn in that classroom with more clarity than I can remember most events of my childhood. He was so handsome and had such a smile! In early childhood, *wanting* something to be true can make it more real than any actual happening.

When my own child was young I tried to remember this experience: It is frightening to parents when a child tells a story we know to be quite impossible. We wonder if we're raising a habitual liar, but we needn't worry. Learning the distinction between fantasy and reality is one of the most difficult tasks a young child faces. What, then, can one do about the 4-year-old who comes home from school, a toy go-car stuffed into his pocket that he says the teacher gave him as a present? The most useless and unnecessarily hurtful thing one could say is, "You are lying to me." Such a response presupposes that the child has control over what he has done. A far more helpful comment might be, "I think we'd better check with Mrs. Bateman about that. Maybe you misunderstood —or maybe you just wanted it so badly that you imagined she gave it to you."

Avoiding the use of the word *liar* doesn't imply indifference or irresponsibility; at times we have to set the record straight and redress wrongs. It is *not* all right to take things that don't belong to you; it is *not* all right to report that an older sister hit the baby-sitter when she didn't; it is *not* even all right to make up stories about wild exploits in killing a lion who escaped from the zoo and insisting this is the truth. But if we define this as lying and scold and punish the child, we are unnecessarily damaging his self-esteem as well as losing an opportunity for learning.

What we can do is help children to understand how much our wishes can influence our thoughts. For instance, you might say, "I can imagine how much you wanted Carol's new doll, and I guess you really believed she gave it to you. But that was just a big hope, and we have to take it back." Or after a false baby-sitting report, "Children often get mad at big sisters and want them to get into trouble. I guess you imagined she hit the sitter." In response to a tall tale, "Lots of things are scary when you're little. It makes you feel bigger and stronger to imagine capturing a lion."

Answers like these tell the child we understand that wishes are powerful feelings with a strong effect on the imagination. They also help to define the distinction between those wishes and reality. Most of all, they don't attack the child's sense of himself; they don't suggest that he is bad, only that he is young and needs a chance to learn and grow.

If we insist on an open confrontation, on the other hand, we create unnecessary battle lines. Since children of all ages are struggling for greater freedom and autonomy, the issue of whether or not one is lying becomes a struggle for power. No kid worth his salt gives up without a fight; he just digs himself into a deeper and deeper hole. Nobody ever wins.

The inability to distinguish between fantasy and reality continues until a child is at least 7 or 8 years old, but the problem may remain much longer. When I was about 13, I went to dancing school on Friday nights. It was one of the more horrendous nightmares of my adolescence. Even now, some forty years later, it chills me to remember the panic and desolation of not being chosen for a dance. One night I brought home a big box of candy. I told my parents that one of the handsomest and most popular boys had escorted me home and bought me the candy.

My parents were mystified, but the truth didn't come out until the end of the month when the candy appeared as a charge (by me) on the monthly drugstore bill. My mortification matched my Friday night misery. I knew the difference between fantasy and reality, all right, but emotional needs are sometimes so strong it's impossible to control the impulse to improve on reality. I was not punished for my deception, and my parents' understanding of why I'd done it taught me more than many of the courses I later took in child psychology.

As children mature, they gain greater control over the need to change reality, especially if their life experiences bring greater satisfaction and fulfillment. But that's a big "if." In talking with a group of young ex-convicts about their childhood experiences I was fascinated to discover that when reality is almost beyond endurance a child can become fixated in a world of fantasy. Many of these men and women agreed that fantasy and reality had become so completely fused in their minds that they sometimes had only the vaguest recollection of why they were in prison.

When fantasy becomes almost a total preoccupation, replacing relationships and action in the world of reality, it enslaves. There is no question that under such circumstances, professional help is necessary. But that is only a small part of the story of fantasy in the human experience. It would be very sad—and totally inaccurate—if we were to view fantasy as something a child would hopefully outgrow. It is much more than that. It is the source of the most profound and creative inner nourishment as well.

When I was leading parent discussion groups, few things made me angrier than a parent who came in looking utterly devastated after a teacher had complained that a child was "a daydreamer." Seeing this as a serious indictment, these parents became thoroughly confused when I responded, "How perfectly *marvelous!*" Without daydreamers what a sorry lot we would all be—no music, no art, no science, no love! Before we dismiss the child who daydreams as a candidate for our anxiety and disapproval, it might be helpful to consider some of the positive aspects of fantasy in the human experience:

1. Fantasy helps us get in touch with our real feelings.

As parents, it can help us to understand our children better. A father notices that his son David, aged 7, reports almost daily, at the dinner table, on his exploits in "beating up" somebody on the playground or on his way home from school. A mother notices that whenever the teacher asks the class to write a story, her 11-year-old daughter, Virginia, almost always writes about boys and men who have daring and exciting adventures. It is possible that David feels that because he is really somewhat shy and quiet, he is a disappointment to his father, who wishes for a more aggressive and physical kind of son, and that Virginia has a strong feeling that because she is a girl she can only look forward to doing the things her mother seems to enjoy—cooking and sewing and taking care of babies. In such cases a child's preoccupation with certain kinds of fantasies gives a parent the opportunity to help him or her examine some feelings that may be quite inaccurate. David's father might show more interest in David's enjoyment of mathematics or music; Virginia's mother might make it clear that today girls and women can be adventurers in many areas.

2. Fantasy helps us to acknowledge and accept some feelings that make us feel ashamed and guilty.

"I dreamed last night that you and Daddy both got killed dead, and I was very scared," reports 5-year-old Lynn at breakfast. A day or two later Lynn says, "I got scared at school today. I was drawing a picture and all of a sudden I thought you and Daddy were in a terrible car accident." By the third or fourth such report, a parent might begin to speculate that maybe, just maybe, Lynn is feeling pretty mad about something and is too frightened to face her angry feelings directly. Fantasy has become the safety valve through which she expresses feelings she cannot acknowledge directly. Without practicing psychiatry without a license, it might be appropriate for Lynn's mother or father to say, "Sometimes I wonder if you feel angry at us because we now must spend so much time with the new baby." Chances are that if this kind of anger and jealousy seem acceptable to her parents, Lynn's fantasies of homicide will diminish.

3. Fantasy helps us to survive periods of unavoidable deprivation.

I know of no story that demonstrates this fact more poignantly than the diary of Anne Frank, a youngster who, deprived of the normal life of childhood, dreamed dreams, wrote stories, and developed a rich inner life. She reached heights of human awareness and sensitivity that have inspired millions of people. On a less dramatic scale, all of us experience periods of frustration and pain, and fantasy helps us to endure and continue growing. Jonathan, aged 7, has moved three times in as many years because of his father's job changes. Jonathan daydreams about having wonderful friends as a prelude to facing the task of starting all over in a new school and a new neighborhood. The fantasy makes him feel less lonely and bereft. Sylvia, aged 9, lies in a hospital bed after a hip operation; she daydreams of being at home, eating breakfast with her family, of running or jumping rope with her friends. This inner nourishment helps her to accept the discomfort and isolation of a painful real experience. When we are sad or have problems that seem insurmountable, fantasy gives us hope, keeps us from despair.

4. Fantasy gives us privacy.

We live in a crowded, noisy, hectic world, with constant assaults on our thoughts and feelings. Competition is a fact of life, especially in the lives of our children. The world in which children wandered freely through fields and woods has become a legend in our own time. Even as we help the child who seems lost in fantasy, we also need to try to develop the sensitivity to know when *not* to interfere. Each of us needs some freedom inside our own heads.

For the child who seems to be growing well, who is not cut off from enjoyable activities and relationships, time alone, time to dream one's private dreams, is a vital part of developing the inner resources that make it possible to enjoy being oneself.

Too many parents have little tolerance for a child alone with his thoughts. At the sight of a 10-year-old lying on his bed after school staring at the ceiling, we may say, "Don't just lie there, *do* something!" Or if a teenager is swinging in a hammock lost in thought while we mow the lawn or paint the fence, we wonder loudly how we came to produce such a lazy good-for-nothing. We need to remember that today's children lead lives of frenetic activity most of the time, and they need periods of daydreaming to refill the inner reservoir. Fantasy is also a necessary escape from constant adult supervision and intrusion. The truth is that the most creative and constructive periods in the lives of both adults and children frequently follow the chance to lie fallow for a while.

5. Fantasy is one of the most important ways of learning how to handle reality.

Another vivid memory I have of childhood is sitting up in bed at night pretending to be a grown-up at one of my parents' dinner parties. I was very poised and sophisticated in these conversations, and every once in a while, as an adult attending a party with unusually stimulating and congenial people, I have suddenly had that feeling of déjà vu—I've been here before! In my private games I was practicing for a grown-up life that has really happened.

The dramatic play of young children represents the same sort of preparation for future events. Pretending to be a mommy, a daddy, a doctor, a policeman, or a pilot enables a young child to get the feel of what these adult roles are all about. Playacting also helps a child cope with new situations and relationships. Five-year-old Jill, for instance, is scheduled to go to the hospital for a tonsillectomy in a few days. Playing with her brother and sister, she says, "Larry, you be the doctor. Joanne will be the little girl and I'll be the mommy. The little girl is scared and crying. The mommy says, 'Good-bye, I'll be back tomorrow with some ice cream for you.' The doctor says, 'It's time to go to sleep; when you wake up your throat will hurt a lot.' " By the time the actual event occurs, Jill will have mastered many of the attendant fears and anxieties through fantasy.

It is impossible to prepare for all painful experiences, but dramatic play can help take the sting out of them. When our daughter was about 4 she fell and cut her hand on a rusty can. It was a deep cut that bled badly, and I was very frightened as we rushed her to the crowded hospital emergency room. During the following week when Wendy began having nightmares and became very fearful, we played "hospital" every afternoon. We used hand puppets for the scared child, the hysterical mother, the stupid nurse who kept saying "You're too big to cry," and the harassed doctor who didn't explain anything. Slowly but surely this playacting helped undo the terrors.

6. Fantasy is a necessary ingredient of creativity.

It's certainly important for reality and fantasy to become reasonably distinct in a child's mind, but if that distinction ever became too sharp, human progress would halt. The scientist must dream of the impossible; the artist must help others dream of it; and all lovers prove that the impossible is true! Dreamers are world shakers and world changers.

In a charming and beautiful children's storybook, *The Velveteen Rabbit* by Margery Williams, a stuffed rabbit asks a toy horse how one knows if one is real—has it anything to do with how one is put together? The toy horse replies, "Real isn't how you're made, it's a thing that happens to you. When a child loves you for a long, long time, not just to play with, but *really* loves you, then you become real."

In the final analysis, there's an inescapable and necessary relationship between fantasy and the human capacity for loving—and that's the most important of all human realities.

The Integrity
of Saying "No!"

❈ If you are an average sort of a parent, you were probably insufferably smug and proud when your child first recognized himself in the mirror, but you were ready to bop his smart little head in when, at about 2½, he began to greet even your most cheerful and winsome comments with a loudly resounding "No!" It may very well have seemed that the first event was grounds for celebration, and the second a sign of hard times a-comin', evoking at least faint feelings of dread, if not open fury.

The strange thing about these two stages in growing is not that they are different but that they are the same thing. In their own way each event heralds just about the most exciting and miraculous of wonders: a child's growing awareness of himself as a person.

Becoming a person is what growing up is all about, and much of this process of self-discovery is pleasurable for parents. We are pleased when Johnny says, "Johnny want," and more pleased when he is able to conceptualize himself enough to say, "Me want." When he gets to that dramatic moment of "I want," we exult in his growing.

The trouble is that "I want some carrots" must, by the laws of nature, sooner or later become "I *don't* want any carrots." To be a person is to have ideas, preferences, opinions about things.

It's wonderful to say "Yes!" to life and the world, of course, but when you are very little, all those yesses are to things that someone else is deciding for you. The first "No!" is probably the loudest affirmation a child will ever make, for it is the moment at which the self emerges to say, "I must begin to direct my own life."

While caught in that twilight zone with a child who is drunk with newfound power, it may help a parent to keep his cool if he can recognize the enormous courage it takes for a child to enter the "No!" stage. There you are, cute and small, comfortably living off the fat of the land with most people eating out of your hand if you'll just smile, coo a bit, and let them decide just about everything for you. There is no conflict about whether to wear the blue or the green playsuit; no need to try to plan your day; no major decisions to take under consideration, such as whether or not you like softboiled eggs. Just sitting in the noonday sun with not a care in the world. Then, gradually, there is this strange, recurring feeling that somehow there is more to living than this state of indolence—that somehow you are really supposed to move on. There is, by God, a *YOU* who isn't Mommy or Daddy or Aunt Sue or Grandpa or a sister and who hates the blue pajamas but loves blueberry pie and can go down the slide sideways and wants a fire truck and doesn't like being put to bed ahead of everyone else. It seems to be time to make this all clear to the rest of the world—and in so doing, to oneself. Here is a *person* to be reckoned with.

"Drunk with power" is exactly what happens for a while. That first "No!" almost always causes a reaction of panic, consternation, and a regrouping of armed forces in the household. Mommy's eyes widen and her lips get tight; Daddy's face gets red, and his eyes get that "I'm in the mood to spank" look; the baby-sitter threatens never to come back; and Grandma says, "That doesn't sound like my sweet boy." This business of saying "No!" is pretty heady stuff! For a while it seems that saying "No!" may be all there is to this business of being an "I." But it gets confusing. Mother says, "Darling, do you want another of your favorite cream-filled cupcakes?" and this madman before her shouts "No!" in a tone of voice that suggests that she has just told him to walk the plank. It's "No!" to scrambled eggs and Dr. Seuss and going to the supermarket in addition to all the things he doesn't like. In the confusion and immaturity of its beginnings, saying "No!" and being a person seem to be the same thing.

Of course this isn't so, and this confusion begins to clear up before long if parents don't panic. If a child's saying "No!" about 90 percent of the time really gets you awfully sore, if you feel that there is a moral imperative involved, if you settle for two armed camps who stop trying to communicate with each other, then your adversary, as a matter of pride, must continue to struggle for his autonomy and selfhood in this crude way, without having the time needed to explore other possibilities.

If, on the other hand, a parent can respect the courage it takes to go through one's first identity crisis, and if he or she can treat it with a dash of wit and humor, the child will soon be able to go on to the discovery that selfhood takes a whole lot more than mere negation.

Saying "No!" can become fun and games for everyone. It takes the sting out if Mommy can say "No!" before you do—if she can say, "How about having some tuna fish for lunch, Johnny?" and then answer herself in mimickry: "No, No, No!" Saying "No!" to everything a child says to you sometimes makes the point that there is more to growing up than that silly business. The light touch is what is called for. It gives a child perspective on what he's really up to. My technique was often, "You absolutely cannot, under any circumstances, brush your teeth, and you must *not* go to bed until midnight!" Said with a broad grin, it somehow establishes the reasonableness of parental authority about some matters.

Respecting a child's push toward autonomy also means finding genuine, bona fide ways of showing him that you, too, recognize that he is growing into his own person, with expanding rights and privileges. He can't see that this transition from helpless babyhood to responsible adulthood takes a long, long time and comes gradually, but you can help him to come to this understanding.

"You are not big enough to cross the street alone, but now you *are* big enough to choose cold cereal or bacon and eggs for breakfast." "You aren't old enough to decide when you want to go to sleep, but you *are* big enough now to choose where you want to play in the afternoon—in the park or at Tommy's house." The first

"No!" calls for an immediate awareness that it is time for more legitimate choices, for more opportunities to continue defining who and what this little person is and needs as he stands there so bravely and defiantly, saying, "I *do so* exist!"

The "No" stage becomes a negative one only if we sound a clarion call and make it a battle of wills. It becomes an affirmative stage if we can enjoy and respect that emergence of a new individual whose preferences and feelings must be considered in mutual decision-making. There you stand, trembling with fury, sure that you have lost not only the battle but the war, because Johnny says "No!" to his bath and "No!" to eating his string beans and "No!" to taking his shoes off. At that moment it might help you to keep your perspective—and even enjoy the wonders of Johnny—if you think to yourself, "What are some of the other things I hope he'll say 'No!' to someday?" "No!" to the gang of kids who want to break basement windows on the way home from school; "No!" to the dope peddler; "No!" to getting into a fight; "No!" to the demagogue who may someday want his vote.

You can't end up with someone who has pride, dignity, and good judgment unless you start letting him learn about saying "No!" when he thinks it's the right time to start learning. A person has to *practice* being a person.

A Child Needs Tears
as Well as Laughter

❋ Leslie was 4 and my next-door neighbor at the Jersey shore. She and I had become good friends. We picked flowers and carrots together in my garden and she took them home to her mother every few days. She liked to come in and inspect my house, and she wasn't always pleased with what she saw. She could get a very stern look about her if, at three in the afternoon, she found an unmade bed. She knew I was crazy about her, and the feeling seemed to be mutual, but we had never talked about it.

I walked into her kitchen one morning to say good-bye to Leslie and her family; I was going back to New York for several weeks. Leslie burst into tears on hearing about my departure. Her mother hugged her and said, "Don't be sad, Eda's coming back. I can't bear it when she's unhappy."

Without thinking I blurted out, "I'm *glad* she feels sad. I feel sad, too. We're going to miss each other." A moment later I was sorry I'd said it because I knew that such a response made many people think I was cruel and unfeeling. But Leslie had a very smart mother. She looked surprised for a moment, then thoughtful, and finally said, "You're right; if I don't let her have her sad feelings, she won't be able to have the happy ones either. Crying and laughing are the other side of each other."

Leslie and I hugged and kissed each other and talked for a few minutes about how hard it was to say good-bye. When I left I really felt rotten. I wondered why I'd insisted on going through all this, then I remembered that it was always going on, whether we acknowledged it openly or not, and that was the real issue.

Too often when we ask a child to mask his genuine feelings, we do so in order to reassure ourselves; most of us cannot bear to see an unhappy child. It's a nice, healthy instinct—but it's wrong. I have seen this operate most frequently during the time when I was working as a consultant in a nursery school and supervised the training of teachers. The teachers and I got along very well most of the time, but there were two situations in which the message would come through loud and clear that the teachers wished I'd mind my own business and leave them to their own techniques. One was the separation of a reluctant child from a parent; the other was when a child hurt himself.

According to their system, for example, after perhaps a week of Mama staying all morning, it would then be decided that it was time to ask her to go shopping for an hour. Johnny would begin to wail as soon as this dastardly plot was explained to him, and the kind, softhearted teacher would immediately pick him up and say, "Now, Johnny, there's nothing to cry about." It is certainly a natural and worthy instinct to want to comfort a child in pain, but it seems to me that the price is too high if you do it in this particular way and deny him the right to experience his pain. I would butt in at this point and say, "Of *course* you want to cry, Johnny. And you have a very good reason. You feel scared and sad, and you can cry as much as you want to. If you feel like sitting in my lap while you cry, that would be fine."

Very often children given this message would look at me as if I were crazy. They'd never heard a grown-up talk this way, and it scared them. The wailing would only get louder, and the secret looks of triumph between the teachers shouted loud and clear, "Do you see what you've done? You've made things much worse. So much for fancy theories."

But when I insisted that they reflect on what a child was really experiencing, that was not the end of the story. Johnny might well cry louder for a minute or two, but if I kept on supporting his right to express his pain, sooner or later he would come sit in my lap and quiet down. After sighing deeply and sucking his thumb for a while, some activity would catch his attention and he'd climb down and run off. After a while the teachers began to admit that acknowledged feelings went away sooner and better than feelings that were denied.

We had to go through the same procedure when a child hurt himself. Suzy would scrape her knee badly, and there would be lots of blood and sand to deal with. She'd be howling loudly, while one teacher would be saying, "Think of how you must have hurt that bad old rock," while another would say, "There's nothing to cry about; let's go get a Band-Aid." At this point they would both look despairingly at me, knowing I was about to increase the drama. I tried never to disappoint them, and butting in again, I would say, "Suzy's got a very good reason to cry; it hurts, and it looks very scary with all that blood." And Suzy would look at me as if I were crazy and yell harder than ever. I had the strong feeling that there were at least two adults in that room who wished I'd drop dead!

By the time we would get a chance to meet together, in a teachers' workshop, there tended to be a polite distance between myself and the teachers who had to put up with my interference, so I would start out by saying, "You're mad as hell at me, so let's talk about it." They were surprised at first, then, seeing that I wasn't upset, they would tell me what they were feeling: What was the point of stirring things up? Wasn't it kinder to distract a child and reassure him? Wasn't I encouraging a child to feel much worse than he needed to feel? Wasn't I putting feelings into his head that he hadn't really thought of himself? As we talked it out, it usually became clear that the teachers were not really sorry I had concentrated on their anger at me. Talking things out honestly cleared the air and made it possible for us to understand and like one another better. At one such conference a teacher finally said, "I think I get the point. If a feeling is there, anyway, you might as well let it happen, because then, when it's over, it's really over." And that's exactly the point. Feelings don't go away just because you try to deny them; they stick around much longer than they would if you accepted them, gave them room to breathe, and got done with them.

The most loving thing an adult can do for a child, despite temporary discomfort and pain, is allow him to experience his feelings as fully as possible. Rather than encouraging or fostering more misery, this approach helps to alleviate it.

Not only is it a good idea to allow feelings to be experienced because this deepens our sense of self and allows us to express positive feelings, but in addition, the acknowledging of pain is comforting to a child. In the long run, this acknowledgment allows him to use his inner resources to meet the challenge at hand. We say, "Now be brave. There's nothing to cry about; Dr. Lane isn't going to hurt you at all," and the child howls for half an hour. On the other hand, if we say, "I know you're scared—you'll probably need to cry a little, but then it will be over quickly," we find ourselves in the presence of a two-minute whimper. It isn't stoicism that accounts for the difference—we haven't demanded that—it is that once a feeling has been understood and acknowledged by an adult, a child feels less burdened by it. He can focus more of his energy and attention on dealing with it.

It is perfectly natural to feel sad when someone you care about is going away for a while; it is natural and intelligent to be scared when you get hurt; it shows sensitivity and love not to want your mother to leave you in a strange, new place. What children need from us is permission, even encouragement, to experience their feelings, to recognize and accept them, and to learn that feelings change. It is perfectly true that in many cases you *can* distract a child's attention, you *can* reduce his discomfort—but what have you really accomplished? I think all you have done is made life easier for the adults in the situation. A good example of this is the mother who cannot endure her child's tears when she leaves him with a baby-sitter, so she arranges to make her departure while her child is taking a nap. Not only is she interfering with the normal and necessary "work" of separation, but she may also lose her child's trust.

In recent years, psychologists and psychiatrists, in working with adults, have discovered that tension, irrational fears, medically unexplainable aches and pains often seem to indicate that some people "have a lot of crying to do." As children, most of us were taught, "There's nothing to cry about." That's one reason it's so easy to follow this pattern with our own children. But when we were told that, it wasn't really true; there *was* something we needed to cry about—and unshed tears can go on to plague us in adulthood. One group of psychotherapists have been discovering that a residue of unexpressed feelings may cause severe muscle tension. A friend told me about a professional seminar of psychologists and psychiatrists in which this was demonstrated very dramatically. One of the current theories is that as children, when we were about to start crying our chins would quiver, but when an adult assured us that we had nothing to cry about, we unconsciously controlled our feelings by gritting our teeth and keeping our faces immobilized. At this seminar there was a brilliant and successful psychoanalyst, hard-driving, controlled, somewhat cold in his demeanor toward his colleagues. A psychologist who was discussing the way tension from unacknowledged feelings affects our bodies asked for a volunteer, and the psychoanalyst, who thought the whole thing was pretty silly, volunteered. The treatment started with carefully planned massaging of muscles in many parts of the body. After about fifteen minutes of this process, the doctor's chin began to quiver uncontrollably, and he began to cry. The observer, who told me about this, said, "What happened then is that two great big, sad tears rolled down John's face, and he looked about four years old and as if his heart were breaking. For the first time, I really understood what is meant by the unfinished business of childhood needs that were pushed aside but remain inside us."

As more and more research and experimentation goes on, it becomes evident that most people in our culture—especially men who were taught that it is sissyish to cry—have paid a heavy price for their stoicism, in backaches, fatigue, in keeping themselves aloof from close relationships, and a horde of other neurotic symptoms that limit their growth and fulfillment. This is a terrible price to pay for unshed tears.

Sometimes it isn't that someone tells you to stop expressing your emotions but that they don't help you find outlets for them. I had such an experience as a child when my grandfather died. We had lived in his house when I was quite young, and I was very attached to him. I was 8 when he died, and I was not taken to the funeral because my parents undoubtedly wanted to protect me from this painful side of life. I remember standing at the window of my bedroom, watching the cars and the people go by, and wondering what to do. I felt excluded from the crying relatives in the next room; I was isolated and immobilized in my grief. I could not cry all by myself. More than twenty years later, in the course of my own psychotherapy, we came to the place where Grandpa had been in my life—and I cried for most of the next week. I went into the mourning I had not consciously experienced at the appropriate time of his death.

It is these personal and professional observations that made me respond spontaneously, without thinking, to Leslie's tears and her right to experience them. It was not that I want to encourage children to wallow in unnecessary misery or be exposed to unnecessary pain, only that we respect the feelings that are already there. Separation from someone you love, a bloody knee, the scary injection, the death of a grandparent, the illness or disappearance of a pet—these are painful and sad experiences and we have been learning about the heavy price we pay, as adults, when we leave unlived feelings unacknowledged deep inside us. Every time we say, "Yes, I know you hurt," we are making it possible for a child to finish whatever business is at hand without leaving an inner residue to be dealt with in adulthood or not at all. And we are also deepening the child's capacity to feel *all* of his feelings—joy and exultation as well as sorrow and woe.

One of the things our children can discover when we give them permission to feel their feelings is that feelings change. The day I came back to the shore Leslie was delighted. She raced across to my house and we had cookies and milk and discussed the condition of my rose bushes after a bad storm. She told me that she and her mother needed some carrots, and after we picked some and she was about to run back to her house, I said, "Boy, do I feel happy to see you again!" Leslie turned, looked at me with her mother's wise eyes, and said, "I know exactly what you mean."

The Ten Most Important Things Parents Can Teach a Little Child

✳ It's Peter's first day in kindergarten. He has a fresh haircut and a new red shirt—and looks scared to death. Peter's mother doesn't understand this, for she's sure Peter is as well prepared for school as any 5-year-old could be. "Why," she told Peter's teacher, "he knows the alphabet, counts to one hundred, and can write his name, too!" But as the teacher soon discovered, Peter was *not* ready. He seemed uneasy around the other children and spent most of the day cowering in a corner with his thumb in his mouth.

Michael, who started kindergarten on the same day as Peter, doesn't know nearly as much. He can barely count to ten and confuses many of the letters in the alphabet. But when his mother leaves him, he skips into the room, smiles shyly at the teacher, walks over to a group of children playing with trucks and asks, "Can I be the garage mechanic?" The teacher is delighted by Michael's self-confidence and ease with new children and says to herself, "Now there's a kid who's ready to learn to read and write!"

In the forty years I've been studying preschoolers, I've become increasingly alarmed over the number of parents who think that preparation for school is a matter of memorization and mental skills. It just isn't so. I have nothing against learning these essential skills but I've learned that they're more appropriately taught—and easier to learn—after other important kinds of growing have gotten a good start.

Earlier concentration on academic tasks can also inhibit normal development. We sometimes forget that nature has its own timetable for growth. Trying to teach the average 3-year-old to write is like trying to teach a 3-month-old baby to walk. The damage could be permanent.

If a child enters kindergarten feeling happy, self-confident, optimistic, curious, and friendly, I'm convinced that he will learn. But if he is nervous, frightened, angry, and preoccupied with unmet needs he won't be able to make use of the intellectual stimulation available to him. In my opinion, a child is not really prepared for school—or for life—until he learns the following ten skills:

1. To Love Himself

Self-love is the most pervasive and essential of all skills. Unless you have the capacity to cherish your own life, you can never become deeply alive—or even fulfill your own capacities. It is the first lesson we learn from the moment we are born, and we learn it from the way we're treated by the first people who care for us.

In view of how much we love our children, it should be easy to give them a sense of self-love, but it doesn't seem to work out that way. Part of the problem is the way we were raised by our own parents. Try to remember what you thought of yourself when you were 5. My guess is that most of us thought we were dumb or ugly. We were furious at *ourselves* if we were scared at night; we were ashamed of *ourselves* if we didn't want to let a younger cousin share a new doll. We were disappointed in *ourselves* if we were awkward or shy or clumsy when Mommy had so hoped for a ballet dancer.

Sometimes we can't help a child love himself until we reevaluate some of our own attitudes—burdens we've been lugging around all the years of our lives. It may take the kind of painful self-exploration that brings us to say, "Yes, brown eyes and olive skin really turn me off. My parents made me feel inferior because I looked like their Italian ancestors and they wanted to be American WASPs. Now that I have this baby with olive skin and brown eyes, can I behave like a grown-up and see how beautiful she is—and let her know it?"

Irrational prejudices passed on to us in our cribs are only one impediment to helping our children love themselves. Some of us also have difficulty communicating the difference between being "bad" and being "human." It makes all the difference in the world if instead of saying, "Stop being such a baby," we say, "You aren't big enough yet to be quiet in a restaurant. We'll have to try again when you're a little older." There's also a big difference between saying, "You're a selfish brat," and "It's very hard to learn to share, so I'm going to help you. If you let Donna use your pail, she will let you have a turn with her dump truck."

The puritanical notion that everyone is either good or bad and that children must therefore be taught to be good has probably caused more human misery than anything else. We are all born with fairly equal parts of devil and angel, and what matters is learning to live with that truth. Of course, we say, "No, you may not hit the baby," but we also say "You're too young to stop yourself when you are angry. I must help you." Learning to accept our angers, jealousies, and unsocial impulses is part of growing up. We must also learn controls, of course, but not by denying that impulses exist or by making our children feel like sinners. The child who's made to feel bad develops self-hatred—and that interferes with learning, living, and loving more than any other psychological problem.

Once a child feels cherished and protected, he can begin to feel compassion for others. One of the earliest experiences of this sort comes from loving a pet of some kind. The youngster who's had the direct personal experience of being cared for tenderly is able to hold a stray kitten gently or call for parental interference if someone is mistreating a dog. Any 5-year-old who can spontaneously exclaim to a bird with a broken wing, "Oh, you poor little thing!" has learned one of the most basic skills necessary for changing the whole quality of life on this planet!

2. To Read Behavior

The child who enters school thinking he is a pretty wonderful person can still get sidetracked from learning if he doesn't know how to interpret behavior—other people's as well as his own. He might for example become so preoccupied with the two girls in the front row who've teamed up against him that he can't concentrate on adding two and five. Or if the teacher yells at him one morning he might feel so embarrassed and frightened that he's unable to pay attention to his lessons for the rest of the day.

But if the child has learned something about moods and human frailty, if he's been taught to interpret certain types of behavior, he's not apt to be so upset by these experiences. He will understand that the two girls are probably feeling scared in a new school and need a common enemy in order to feel more secure. And he'll realize that his teacher is just in a bad mood—due to a fight with her husband or a bad traffic jam on the way to work, perhaps—and will probably apologize tomorrow.

In addition to reading the behavior of others, a child needs to learn how to interpret his own behavior. This, too, can have a big effect on the amount of energy he has available for academic pursuits. If Junior yells at Mom at the breakfast table—if he takes one look at the scrambled eggs and says, "You *know* I hate them watery; I'm going to throw them in the garbage!"—then dashes out of the house, one of two things is likely to happen in second grade that day. He may be so full of guilt and terror that he can't hear a word the teacher is saying. Or he may ask himself why he blew his top, wonder if he was still mad at his dad for yelling at him the night before, and decide to apologize when he gets home. In the latter response he's able to forget about it while he's in school. And with no anger and confusion on his mind, he hears his teacher loud and clear.

3. To Communicate With Words

After gaining insight into the real meaning of their behavior, children need to develop the skill of helping other people read it. If a girl can say to a teacher, "I was so scared I'd get it wrong, I just couldn't think," the teacher may realize that anxiety is no route to learning and provide the necessary reassurance. If a child can tell his father, "You scare me when you yell so loud," chances are good that Father will try to reason with him calmly instead. Any 5-year-old who can comfortably and spontaneously communicate his feelings by saying, "I'm scared," "I love you a lot!" or "There's a rumbly, tingly feeling in my middle that makes me think maybe I'm not ready for a two-wheeler" has skills that will give him the freedom he needs to think, to wonder, and to learn.

4. To Understand the Difference Between Thoughts and Actions

Without this skill, which can be well established by the age of 5, a child may find it extremely difficult to concentrate in school. Gregory, for example, looks out the window and dreams of being a fighter pilot while his first-grade teacher explains the basics of arithmetic. He never hears what his teacher says because deep down he is a very angry boy. His parents have just divorced, and if he lets his real feelings surface they might well be, "I hate them both! I wish they'd drop dead!" These are such terrible thoughts that Gregory has to use all his powers of concentration to keep them *out* of his conscious mind.

But if, in his first five or six years, Gregory had been helped to understand that thoughts are not the same as actions and that feelings appropriately expressed never hurt anybody, he could let the feelings happen. And all that energy he's using to avoid his feelings could be turned to other pursuits—including the fascinating possibilities of adding and subtracting. He needs help in living through this very real crisis, of course, but he should be taught that it's natural to have scary feelings when you hurt, when you are worried, when life is very painful. It's impossible for a child to pay attention and learn if he's harboring feelings that he thinks are dangerous and bad.

5. To Wonder and Ask Why

All the popular books and the talk about the facts and skills we must teach preschool children have obscured—and almost ruined—their natural, instinctive intellectual curiosity. Often we become so preoccupied with number rods and flannel boards that we stop listening to the marvelous questions children ask all by themselves: "Why do leaves change color? . . . What makes grass grow? . . . Where does snow come from? . . . How can an egg become a baby? . . . What is dying? . . . Why do I grow bigger? . . . How does milk get to the supermarket? . . . Why are some children hungry? . . . How does a submarine stay under the water and not get drowned?"

If we want to encourage this instinct to wonder and ask why—to learn—we must make sure that by the time a child is 5, he glories in his wonderings and knows that there are ways to find some answers. He must also learn, of course, that some questions still don't have answers, that some questions have lots of different answers, and that sometimes he has to make an effort to find his own special answers.

In her book *The Learning Child*, the late Dr. Dorothy H. Cohen, professor of education at Bank Street College, makes a profoundly important distinction between giving a child fish to eat and teaching him how to fish. If we give him fish to eat we may satisfy his hunger momentarily, but what will happen when we are not around to feed him? It is the same with facts and information; if we always give them to a child ready-made, he'll never learn how to find them on his own. Children must be taught how to fish for their own answers.

When we say, "I don't know," "I'm busy now," "Ask Daddy," or "That's not a nice subject to talk about," we discourage a child's wish to do his own fishing and learning. If, on the other hand, we share his curiosity and offer guidance in finding the answers we encourage the kind of intellectual development that is most meaningful throughout a person's life.

6. To Understand That Complicated Questions Do Not Have Simple Answers

Our children's generation will have to face some very tough questions. There are no easy solutions to such problems as the lost balance in nature, the population explosion, the proliferation of weapons that can wipe all human life. If they are going to be wise and mature adults, children need to start understanding—at 2 and 3 and 4—that simple solutions never solve problems, that you really have to dig deeper and work harder. This means that if Fred takes a toy away from Pam on the playground, we don't explain it by saying, "Fred's Jewish." When a city block shows signs of decay, we don't say, "That's what happens when blacks or Puerto Ricans or Mexican-Americans move into a neighborhood." Such simple answers, given to children generation after generation, have led to a life of danger and despair in many parts of our land.

We need to train children to look for root causes. "Well, maybe Joe was mean today because he came to school hungry," or "If Sarah keeps breaking the clay things you make in school, we'd better talk to the teacher. She may have to talk to Sarah's mommy and daddy to find out why Sarah is unhappy and what we can all do to help her." This is the complicated way, but it does far more for a child than "I guess Sarah is a bad girl and you better keep away from her."

There are no simple solutions to social problems, and we do a terrible disservice to our children, to ourselves, and to the future when we mislead young children about this. We start children off on the wrong track when we emphasize questions for which simple right and wrong answers do exist ("How much are three and six? What's the third letter of the alphabet?"). Children need to experience complexity first, so they'll be prepared to face the confusion, the uncertainty, and the basic inconsistencies of real life.

7. To Risk Failure as a Necessary Part of Growing

In order to learn you need the courage to make mistakes—even to fail. The first book you check may not have the answer to why birds migrate; you may have to look someplace else. The first table you make out of wood may be ugly and lopsided, but if you're able to learn from your mistakes the second one will turn out much better. Children need help in understanding that learning is often a long, slow process of trial and error. No great invention or scientific discovery was ever made without a great deal of experimentation and failure first.

We must make it quite clear to our children that, despite what our modern educational system seems to indicate, passing and failing are *not* what learning is all about. In the words of a wise second-grade teacher, "Schools really should teach children to be gamblers! The only way to find out what you know or don't know, the only way to learn more, is to gamble a little. We scare kids to death. Who wants to take a chance on answering a question or struggling to learn something new if they're graded on success or failure instead of on effort?"

8. To Trust Grown-ups

The 5-year-old needs to have a fundamental trust in the adults in his life if he is to devote much of his attention to academic skills. And it is difficult to trust people if they lie to you—if they tell you they'll be there when you wake up and instead you find a baby-sitter; if they tell you the doctor won't hurt you when he does. We pay a very heavy price when we play games with children in order to avoid tears. If you want to be trusted, it's better to say, "I'm going out for a few hours while you're taking your nap," even if we have to endure a miserable good-bye. And, at the doctor's, "This will probably hurt a little, but it will be over soon. You can sit on my lap and cry if you feel like it."

Many parents think consistency is what makes an adult trust-worthy, but I think that's a big mistake. There is a very fine line between consistency and rigidity, and I believe it's important to trust people even though their feelings fluctuate and they change their minds. Growing makes people change, and we are all subject to swings in mood. The only consistencies that are important to a child are our attempts to be honest with him, to explain our inconsistencies as best we can, and to apologize when they don't make sense.

It is possible to help a child understand that not all people are loving and kind, and still give him the feeling that most of his experiences with adults will be good. The development of faith depends partly on the degree to which we are willing to share a child's feelings about people. We have to be straightforward with a child in saying such things as, "Yes, you're right; your nursery school teacher *does* make too much of a fuss about clean hands," or "Yes, I see what you mean about Aunt Clara; she is too bossy when we visit." Distrust results from feeling you're the only one who sees the unpleasant or difficult qualities in other people, and this is a common experience for children. We won't destroy a child's faith if we acknowledge human imperfection; it works the other way around.

9. To Have a Mind of His Own

Saying "No" is really saying "I am." It starts as a child begins to have some self-image, some sense that he is really a separate person. Many parents become scared and angry over this eventuality when they ought to exult in it. The sense of being unique and having the power to make choices is a vital part of being human.

If a child has some sense of who he is, he'll certainly have preferences and opinions by the time he's 5. It is a skill that is very easy to teach—you just encourage your child to express his opinions without the fear of reprisal. None of us wants to raise intellectual or spiritual weaklings; we want our children to make critical decisions, to have good judgment and inner convictions. And we can't wait until they get to college to begin developing these skills. The principle is already actively at work when we say, "Now that you're almost three, Jeff, I think you should decide whether we buy the blue or the red overalls." Or "Everybody likes some things and not others. Mary, when we have cold cereal for breakfast you can make yourself a peanut butter and jelly sandwich." Or "Well I don't hate Mrs. Freeley, but you have a right to your opinion."

When we indicate respect for a child's personality, his developing views, likes and dislikes, we prepare him for situations in which he has to make a spontaneous decision on his own—such as whether to join a group of children who decide to explore a condemned building or whether to accept a ride from a stranger who says he knows his father. When we are exasperated with the "Nos" at 2½, we might do well to remember that there will be times when we're grateful for a child's ability to say "No." Judgment improves with practice.

10. To Know When to Lean on Adults

By the time a child is 5, I believe he should know that there are many situations he simply cannot handle by himself or with his classmates. He cannot handle gangs of older children, teenage drug pushers, the man who exposes himself in the playground, the wild behavior of a class with an inexperienced new teacher. Part of trusting adults is knowing when you need help—and being able to ask for it. That may sound simple, but surprisingly few children come into kindergarten and first grade with the ability to make this choice. As a result, many are quickly caught up in situations that are so overwhelming and frightening that learning is impossible. We need to make it clear to children that *we* can be friends; that *we* can help them without being overprotective or babying them; that *we* can understand their world. We say we believe in the rights of the weak and the small, but too often we don't include our children in this idealistic philosophy.

Learning is much easier when there's no unfinished business in a child's early development. What's more, I know that a child who has help in working toward mastery in these ten areas will rarely be wantonly cruel or knowingly exploitative of others. If we direct more of our attention to these deeper human values, we can raise a generation of wise and loving human beings who will have the capacity to accept change and to make the world a better and safer place in which to live.

The Importance of
Learning to Say Good-bye

✳ The other day I called a friend I hadn't spoken to for several months. She sounded very depressed. She is very active in church work and had been asked to go to a national conference for a week, to lead an important workshop. She wanted desperately to go but told me it was impossible. "I can't leave Ginny for five days—she screams if I go to the supermarket for half an hour!"

Ginny is 4 years old. Her father is a free-lance writer who works at home. She has an adoring grandmother who is ready to baby-sit almost at a moment's notice. If I hadn't heard the same story hundreds of times before I wouldn't have believed my ears. "You gotta be kidding!" I said. The conversation seemed to cool a bit. After she had hung up quite abruptly, I began to try to put Ginny and her mother into focus. Ginny is an only child, born when her mother was 38 years old. Helen had a well-established teaching career by that time, but she had wanted a baby so much, for such a long time, that in her excitement and enthusiasm she quit her job and became a full-time mother. I sometimes wondered whether she'd regretted such an impetuous decision. Helen's reluctance to leave Ginny began to sound to me like unresolved ambivalence— a lot of *very* mixed feelings. Sometimes when a child clings a great deal and a parent seems to encourage and reinforce this behavior by total passive acceptance, it may mean that the parent has strong wishes to go but feels guilty about it. The child gets the subtle message, "If you cry a lot and I stay with you, that proves I don't really want to go."

Separation between parents and children is a normal and necessary aspect of growing up. But one of the things that can sometimes create extra stumbling blocks in this process is the fact that we may be afraid to examine our ambivalent feelings. Dr. David Mace, a wise and experienced marriage counselor, once said that the problems in family living are like the dilemma of the poor porcupine. There he is, alone and cold in the woods; he meets a nice lady porcupine and they huddle together for warmth and comfort. But after a while their quills get prickly and they have to move apart —until they get cold and lonely and move back together again. This seems to be the nature of human nature: to want love and closeness and to also want individual freedom and autonomy. All through our lives we struggle to find a balance.

It seems to me that if one is going to try to be most helpful to a young child who is going through separation experiences, it is first of all necessary to explore one's own feelings. Even the tiniest baby seems to have a built-in radar system; he knows what his parents are feeling even when they don't! It is perfectly normal to have ambivalent feelings. Every parent both loves and hates the baby who clings, who is so dependent. At one minute (and I remember the feeling well!) you feel as if your life is over; this helpless, screaming little mass of humanity will control the rest of your life —you are eternally imprisoned. I wanted to scream, "Let me out of here! What have I done to my life?" I guess I did scream. There were also moments of pure joy—that tiny golden head, that gurgle of pleasure, that smile of recognition; the waves of love and joy I felt in holding the tiny soft warm life against my body.

The feelings of hello and I-want-to-say-good-bye come and go. They confuse us as well as the baby. We both do better if the negative feelings are not kept a deep dark secret. It is not fashionable in some circles to acknowledge the desire to stay home with a baby, which is considered an imposition on one's personhood.

Only when a parent is able to face the range of his or her feelings can decisions be made more objectively. Going through early separation is painful for children, but if these experiences are carried out gradually, patiently—but firmly—new levels of growth and mastery are possible.

We know, from the suffering of adults who look back into their early experiences, that too often we all tried too hard to control our feelings. We stopped crying in order to get love and approval, but we also ended up with nervous tensions, too many headaches, sinus trouble, a spastic colon. I have learned through thirty years of working with children and almost as many years researching my own childhood that we need to experience our feelings while we are having them in order to grow up whole. What the teachers discovered after a while was that the children who ventilated their feelings usually mastered their anxieties more easily and permanently.

During the course of many years of psychotherapy I was finally able to reexperience some of my earliest infantile feelings. They were *awful*. They taught me something I wish I'd known when my daughter was an infant. The child who clings most desperately is often the one who feels most thrust away, who finds himself isolated, terrified, and alone. This is often the way a young child feels when he cries in the night. He has no sense of time or space, no knowledge of night or day, or of the fact that there are people who hear him. All he knows is that he is alone and that it might be forever.

It is no accident that one of the early games of infancy is peekaboo. It is the way in which the young child tries to cope with separation anxiety. For a moment a parent disappears behind the couch; then suddenly he or she pops up. For the child it is practice in accepting the idea that a parent can disappear but always reappears. The repetition brings reassurance. But it is a slow process and rarely if ever comes without a struggle. Young children will inevitably go through periods of crying when a parent leaves. The problem is that almost as inevitably, parents tend to feel guilty and then angry when this happens. We need to understand that separation experiences are essential to growth—from the womb to the world —and it takes about twenty years to work it through!

When a need is satisfied, it gradually disappears. Once a child has felt loving boundaries and there has been body comfort when needed, curiosity and a spirit of adventure come more easily. It is certainly pleasant to tuck one's head into a nice warm neck-and-shoulder niche—but if only this friendly lady would let you go, you would rather be on the floor banging all those pots and pans!

One of the most difficult problems occurs when an ambivalent parent burdened with unacknowledged feelings of guilt allows a child to take over. I recall the time when my husband and I were supposed to have dinner and then go to the theater with another couple. They never arrived at the restaurant and walked into the theater in the middle of the first act whispering to us, "Martha just wouldn't let us go!" Martha was just 2 at the time; I had visions of her handcuffing them to the bed or holding a whip over their heads! Children need to know that grown-ups are in charge. If they aren't, a child feels caught in a terrifying tide of chaotic confusion. It is *not* a matter of saying, "Look here, you stop that fussing. We are going out and that's all there is to it. If you don't stop crying, you are going to get a spanking." Rather it is a matter of getting across a message of acceptance and firmness. "Daddy and I know you feel upset when we go out, but we want to see our friends (or we want to have some time by ourselves). You'll have a good time with the baby-sitter. We'll see you in the morning." If a child seems very anxious it may be necessary to say, "I know you're angry or scared and maybe you need to cry—that's okay. Maybe it will help if we call to say good night at bedtime. We'd be glad to do that. But we are going out."

Separation is not difficult only for children; the tables do turn. Ellen comes in and announces, "Kathy's parents are taking her on a camping trip to Yellowstone Park and they invited me, too. I want to go." There is a new note of independence in Ellen's voice —you suddenly realize that your "cute little baby" is a grown-up young lady. When did it happen? Does it have to happen so soon? Your impulse is to say, "Don't be silly—you are much too young to be away for a whole month." You may need instead to say to yourself that although separation hurts, it must be allowed to happen.

Some children move out into the world with relative ease; they seem always ready for some new adventure. Others remain fearful and cautious no matter how positive their life experiences may be. For these children saying good-bye becomes agonizing if we make them feel they are failing at an important task. Feelings of inferiority use up all their energy, and there is little left over with which to meet a new challenge.

David was scared when he started nursery school; he was scared when he went to first grade; he was scared when he started day camp. Now it is the day before he goes off to sleep-away camp. He is 10 years old and has announced that he is not leaving tomorrow. If he is told that he's acting like a baby he will be more frightened. What he needs is reassurance of who he is, someone to affirm, "David darling, you're *always* scared before something new happens. That's just the way you are. You were like that when you were a baby and you will probably still be like that sometimes when you are a grown man. It's okay to feel that way—lots of people do. But we both know it doesn't take too long before you begin to enjoy yourself, so let's see how it goes for a week or two. It's not a matter of life or death. If you're still unhappy, you can come home."

When children go off to their first birthday parties, overnight visits to grandparents, nursery school—even away to college—a part of us is overjoyed. Freedom at last! But there is also a part of us that feels the loss of a vital connection. There is no reason a mother or father shouldn't be delighted about getting to work on time again, or going back to school. There is nothing shameful about feeling angry at the child who doesn't want to go. It is what a parent *does* that matters. Anger and disappointment are natural, but it helps if we are mature and responsible enough to handle these feelings by behaving in a compassionate way. It would be nice to be able to say good-bye on the first day of school, but there's Sue feeling lost and afraid, or there's Josh, always shy and fearful in new situations. They need our help. We need to act like grown-ups, ready to help with the letting-go process sensitively, patiently, and lovingly.

It often seems impossible to clue in to a child's inner timetable. You think to yourself, 'Andrea has so many friends this year, she's doing so well at school—of course she's ready to take a plane trip alone to go and visit her grandparents.' But the time approaches, and Andrea, who is usually confident and adventurous, gets very quiet. It is possible that for her 8 is still too young for such a trip.

Or there is Jeremy, who wants to go mountain climbing with two friends. They are all just 13 and you are sure he's much too young for so much responsibility, even though there are student hostels all the way up the trail. You say, "Nothing doing!" and are met with an anguished cry and more rebellion and fury than you've ever seen. Maybe you need to reconsider; maybe he's gotten older and more mature than you have noticed lately.

The important thing is sensitive observation and a willingness to experiment. We all make mistakes in judgment about a child's readiness for different levels of separation experiences. Both parents and children vacillate, which is natural; all we need to do is talk to each other about it and experiment with different alternatives.

The choice of baby-sitter is an important ingredient in helping a child deal with separation. When my daughter was young, beyond the essentials of a decent, responsible, loving person, I wanted someone who would not make too many demands or be a disciplinarian; that was my job. Of course a baby-sitter cannot let a child do anything that is dangerous or unkind but I never asked a babysitter to be sure my child ate a balanced meal or went to bed exactly on time. I wanted my daughter to have fun. This makes the separation more tolerable. Once when our daughter heard that we were going out, she exclaimed, "Oh, good! Mrs. Smith lets me watch more television and lets me have *two* Hostess cupcakes!" This is a reasonable reward for learning about letting go.

One factor that contributes to mixed feelings about separation is that the young child has no perspective on his or her feelings—and parents often lose theirs. I well remember the feeling that my child would never let me go. Even after she had learned to accept baby-sitters and going to school she would assure me that she would never grow up and leave us. She did not like to hear talk about her growing up and getting married. When she was 6 or 7 she asked, "Can't I just stay here and live with you and Daddy?" I told her she could until she wanted to go. She looked at me as if I was retarded; what could ever make her want to go? "Someday when you are a grown-up person," I said, "I think I will tell you what you used to say when you were a little girl. You know what? You won't believe me!" No child can anticipate feelings he or she hasn't yet experienced. We need not be frightened by this. We can express our own awareness of growing and changing without insisting.

At 18, our daughter announced that she was moving out. Not a question—a statement. It was my turn to be shocked, unready. She was very kind; she let me go shopping with her, buy a broom and a mop and a bath mat; let me advise her as to the best scouring powders and laundry soaps. She allowed me to handle my separation anxiety by participating in the process. Standing in a hardware store I said, "You know, I once told you that someday, when you were grown up, I would remind you that at one time you wanted to live with me and Daddy forever." She stared at me, disbelieving. "You gotta be kidding!" she said, and the look in her eyes again suggested some suspicion that I was not exactly bright.

A friend told me recently, "On Annie's wedding day I was close to tears, afraid I'd behave like an idiot at the ceremony. She was our baby—now we'd be alone again after thirty years of parenthood. I felt so relieved when she began to cry while she was putting on her wedding dress; we had a good cry together and I felt so comforted by *her* mixed feelings!"

I can still remember my first day in kindergarten, fifty-seven years ago! I can see a tremendous, cavernous room with very tall, giantlike strangers walking around. Everything seems out of proportion; there is a slide that looks thirty feet high, a jungle gym four stories high. I know it was a tiny, cramped school, but I was seeing it through the eyes of a terrified little girl in a strange land. Even as I write about it I get a hollow feeling in the pit of my stomach. What if my mother never came back? Did anybody know where I lived? Suppose I had to stay there forever? Forever is an empty, black, bottomless pit of terror. No matter how much I may have been reassured, no matter how sure I may have been that I was loved, the fear of desertion, of helplessness, is never far away when one is small.

We learn slowly; life teaches us. Each year at school I was better able to leave my parents behind. Slowly but surely I moved toward my own generation, my own world. I still experienced waves of homesickness when I went away—even when I went to college. But by the end of high school the ultimate choice had been made. On graduation day I wrote my parents: "I don't know how I can bear to leave this school and these friends. They are *my whole life!*"

Separation from those we love is always difficult, painful. It is natural to worry when you care so much, to be apprehensive, to wonder if you will ever see each other again. Right now my husband is about to leave for California. I worry about the plane, can already foresee the loneliness, and know that phone calls may leave me feeling even more alone. But we learn early and late that separation is a part of life, part of loving. The more we care, the more the pain. But there are gains in having to experience one's separate identity. In nursery school being separated from home brings secondary gains; you learn about the glory of finger paints; you learn that a teacher's lap can be comforting; there are pictures to be painted and songs to be sung and fantastic discoveries to be made.

For me separation now means quiet days of introspection, uninterrupted stretches of writing I want to do, listening to music whenever I feel like it, reading in the middle of the night, seeing friends my husband doesn't share with me. The school bus *does* take you back to your own house; Mom and Dad *do* come to visitors' weekend at camp and to the school bazaar. And my husband will come back from his trip, full of new ideas and very glad to see me. Learning to say good-bye is only the other half of the lovely business of saying hello all over again.

How to Live With Three Under Three

✿ Johnny is 2½ years old. He has two sisters, Susan, aged 19 months, and Cathy, 8 months. His mother says that he reacted quite badly when Cathy was born. Since that time eight months ago he has become more and more withdrawn and unsure of himself. He has had one respiratory infection after another, although he was previously a healthy little boy. He has also developed severe sleeping problems.

His mother describes the situation by reporting: "My husband and I have always felt warmly toward the coming of each child. Unfortunately Johnny took the arrival of the new baby very hard. His older sister, Susan, was at an extremely cute state when Cathy arrived on the scene, and of course a new baby is also very captivating. Johnny sensed all this and began to make many demands for our attention. It was almost impossible to give him as much attention as he wanted because we had to care for the other two. He seemed more and more unhappy and more and more demanding.

"Accompanying his recent illnesses, Johnny has developed a sleeping problem. He screams and cries at night, and climbs out of his crib no matter how many times we put him to bed. Finally we tried letting him fall asleep on the living-room couch and then putting him into his crib after he was asleep. But most of the time he would wake up and come back out to us. We tried being gentle but firm in getting him to bed, but this only worked once in a while.

We tried completely ignoring him or spanking him, and neither method was any more effective. He reached the point where he was seeing us off to bed at 11:00 P.M. and would fall asleep in the doorway of our bedroom.

"Thinking he might not like the crib, we bought him a youth bed. We put it in the baby's room and moved her into his crib, but the situation has gone from bad to worse.

"Cutting out his nap doesn't help either. He falls asleep out of sheer exhaustion by six-thirty P.M. and within a few hours wakes up and is set for the night shift! With two younger children to care for, I am beside myself with worry and fatigue."

Of course there are enormous differences in all families where three or four or more children have been born in fairly rapid succession. Different circumstances create great variations in the picture. For example, the personalities of the parents involved— are they usually easygoing and relaxed or inclined to be somewhat tense and anxious? Does Daddy help with the ordinary routines, and does he enjoy helping? Are there loving grandparents or other relatives who can help to ease the parents' burden? Do household facilities help or hinder? Can the family afford household help, a baby-sitter? Do friends and neighbors help with things like shopping?

The problems of having several very young children are *not* insurmountable, but parents should examine the special nature of this situation so they can meet it more effectively—with less unhappiness for the youngsters and less weariness and bewilderment for themselves.

To get back to Johnny, his sleeping difficulties are not really the core of our concern. In the first place this symptom doesn't tell us very much about Johnny; almost every child has a "sleeping problem" at some time during his early years. The range of possible causes is considerable—from a reaction to having moved recently to the normal anger of having to go to bed when you don't feel tired and it seems as if the fun is just beginning. Perhaps Johnny had bad dreams and is afraid of more, or he might just be trying to sleep with Mommy and Daddy, a common phase. These and many other circumstances have made most parents all too familiar with occasional sleeping problems. If we think of Johnny's behavior as a "sleeping problem" we may lose sight of the fact that it's only a symptom through which Johnny is trying to tell us something about his feelings in meeting the realities of his special life situation. Not only can sleeping difficulties mean totally different things to different children at different times, but each child can have different symptoms even when the basic problem is the same. Sally will have temper tantrums; Brian may refuse to eat; and Tommy may go back to bedwetting. Each child reacts to his environment in his own unique way, but whatever form the behavior may take, it is a warning signal, a plea for help.

So for the moment let's forget Johnny's behavior and take a closer look at his life situation. What could be bothering this 2½-year-old who used to be healthy and happy and able to take life in his stride? Johnny was a most welcome, wanted, and loved baby. As the first child, his early months were filled with a special attentiveness on the part of his parents and relatives. Every event in his growth was exciting—the first time he rolled over, the first tooth, the first word, the first step. He must have had a strong feeling of well-being, of being cute and satisfying and smart, and very much the center of his parents' world.

When Johnny was 11 months old, he got quite a jolt; he wasn't the only baby in the world after all! Too young to put his feelings into words or to have understood or anticipated a change in his life, he could only respond with generalized sensations, perhaps of bewilderment or anger, or a feeling of not being so very wonderful and satisfying to his parents after all. His babyhood was cut short; from now on his needs would not be met as quickly or perhaps as satisfyingly. Babies make a great many demands on adults; they have no patience for waiting, and they have little or no tolerance for the ordinary frustrations that they learn to handle when they're older. It's hard to give up infantile needs and satisfactions, even gradually; it's even harder to accept a change that comes abruptly.

If Johnny had been 3 or 4 or 5 years old, he might have had a chance to know about and expect the arrival of a baby sister. He might have had some share in the plans, such as helping to choose the crib or the layette. His parents would have been able to help him anticipate the new arrival in fairly realistic terms—that it would be fun, but not all the time; that he would love the baby, but not all the time; that he might feel a little jealous at first, and that this was a normal and natural way for a little boy to feel. He also might have been able to understand that Mother needed more rest, was sometimes tired or cross, or unable to play with him. We have learned so much about the normality of mixed feelings in somewhat older children that in most cases parents are now able to successfully ease a child through his initial experiences with a new baby.

But Johnny wasn't old enough to understood any of these things, and he could not react with thoughts and language, only with vague feelings. We have sometimes tended to think that this should make a situation easier rather than harder for a child to handle, but often the reverse is true. The child who meets a difficult life situation during what is called the "pre-verbal" period is often more upset and disturbed than he might have been later on.

When Johnny was 22 months old, it happened all over again. One cute and enchanting little girl had undoubtedly been competition enough, and now there was another. Did all this attention and interest in baby girls mean that boys weren't much good? Was he a bad boy because he just didn't like what was happening? Were Mommy and Daddy so busy with the others because he wasn't lovable? By the time he was 2, Johnny was probably able to translate some of his feelings into words. But how could his parents help him? He wasn't old enough even the second time to be prepared in advance for the new baby's arrival. He wasn't old enough to feel that he might have a vital and responsible role as the oldest or share in caring for the baby. He wasn't old enough to have begun to find satisfactions of his own outside the family—experiences that could help him feel special, stronger, freer. He was still very much a baby himself.

Whatever Johnny's own special uncertainties, he needed reassurance, and he needed to be near his parents. Darkness and sleep may have represented a sense of isolation, of loneliness. Did his confusion, his anger, his loss of self-esteem become particularly unbearable at night? Did his parents' disapproval of his behavior confirm his sense of no longer being needed and loved? It may be that seeing the new baby in his old crib represented a final confirmation of displacement.

These are all merely conjectures; we can't be sure exactly what any child is thinking or feeling, but we can look at circumstances and behavior and make some general observations about the kinds of things that are *probably* happening. Once we have this general, tentative frame of reference, we can begin to look for answers.

Many parents are now opting to have their children close in age so that they can really enjoy each other's companionship, share similar interests and experiences, and grow up together with a special closeness and sense of family identification. Parents need to think a little about the "cons" as well as the "pros" of this approach. If the oldest children will be too young to understand or be prepared for new siblings, how can we help them meet this experience without anxiety and shock? Some parents have said, "We want to have all of our children one right after the other, because that way they will be too young to know the difference. They won't be aware of what's going on and will just assume this is the way things are."

Perhaps the most important thing we can learn from children like Johnny is that this is *not* likely to be the case. While it's true that all children express their feelings through their behavior, this is particularly true of younger children. The younger a child is, the less he can *express* feelings of rivalry directly. But he can and does *notice* and *react*, not with words but with general sensations and feelings. These reactions are expressed through the language of behavior, such as Johnny's sleeping difficulties. If we accept the fact that it isn't easy for a child to give up being a baby, especially when he still is one, and if we accept the idea that babies are vulnerable to change and sensitive to all the nuances of life, then we can plan for these youngsters more effectively.

One father arranges his schedule so that his first half hour at home in the evening is spent with his four-year-old son, building with blocks, playing a game, or reading a story; then he helps his wife bathe the two younger children. A mother lets her three-year-old daughter make believe that she's a little baby; she's allowed to have a bottle just like her baby brother's, and she can cuddle on Mommy's lap and talk baby talk in their few moments alone while the younger babies are napping. A grandmother comes to baby-sit one afternoon a week so that two-year-old Billy and his mother can go off on a spree to the grocery store or playground, leaving the younger children at home. Families are making allowances for feelings and needs that cannot be expressed in words, but that are present all the same.

Under strain, young children often regress, becoming more babyish and demanding. When we are prepared for this and are able to accept it without anxiety, we can permit a child to work out his needs in this way, finding that he soon returns to a more mature level of development. When we permit a child to talk baby talk, to suck on a bottle, and imitate the baby's way of eating, strained foods and all, we are giving him the support he needs in order to regain strength and resourcefulness. Instead of increasing his sense of defeat and unworthiness, we are letting him know by our attitude that he's still wonderful but just a little bothered by the events of life. When the needed satisfactions and reassurances come about in this way, we can usually set reasonable limits for bedtime and other routines without these becoming the avenue for expressing discomfort and unhappiness.

In addition to the problem of sharing parental attention and care, sometimes the oldest child in a family such as Johnny's is reacting to the lack of opportunity for healthy growth, for exploration and experimentation in the world around him. When a child remains the only child until he is 4 or 5, his parents are usually able to let him roam more freely; there is more time to watch him so that he doesn't get hurt, to permit him to begin to run and climb and explore. Someone can be near him when he first investigates the swings and slides in the playground. There's more time to put things back when he begins to explore the fascinating world of pots and pans in the closet under the sink; he can run in the park because Mommy or Daddy is following close behind.

Things are different when Johnny's mother is wheeling a baby carriage, is already pregnant with her third child, and both parents are so busy with formulas, washing, and other household chores. It may be that the very thing that could most help Johnny easily accept his younger sisters—his sense of being older, wiser, stronger, more independent—is hampered by restrictions on his own activity. In order to foster the sense that there are compensations for being the oldest, it may be wise to try and plan for special times, when Johnny can enjoy the new challenges of growing. A Saturday-morning excursion alone with Daddy, a special visit with Mommy at a friend's house where there may be other children of his own age, or an outing with his grandparents on a Sunday may help a youngster see the benefits and satisfactions in his *own* world and make it easier to give up wanting to be like the babies.

Parents need to realize that the early years with several babies are going to mean a great investment of time and energy. They must also remain attentive to the special problems that may emerge for the oldest or older children. But take heart: These difficulties, whatever form they may take, are temporary. Slowly but surely Johnny's parents can give him enough reassurance during the day to alleviate his anxiety at night. By allowing him be babyish when he feels like it, by giving him some special times without the others to pursue his own interests, and by including him in the care of the baby if he enjoys this sense of involvement and responsibility, he will begin to feel better about himself and the world around him. As he becomes old enough to play with other children his own age, perhaps attend a nursery school, he will begin to have interests and experiences of his own that will reinforce his sense of well-being.

There is an expression, current in our atomic age, "Don't push the panic button!" This may well be a good motto for families in which the oldest of several children is still pretty much a baby himself. If parents can accept the fact that reactions to any changes in the family constellation are often dramatic and just as important and meaningful for 1- and 2-year-olds as for older children, they will be able to meet the challenge more effectively. If Johnny had been 5 years old when the next baby was expected, his mother, under the influence of all she has heard and read about sibling rivalry, probably would have planned carefully and intelligently to help Johnny expect the new arrival and understand some of the mixed feelings he might have. The only modification for Johnny and his parents when he is a 2½-year-old, with two younger sisters, is to plan *differently*. His parents can face the fact that he will have feelings and reactions that he cannot communicate through language, but that he can be reached by the kinds of reassuring behavior that are understood by an almost-baby who is also a big brother.

Children Who Won't Eat

❋ If you work with parents of nursery-school-age children, there is one phrase you can be absolutely certain you will hear repeated endlessly: "That child doesn't eat enough to keep a bird alive!"

I don't know much about birds, but I do know that these children whose parents believe they are starving to death somehow manage to feebly stagger their way into becoming the tallest, strongest, and, unhappily, too often, the fattest school-age children in human history!

In Ellen's house the situation was considered to be so desperate that her mother called the school and asked if we could make a very early morning appointment so that both she and her husband could discuss their daughter's problem. Ellen, at almost 4, looked like a string bean. And according to her frightened parents, no self-respecting bird could have survived for 24 hours on what Ellen managed to consume in a week. Every meal had become a battleground—and Ellen was winning hands down. "When she began to throw up when I got her to eat at all, I knew I was licked," her mother said.

Whether a parent opens a book by Dr. Spock or consults her "real-life" pediatrician, she is almost certainly advised that between the ages of 2½ and 5, give or take a year on either end, children seem to need very little food not only to sustain them but even for normal growth. So why is this such a common source of worry? I remember my own experience with this when my daughter was about 4 years old. I certainly *should* have known better. I had been a nursery school teacher and a child psychologist for a number of years by that time. Our pediatrician, one of the calmest and most reassuring people I'd ever met, gently suggested that I take a good look at my daughter—a living dynamo, full of more pep and vitality than I could reasonably tolerate as I staggered after her in merry chase from sunup to sundown. Well, I countered, she did get a lot of colds. "She's being exposed to germs among other children at nursery school now," I was told—and which I darn well knew anyway. I also couldn't deny that she was tall for her age, which left me with no ready comeback for the good doctor's query, "Would she be growing so tall if she was suffering from malnutrition?" As we parted the doctor made a profound and entirely brilliant prediction of things to come. "When Wendy is about seven years old," she said, "she will develop a hollow leg, and for all the rest of her growing years you will regret your present anxieties and wish she'd stop eating you out of house and home." I had good reason to remember that statement for many a long year as I dragged home freight car loads of groceries to a female sieve with *two* hollow legs.

When most of us were babies our mothers still lived in a world in which the large majority of people had every reason to believe that a fat baby was a healthy baby. It is no accident that so many ethnic strains in American society have emphasized a relationship between fat and health. Some years ago I listened in on a conversation among a group of soldiers on a train who were comparing notes on their mothers' cooking. There was general agreement that the greatest possible joy they could bring to their mothers would be to go home and say, "Ma, I'm starving for some decent food" and then to spend their two weeks' leave at the dining-room table, retiring only for short rest periods! Among this group were Jewish, Italian, black, Polish, and Greek Americans.

The history of civilization is the history of human beings trying to overcome the never-ending terror of starvation. Because having enough food has always represented human survival, it has naturally become associated with giving love. Providing enough food for one's children to grow big—and fat—has always been a major expression of maternal love. If you mention a child who is "a feeding problem" to people from other countries less richly endowed than ours, they really won't know what you're talking about; you have to explain, to their wide-eyed amazement, that in the United States some parents bribe, cajole, threaten, and punish their children for not eating. Certainly one aspect of our parent-child battles over food stems from the fact that food may no longer be as precious and hard to come by as it was in our childhood, and we have not been able to make our feelings and attitudes keep pace with an environment of overabundance.

But there are many other reasons for our difficulties in this area. One of them is that the decrease in a child's appetite often comes just at the time he has to make it known that he will not let us be in charge all the time. That adorable, pliable, cuddly baby has turned into a person—how dare he!—who has learned one word that will change the whole course of his life: "NO!" This is a drama that shakes many an otherwise well-balanced and stable parent. Of course we want our children to become increasingly independent; we want them to be curious, adventurous, and bright. And we really do know, deep down in our hearts, that the emerging defiance, the strong will, the demand to be heard, is a necessary step toward all those other things—but we're not too sure we like the price. Our gorge begins to rise; this 2½-foot pip-squeak has some nerve telling *us* he's not hungry!

It is interesting to watch different families as the beginning of real self-assertion gets under way. There are some mothers and fathers whose own life experiences have been more relaxed about eating; they don't get either angry or anxious when a child says he's not hungry. They ignore the protests and say, "Okay, let me know when you get hungry. I'm not going to start cooking a whole new meal for you, but I'll fix you a peanut butter sandwich and a glass of milk." The large majority of preschoolers in these homes do not become feeding problems. But don't feel too envious of these parents' good fortune; you may be sure that they have their own special and individual idiosyncrasies. Mother cannot stand disorder, and she has made up her mind that by the time her children are in first grade every one of them is going to be "habit-trained" to fold his pajamas, make his bed, and put away his toys. Chances are that the time she saves on feeding problems is spent on bribing, punishing, cajoling, and yelling at her children to clean up! Most of us have our own Achilles' heel—and young children, with that marvelous and sensitive radar equipment with which they seem so highly endowed at 3 or 4, are able to circle in and land on exactly the issue that will bother us most, making that the battleground on which they will fight or die for autonomy and freedom.

It is too bad that we permit a matter such as eating, which ought to be pleasurable, to serve as a call to war. We need to recognize two things primarily: first, our anxiety and concern about what a child is eating is almost always excessive, and secondly, there is really no earthly reason for us to go along with the child in letting this area of life throw us both into opposing armed camps. Knowing that children do need us to become more and more aware of their growth and readiness to make decisions, we can and must find reasonable and practical ways to let them know that yes, we *do* see how big they are getting, and we *are* delighted, and we *will* let them make more decisions for themselves. If we are going to do this in the area of eating, we will have to become more flexible in our ideas of right and wrong.

Is there anyone among us who isn't absolutely certain that it is necessary and good to have three meals a day? Don't you have the vague feeling that "breakfast, lunch, and dinner" were somehow handed down to us as fundamental laws of the universe? That's what comes of getting overcivilized, I suppose. It is easy to have this notion shaken by a quick review of any book on cultural anthropology, which will testify to the fact that, subversive as that thought may seem, there are cultures in many parts of the world with totally different eating habits than ours.

Children are not born with the notion or appreciation of social eating. As we remember all too well, some of them preferred eating all night and sleeping all day! While they are remarkably good-natured about adapting to our daily schedules by the time they are 3 or 4, they are still very little, and there is no reason to assume that packing in a lot of food three times a day is half so jolly for them as it would be to have six or eight tiny snacks on the run (since running is so much more natural at 4 than sitting still).

"But you're encouraging us to let our children become little savages," I can hear some parent screaming. And another is muttering to himself, "This woman wants us to be waiting on our children like a short-order cook, twelve hours a day." And a prim voice over in the corner adds, "Table manners are essential to good social relations and must be instilled in a child as early as possible."

Most of us don't like to do what we can't do well, nor can we become absorbed in something that doesn't interest us in the slightest. Sitting down together for a meal *does* have social meaning for adults and for children who are old enough to have mastered the art of conversation, and who enjoy expressing their own ideas, describing their experiences, and listening to others' reactions. But no child under the age of 7 or 8, no matter how brilliant, can even faintly approach this art.

When a child is mature enough for a new experience, he *wants* it and takes to it like a duck to water, and without any advance training. When my daughter was 1 year old and preferred to inspect the world on all fours, nobody said to me, "Eda, for heaven's sake, get that child up on two feet. How will she ever learn the habit of walking where she wants to go if you let her go on thinking she's an orangutan?" We believe in physical growth; we know that a healthy baby will learn to walk in his own good time, and we don't try to train him a year ahead of time. However, when I let my little girl eat most of her meals in front of the television set at age 5, believe me, people screamed! *My* mother, *his* mother, four out of five baby-sitters, two out of three neighbors—and even the television repair man. "What are you teaching that child about mealtimes?" they howled (in their own variation on the theme). "It's bad for her eyes, for her stomach—it's bad for her psyche." It got to be pretty bad for me, too. But I somehow mustered the courage to stick to my guns. Food was simply not terribly interesting at this time, and eating with others, making a social occasion of mealtimes, was superimposing a custom for people who enjoy and have a talent for sharing their ideas and experiences through conversation on a child who simply couldn't care less. By the time our daughter was 8 or 9, she was very much a member of the table. In fact, from that time until she went to a home of her own, my husband and I had a hard time getting a word in ourselves at dinner. She began to enjoy gourmet tastes and flavors; her ability to converse developed by leaps and bounds; she became interested in the subjects we talked about, and she was dying to tell us what she thought, too. If we could relax a little and wait with some faith, we would be able to help our younger children live more comfortably during the period when they are not at all motivated to eating regularly socially.

The family who came to see us at the nursery school—as did hundreds of others—learned to see that their anxiety and inflexible expectations had made eating a power struggle. Ellen knew that if she asserted herself in this area she would certainly make an impression. Before anyone knew for sure just what had happened, food had become associated with a struggle for independence, and mealtimes had become an avenue for the expression of anxiety, anger, the head-on collision of wills. We suggested the following regime: When Ellen arrived home from nursery school at noon, she was probably pretty worn out since she played hard. There was really no reason to assume that she wanted to eat right away. If she felt like it, she could take a little rest first. If she said she was hungry, she herself could help in preparing something very simple—a toasted cheese sandwich, a hot dog broiled on a fork over the stove, a box of cereal, munched in front of the TV set. There are all kinds of perfectly appropriate, nourishing foods that can be made available for snacks throughout the afternoon—nuts, raisins, bananas, carrot sticks, peanut butter and bread, cheese, a dish of pudding, a slice of bologna, or some tuna fish, for example. Afternoon play in the backyard might involve some picnic snacks. I remember hating eggs as a child, except when I could take a scrambled egg sandwich outdoors to eat in a secret "house" behind some bushes; there it was ambrosia. During the course of a day, such snacks can provide all the essentials of a nourishing, well-balanced diet, without any tears or storms, and with genuine pleasure in eating-when-you're-hungry. The truth of the matter is, once parents indicate this kind of flexibility and all the tension has been dissipated, children will often, in a very short time, decide that they prefer to eat the things they see the rest of the family eating at mealtimes, thereby "civilizing" themselves with very little help from us.

Another source of rigidity in our thinking about eating habits is the idea that there's a "proper" kind of food for each meal: cereals and eggs for breakfast, meat and vegetables later in the day. I know of one little boy who had an absolute passion for canned spaghetti and meatballs. He lived in a cold climate, and his mother wanted him to have good nourishment for breakfast, but every morning was a torture for all concerned until she hit on the brilliant idea that spaghetti and meatballs provided the same nutrients as most breakfast foods. So for three years, Eric had his spaghetti for breakfast. There is no reason on earth not to have soup, hamburgers, or hot dogs on a bun for breakfast if a young child finds them more appealing. On hot summer days, a large plate of ice cream can be a perfectly appropriate breakfast. In general, we want our children to have fruits and vegetables, meat, and some kind of starch during the course of a day—and they can have all of this in informal snacks, without strain or pain, if we really think about the variety of foods that are available to us and just exercise a little imagination. Nuts, raisins, bananas, and other snacks that are fun to hold can be offered throughout the day. The important point is that we are not permitting a child to fill up on junk. Soda and candy should never be substituted for nourishing foods, but we can offer small amounts of tasty treats that are perfectly good and healthy at odd hours.

In spite of all our ingenuity, we may find ourselves in situations so extreme as to require consultation with the pediatrician. Sometimes the relationship between a parent and child has become so distorted on the subject of food that both will need professional help in getting off to a new start. There are also documented cases of strange nutritional problems that are reflected in the craving for certain foods. In one such case, a mother battled continually with a 4-year-old who always wanted his dessert first. The puzzling thing was that when she capitulated, Junior usually ate a little more than he otherwise would. It was unbearable to watch, but sometimes if he ate a bar of chocolate right before lunch, he also ate more meat and potatoes. It seems that for some children this makes a lot of sense. Eating something sweet when they are overtired causes a sharp rise in blood sugar, followed by a sharp decline, before a leveling-off process takes place. The decline in blood sugar results in increased appetite, which makes these children feel hungrier and more eager to eat other, more valuable foods. This isn't true for every child and, like anything else, it is an approach that can be abused, but it is an indication of the wisdom of the body itself if we will observe and listen to its messages. The same thing is true when a child is overtired or seems to be coming down with some illness. If we force him to eat, he throws up; his body knows better than we do.

Another important fact to keep in mind is that a diet doesn't have to be well-balanced every day. Children tend to like to go on binges, but experiments have shown that they will seek a natural balance over a period of several weeks or a month if eating is not associated with emotional turmoil. A child may want tuna fish for lunch and bananas for supper for five days in a row; then he can't stand the sight of them and goes on a raisins and orange juice binge —followed shortly by a craving for peanuts and cheese. As long as these are real foods that have nutritional value beyond mere calories and sugar, trust the child to provide his own variety.

At age 7, Sally has had fourteen cavities filled within the past two years and is sick more than she is well most of the winter. She is the victim of an overpermissiveness that missed the point entirely. Her mother permitted her to eat whatever she pleased, and Sally pleased to eat candy, brownies, and soda. It is not necessary or wise to abdicate parental responsibility any more than it is helpful to use one's adult power to subdue opposition. Parents certainly are responsible for the health of their youngsters, but that responsibility can be exercised rigidly and inflexibly or with maturity and imagination. We are too big and smart to fight with our children on such issues! Surely we are talented enough to find interesting, novel, and intelligent ways of being flexible and experimental. The fact that such an approach works is evidenced by the way our children eat in other people's homes and in nursery school, when they stay for lunch. In an environment that is free of tension and strenuous demands, most children eat with pleasure. A good example of this is what happens when take a car trip and you really want to get to your destination quickly, without too many stops. You and I know perfectly well that it is just at such times, when we don't want to feed our children, that they become most ravenous!

Several weeks ago, Ellen's mother came back to give us a progress report. It still makes her uncomfortable and uneasy that skinny Ellen is really healthy, and there are anxious moments when Ellen tests her mother to see if she really means it when she says, "Eating is for when you are hungry, and not for anything else." However, there was one glorious moment of satisfaction when Ellen popped in one afternoon after playing in the snow and muttered disagreeably, "The trouble with this house is there's never anything to eat."

Part IV

READING
BEHAVIOR

An Exhaustion
Unto Madness

❋ Recently I went to one of those gigantic cut-rate drugstores, and there was a long line at the checkout counter. It was about 12:45 P.M. Right in front of me, loaded down with purchases, was a young woman. Clinging to her legs, wailing as if the world were coming to an immediate end, was a 3- or 4-year-old girl. Her sobs were coming in deep gulps, and she had a terrified look in her eyes. She was desperately trying to stop crying, but the more she tried, the more awful her crying became.

The young mother was obviously embarrassed by the noise her daughter was making and feeling very harassed. It was late for lunch, her shopping was taking longer than she'd expected, and she knew her child was hungry and tired. I wanted to suggest that she go to the head of the line—and to try to explain this kind of crying —but like most people, I've been thoroughly trained to mind my own business.

How would I have felt if someone had interfered when I was in the same position? At that time—more than thirty years ago—I'd have considered it an invasion of my privacy. But now I wonder if someone could have helped this young mother. The impulse to speak up was so strong that I ran away, down the farthest aisle, as I heard the mother scream, "Stop it! Stop it! Do I have to spank you or are you going to stop that crying?"

Every parent lives through similar situations. They're most common at lunchtime on buses and trains, in supermarkets and airports. They also occur at dusk on Christmas and other holidays as families say their good-byes and face the long trip home. I can recall with absolute clarity my own sense of helpless, embarrassed rage when it happened to me. The more my daughter howled, the more furious I'd become and the worse my threats of punishment. Whenever I witness these scenes now, I deeply regret my lack of understanding then.

I hope I'd behave differently today. In the years since I was a young mother, I've learned many things about childhood. Although I had a degree in child psychology and certainly understood *in my head* that children get cranky and cry, and that the angrier a parent gets the worse the situation becomes, I was frequently unable to behave in ways that related to my understanding. I just felt waves of fury washing over me. At times I wanted to kill that screaming kid.

Since then I've gone on a profound exploration of myself through psychotherapy. And I'm convinced that it's been more useful to the understanding of childhood than ten degrees in psychology. I was studying one child—myself—and in the course of this self-exploration I rediscovered what it feels like to be little. One of the many fascinating things I learned is that under the age of 5 or 6, there is a kind of exhaustion that comes close to madness. The child feels a deep and total fatigue that destroys his limited ability to make sense of the external world. It is a feeling of total disorder and confusion. Reality becomes distorted, and the child's whole being is enveloped in helplessness and terror. All he can do is cry like the infant he feels he's become again. But when adults behave as if the child is just being ornery, total panic ensues. There he is, lost in a terrible anxiety in which he knows he's losing control in every aspect of his being, while grown-ups—his only hope of survival—are screaming at him to stop this nonsense and behave.

The child wants desperately to stop crying. Those adults are his lifeline; displeasing them is what he dreads most in the world, yet he cannot stop. He feels totally out of control, like a plane spinning toward a monstrous crash landing. Many parents say, "That's the time for a good smack on the behind; it clears the air." And I must admit that sometimes that kind of "crash landing" is so much milder than the child's internal fears that he comes out of his fog and experiences relief. But it's usually very temporary; the fatigue soon brings the madness back.

What, then, does a tired parent who's already behind schedule do when caught in traffic or on a long line with a wailing child? The solution depends on the degree to which the parent can get in touch with his own childhood. I felt panic and fury when caught in such situations with my own daughter because she evoked memories that scared me. I became furious at Wendy for reminding me of feelings of helplessness and terror I'd had as a child—and long since repressed. I now believe that we behave most angrily and irrationally toward a child when he or she has reminded us—at a deep, unconscious level—of feelings we had during our own childhood and don't want to remember.

When Wendy was 4, I was 30. I thought I was an adult woman who had left childhood behind forever. It never occurred to me that somewhere inside I still felt like a 4-year-old. I was responsible, well-organized, trying hard to manage my life. The last thing I wanted to feel was helpless. But when my daughter cried those awful, endless, piercing sobs, she aroused in me those same lost feelings of madness—total disintegration, utter helplessness and vulnerability. My rage was my defense against those feelings.

Today I think I could accept the fact that these sounds were hitting me at the deepest level of my own childhood experience. And because I could acknowledge and feel it, I could go beyond it. We feel most trapped by feelings we don't understand. What I'd try to do, therefore, is comfort both myself and my child. "Yes," I'd say to myself, "that's the way I once felt. It was awful, frightening, overwhelming. But now that I'm an adult, I have the capacity to mother both myself and my child. Now that I understand what I once needed, perhaps I can answer that need in my child—and myself." More and more young parents who've kept in touch with their own childhood feelings seem to be able to do this.

One day a young man got on a bus with a child who was screaming and writhing in his arms. It was all he could do to hold on to her. As she wailed at the top of her lungs, he was well aware of the looks of annoyance on the faces of the other passengers. When he finally got seated, the young father kept a firm grip on the screaming mass of humanity in his arms and spoke to her in a low, steady voice. "Jenny darling," he said, "I know just how you feel. You are so hungry and tired; it's a scary feeling. You're all mixed up about everything. You just can't stop crying. I know you can't help it. Let me rock you. I promise we'll soon be home, and you can get into your bed and I'll sing you to sleep. Yes, poor baby. I know you can't stop crying." After a few minutes, as the message of understanding seeped through the exhaustion, Jenny quieted down, sucked her thumb, and fell asleep.

This was a big man, and he could carry Jenny. But what does the petite mommy with bundles to carry and three more blocks to walk do with a child screaming on the sidewalk because she wants to be carried? Few things drive a parent up the wall faster than the tired child who won't walk. The threats I hear range from a spanking to the final terror—"If you don't start walking *this minute*, I'm just going to leave you here!" If I were in that position today, though, I'd try to sit down on the sidewalk and rest with my child for a few minutes.

If a parent tries to empathize with what the child is experiencing —and acknowledges feeling the same way long ago—the whole situation changes. If you think your child is a spoiled brat who is trying to drive you out of your mind, then the wish to strike back becomes overwhelming. If, on the other hand, you think to yourself, "When a little kid gets tired the whole world falls apart—and it must have been that way for me once too," then nurturing that is beneficial to both parent and child can take place. The road to controlling both the child's tears and your own rage is to acknowledge the real feelings that are surfacing. You might say, for instance, "Okay, darling; I know you can't walk another step and you can't stop crying because you're so tired. But I can't pick you up, anymore. I just can't. Perhaps we should both just sit down right here on the street. Or maybe we could get to that bench or the shoe store up the street where we could rest for a minute. And I have a snack in my bag that might help you feel better."

Once a parent begins to feed the child's need, the feelings of embarrassment, guilt, and rage begin to dissipate. By recognizing the child-terror and by nurturing the child-need, both parent and child receive inner nourishment. You make up for the deprivation you suffered as a child by dealing sensitively with your child's similar pain and need. The child crying for comfort inside each of us gets another chance.

I have not forgotten how endless and exhausting child care can be. Some days seem unendurable no matter how much you enjoy parenthood and love your children. I remember the fear, guilt, frustration; the boredom and the feeling of being trapped by the total dependency of a child. I remember days when I wanted to scream, "Let me out of here!" Now I realize that those terrible feelings of having to give more than I could would not have been so strong if I'd only understood that every time I answered my child's needs with patience and kindness, I was also nourishing a secret part of myself. It would have made my life easier if I'd told both of us how hard it is to be young and vulnerable—and how much comforting we need. In that act of loving, I would have given relief from pain to the child in myself as well as to my daughter.

I'd like to think that if I were that young mother in the checkout line, I'd now be able to speak to that fatigue-madness. I hope I'd *ask* to go to the head of the line or just sit right down on the floor and take my child in my arms and comfort her. I'm sure I'd be comforting the child in my own past as well as the child in my arms. Among the three of us—my inner child, my daughter, and my adult self—the nourishment of my understanding would give us the strength to get home and have lunch.

When a Child Lies

✱ "I'm really worried about my eight-year-old daughter," a mother, Joan, told me recently. "She lies all the time and I really can't understand it. We've told Karen over and over that no matter what she does, she'll be forgiven as long as she tells us the truth. But if we find her lying—even about something minor—we'll punish her. So there's really no reason for her to lie."

It sounded logical so I probed a little further. Joan assured me that Karen was very bright and seemed normal in every other way. But when I asked how much time she devoted to Karen, she admitted that she and her husband had both been working very hard for the past year and often didn't get home until after Karen was in bed. "But we always have breakfast together," she said, "and we try to spend most of our weekends with her."

"Let me get this straight," I said. "If Karen tells the truth, nothing happens. But when she lies, all hell breaks loose. Is that right?" "Exactly," said Joan. "We really make an awful fuss about lying because it's something Jack and I both feel very strongly about. Do you suppose that could be what she wants—all that attention?"

It seemed ridiculous to Joan that Karen would rather be spanked than ignored. But from Karen's point of view, punishment may be a small price to pay for being the center of attention—particularly if that's the only way she can get attention. Children operate on a different kind of logic from most adults, and that often makes it difficult for parents to find the reasons for a child's behavior.

In my forty years of talking with parents and trying to understand children, I cannot recall a single instance in which we could not find reasons for lying. This is not to suggest that such behavior is acceptable, but you need to understand it before you can stop it. We can't help our children through the thornier moments of growing up unless we're willing to deal with causes.

It takes a long time for a child to understand the distinction between reality and fantasy, and the impulse to solve reality issues with fantasy solutions is often overwhelming. It is absolutely normal for a 3-year-old to deny spilling the milk and say "Timmy did it" when Timmy is an imaginary squirrel that always gets her into trouble. It feels like such a good idea! And a 3-year-old, caught between the fuzzy worlds of imagination and reality, is not entirely sure that Timmy did *not* do it.

In such cases, a parent can say, "You are a very naughty girl for lying to me," which makes the child feel terrible and unlovable. Or you might say, "I guess you must wish that Timmy did it, because you're sorry it happened," and let it go at that. The second approach is far more helpful, for that happens to be the truth.

In a similar case, 4-year-old Jeffrey comes home from nursery school with a can of Play-Doh. He tells his parents that the teacher gave him a present for being such a good boy. His father is very suspicious—partly because the chances of Jeffrey being *that* good are very slim. He replies, "I think you're lying, Jeff; that Play-Doh belongs in school and tomorrow we're going to take it back." But as reality becomes more painful through disapproval, Jeffrey moves further into fantasy. "She said she's going to give me a present every day, and I'm the only one in the whole class who knows how to sing and she's going to let me play her autoharp." Then, looking at his father's increasingly angry face, Jeffrey knocks over a chair, gives the baby a smack on the head, and runs out of the room. There is now a major crisis that might have been avoided.

At 4, it is still perfectly normal to make up stories and to believe them, sincerely. Preschoolers don't really lie so much as weave reality and fantasy in and out of their daily lives with marvelous abandon. It would have made more sense for Jeffrey's father to have said, "That sounds like a nice idea, Jeff. But I wonder if it really happened that way; let's talk to Mrs. Gardner about it tomorrow when I take you to school." The parent may then discover that the teacher thinks Jeff's increasingly difficult behavior is due to the arrival of a new child who is competing with Jeff to be the leader of the group. The issue isn't so much that Jeff is lying but that he's distorting the truth to relieve some pain.

The young child's motives for lying have nothing to do with the same behavior in adults. A child's motives are related to his or her level of understanding. We need to remember that until the age of 7 or 8 all children are confused about what is true and what is make-believe. Their fears, their dreams, their reactions to stories, are often far more intense than the everyday events of life. Playing that one is a fireman or a policeman, a mommy or a daddy, is often more real to a child than being the "real" Johnny or Susie.

Through play, through observation, through interacting with adults, children slowly begin to make sharper distinctions. They become less easily overpowered by their impulses and can begin to control the wishes that precipitate the tales. Imagination is one of the great gifts of life, and you don't want to destroy it—only channel it. "That's a lovely story, darling," you might say. "Let's write it down and you can draw pictures to go with it." Or, "I know how much you *wish* we had gone to the lake on Saturday, but we didn't. And it isn't fair to tell Jennie we did just because she went to the circus. She's your good friend, and I know you want her to trust you."

We need to teach children that lying is not a matter of being "good" or "bad." It has to do with how people treat each other. Lies get in the way of love and trust; they hurt relationships. By the time children are school-age, they can begin to see how much they want to be respected by others—and how much they in turn need to trust others.

This does not mean that youngsters don't still give in to an occasional overwhelming impulse all through adolescence. I have yet to find an adult who could not recall having lied to a parent —about why she got home late, what happened at a party, or where his money went, perhaps—long after the age when they knew better. Such events should not go unchallenged, of course. Discussion, open confrontation, and restitution are the ways we help our children become civilized. But when such falls from grace are occasional, you needn't worry that your child is headed for a life of crime.

Habitual, almost continual, lying during the years from 10 through adolescence is another matter, however, that cannot be treated with humor or indulgence. Since lying is more inappropriate at 12 or 15 than at 4 or 6, it needs to be examined even more carefully for causes.

The most common causes seem to be feelings of rivalry and jealousy, fear of rejection, the need for more attention and approval. The child who becomes a compulsive liar often cannot see any reasonable alternatives for getting the attention and help he or she craves. Often, unrealistic expectations on the part of parents are to blame. "I'm not smart enough"; "I'm too dumb"; "My father is ashamed of the way I read all the time and don't like football"; "My mother wishes I were prettier and wore dresses instead of jeans." These are typical comments from children who lie a lot.

The manner in which parents handle the early signs of discomfort and disturbance is crucial. When a child first begins to lie often and well, many think that anger and physical punishment will "cure" the aberration. They're dead wrong. If a boy is lying because he needs attention and affection but will settle for attention . . . if a girl is lying because she thinks she's such a nothing that only lies can make her interesting . . . if a child is lying in order to make an impression he can't seem to make in any other way— then being convicted as a "bad person" and punished accordingly only intensifies the needs that started the whole thing in the first place.

One personal experience that sticks in my mind occurred when my daughter was about 13. She took a skirt from a much-loved relative's closet, then lied and said it was given to her. Although I was often a lousy mother who failed to practice what I preached, this time I resisted the impulse to scream invectives and predict a life of crime. Instead I asked, *"Why?"* Wendy didn't know and was too scared and ashamed to say anything. But she and her father and I sat down and talked about her anxieties, her feelings of insecurity, her wish to comfort herself with pretty things, and her need to have something from someone she loved more than she could love us at that stage of her adolescent struggle.

We returned the skirt for her, explaining her mortification. We did not force her to do it herself because we could see she'd suffered enough already. I hope—I believe—that the concern and compassion we were able to demonstrate in that situation was at least partly responsible for the loved and loving human being that our daughter grew up to be.

The key to a child's attitude toward him or herself as well as toward lying is the reaction of adults. The most important thing —and one I wish I'd remembered more often—is, *Don't Get Hysterical!* Childhood lying stems from immaturity—and if you can't be immature when you're a child, when can you be? Later on, lying is the result of a momentary loss of control over your impulses. While the lie cannot be ignored, forgiveness tends to strengthen the controls. Feeling understood and loved encourages the development of necessary moral convictions.

When a child becomes a habitual liar, it is not necessarily the start of a lifelong pattern of behavior. It is an indication that the youngster is going through a rough growing period and has special problems that need looking into. A teacher of deaf children told me that one of the boys in her class announced that he was such a star on his Little League team that a professional baseball scout had called his father to say they were watching his progress. The teacher was so thrilled about Greg's experience that she called his mother. "But," she told me, "the whole thing was fabrication. I was so disappointed I wept. And I wept again when I talked to Greg about it. Years later—after he'd finished high school and college—he told me he'd never forgotten that episode. 'It wasn't what you said,' he explained, 'it was the tears in your eyes. No one had ever understood so well how much I suffered. It helped me to accept my handicap.'"

Even more important than what we say or do about a child's lying, of course, is how we ourselves behave. And there's the rub! Life is so much easier sometimes when we lie a little. It seems so innocuous—but is it? Kenneth, age 10, is told that his grandmother has gone on a trip because she needed a rest. After she dies of cancer, he finds out she was in the hospital all that time. Diana is told she must go to a sleep-away camp for eight weeks because the doctor says she needs more exercise; when she gets home she finds that her parents have separated.

If we want our children to learn that lying interferes with trust and that trust is necessary for loving, we need to reexamine those situations of avoidance and protection that amount to lying. We cannot ask our children to be trustworthy unless we can be trustworthy ourselves. It may be very painful for Kenneth to watch his grandmother die, but at least he'll be able to trust his parents and know that they respect him enough to know he can live through such pain. He had a right to say good-bye to his grandmother, and his feelings of betrayal can only add to his grief. And if a youngster like Diana ever needs to be treated with dignity and trust, it is when her family is in real trouble. Children can and do live through horrendous events, but they do so successfully only when they know what is happening and are given help in understanding the truth.

The biggest problem of all in this regard is the so-called white lie. There are real but very fine lines of distinction between telling the truth at all costs and hurting people unnecessarily. From the moment they're able to understand, children hear us telling lies. We even encourage them to do likewise. "It wasn't nice to tell Aunt Jane she has a big nose; you hurt her feelings," we say to a 3-year-old. But Aunt Jane *does* have a big nose. Our children hear us canceling a dinner engagement because "We all have the flu," when they know it's just because Daddy doesn't want to miss seeing a football game on television.

While I was having lunch recently in an elegant restaurant, an elderly woman passed our table. One of my companions said to the other, "Oh look, Jean, there's Mrs. Allerton. Poor old thing, she can't seem to see where she's going." The second woman got up quickly and put her arm around Mrs. Allerton. "Hello, dear," she said. "I'm Jean Mason and I haven't seen you in such a long time. I heard you were ill. How are you feeling now?"

Mrs. Allerton brightened. She'd had the flu, then got pneumonia and had been hospitalized, she said. "It was really awful and I still feel very shaky." My two friends hugged her, said she looked wonderful, and told her that her new hairdo was lovely. Mrs. Allerton stood up straighter and beamed. "You girls are a tonic," she said, then walked off with far more vitality and self-assurance than she showed when we first saw her.

As she disappeared, Jean said, "Doesn't she look awful, Ellie?" Ellie agreed: "It's so sad; she used to be quite a marvelous lady. Now she looks ridiculous with that awful hair dye." I was startled, then shocked. But after thinking it over, I had to admit that lying is justified when nobody gets hurt and somebody can be made to feel wonderful.

Obviously you can't make rigid and inflexible rules about honesty; it isn't the best policy 100 percent of the time. One friend of mine wished she hadn't made such a point of the truth when her honest Henrietta, age 5, told the next-door neighbor, "My daddy says that all those men who visit you sure aren't your cousins!"

Confusing as it is, we must try to help our children understand the need for flexibility, for exploring the subtlety of feelings. Lying is not wrong when the truth will *unnecessarily* hurt another person. But there are times when although the truth may hurt, it is essential to a loving and trusting relationship. In such cases we try to tell the truth tenderly and sensitively. But we must share our angry feelings or risk poisoning a relationship; we must share crises of illness, separation, death, and unemployment or lose touch with those we need the most at such times. Communication about important issues is essential, but honesty can also be tempered with kindness.

A father told me about a recent experience he had while practicing pitching and catching with his two sons, Mike, 10, and Danny, 7. Mike is a natural athlete, while Danny is obviously meant for other things. Mike had been teasing Danny about his clumsiness, and his father had tried to make him understand how desperately Danny wanted to be like him, and how deeply the teasing hurt him. But despite their talks, Mike continued to tease his brother. When Danny failed to catch an easy ball, their father expected some derision from Mike. Much to his surprise, Mike said, "That was a good try, Danny; you're really improving." Then he turned and winked conspiratorily at his father. "You could say Mike was lying," the father told me, "It was an easy ball and Danny should have caught it. But my reaction was one of delight. It was a sign to me that Mike was growing up, becoming sensitive to another person's feelings."

What we teach our children about lying is of vital importance. It not only involves trust and honest communication between people who care about each other but helps children examine ethical issues as well as such important qualities as love and mercy.

I'm Scared, Mommy

❋ I was standing near an escalator when I noticed a young mother angrily trying to force her small daughter onto the moving steps. The child, who looked about 4, was hanging back, gripping the banister, and howling, "No, no! I'm scared, Mommy, I'm scared!" The mother, whose arms were full of packages, kept tugging at the child. "Stop being such a baby," she told her. "I'm ashamed of you. There's nothing for you to be afraid of."

At that point a tall white-haired man who'd been waiting to get on the escalator bent down to the little girl and said, "You know what these are? These are stairs for bunny rabbits. At night, when the store is closed, they jump up and down the stairs. It's a special rabbit game. But in the daytime all the people scare the rabbits, so they hide and let boys and girls ride on their stairs until nighttime." The little girl looked at him intently. Then, with a serious look on her face, she trustingly took his hand and they rode up the escalator together.

How charming, I thought to myself. That man must have children and grandchildren of his own to be able to distract the little girl so effectively. But something about the episode kept bothering me all day. It was all so sweet—what was wrong with it?

It came to me later that evening. The trouble was that even though the child had been persuaded to go up the escalator, nobody told her that it was all right to be scared. And that was far more important than being distracted. The fears of young children often have so little to do with reality that most adults find themselves saying "There's nothing to be afraid of" repeatedly. I remember doing it quite a lot when my daughter was small. How I wish I had been as smart then as I sometimes think I am now!

What I have learned over the years is that irrational fears are far stronger than real fears, and they're especially prevalent during early childhood. Feelings of inadequacy and unlovableness in adults are related to being told we were silly, dumb, foolish, and babyish about our childhood fears. We never really get over these feelings. Somewhere, deep down inside, lurks a little child who is ashamed of being afraid.

What bothered me about the little girl on the escalator was that I wished *I* had spoken to her. I wished I'd said, "It's all right to be afraid. All little children are afraid sometimes." Then it might have been appropriate to add, "And since you are feeling scared, maybe it would help if I told you a funny story . . . or if I carried you."

Young children need so desperately to know that they are normal and lovable. It's awful to have feelings other people don't seem to understand. It's bad enough to be scared of thunder or the dark, and it's even more scary when the people you love get impatient and angry with you.

A child's fears are similar to feelings of fatigue in that the youngster simply cannot control what is happening. These feelings are overwhelming. If they could be controlled, we'd be dealing with an adult, not a child.

When a young child seems to be constantly afraid, we need to explore where the fears are coming from and what they mean. The most common explanation is *displacement*. The child unconsciously finds a substitute for a fear that is too painful to think about. For example, Jenny is afraid of her father's bad temper—and cowers when it thunders; Jeff fears his hostility toward the new baby—and talks about the "bad, bad monster" in his dreams.

"When I was a little girl," a friend of mine told me, "I was terrified of a lion that came into my room at night. My father tried to reassure me by saying it was impossible; all the lions lived in the zoo. That didn't help at all because I knew he was right; when *he* was around all the lions *were* in the zoo. It was when I was alone in the dark that one lion got out of the zoo and came to torment me! It all seemed so clear and logical to me that I couldn't understand how my father could be so stupid."

Adults need to remember that small children do not see the world from our point of view. When my daughter was about 4 years old, for example, she was terribly frightened of the dark. A nightlight in her room and another light in the hall didn't seem to help. And despite having read all the child psychology books, I behaved like any other tired, harassed, overworked mother. "There's nothing to be afraid of in the dark," I insisted. One night my daughter looked at me with solemn eyes and said, "I'm not afraid of *your* dark; I'm afraid of *my* dark." We cannot dismiss the rich and intense experiences of fantasy as unreal or unimportant. To do so is to cut a child off from his or her deepest feelings.

· Whatever the child on the escalator was afraid of—and when you think about it, a moving staircase does have something reptilian and scary about it, especially if you're only two feet tall—her fear was very real. Telling her it was silly could not make it go away. And implying that she was a bad little girl to embarrass her mother can—if it happens often enough—make her feel that something is wrong with her, that she is unlovable.

Parents are often reluctant to acknowledge a child's fears because they are afraid they'll reinforce existing fears and even encourage new ones. This concern is understandable but entirely wrong. Acknowledging a feeling with genuine compassion is the best way to help it go away. In all my years of working with parents and children I have never seen one case in which sympathy and understanding increased a child's fears.

One mother got very angry with me when I told her crying child, "I know how terrible you feel because Mommy is going to leave you here at nursery school." As the mother explained, "I've been trying so hard to convince Ginny that there is nothing to be afraid of, and now you're undermining all my hard work!" Her anger turned to confusion, however, when Ginny crawled into my lap, sucking her thumb and whimpering a little, but not screaming anymore.

In a similar situation a father was trying to get his son into the ocean. Kenny was crying and looking terrified, but his father kept asking, "What's the matter with you? Why are you acting like such a baby? Do you think I'd let you drown? It's fun in the water!" When I butted in to say, "Boy, those waves sure are scary, I know lots of boys and girls who are afraid of the ocean," Kenny's father obviously had a hard time controlling his impulse to hit me. Kenny ran away to play in the sand and his father said, "So much for your wonderful psychology. You literally told him he's right to be afraid. Now he'll never go into the water,"

I didn't tell Kenny it was right or wrong to be afraid; all I did was acknowledge the reality of his fear. The boy's mother seemed to have understood. A few minutes later she and Kenny were playing a game, running away from "the naughty little waves that are biting us." Kenny was having a marvelous time trying to master his fear as he ran into the waves, then laughed and screamed as he ran out again.

Telling a child that you understand how he feels and that many children feel the same way frees him or her to meet the challenge the fear presents. A child who feels "I'm normal and nice" has the necessary energy to deal with his fears. The bravest child in the doctor's office is the one who has been told, "You will probably be scared and it is all right to cry. I'll hold your hand very tight and it will be over in a minute." With that kind of moral support, there is hardly anything a child can't do!

If Your Child
Threatens to Run Away

❉ Many years ago I happened to be reading a charming story to my then 4-year-old daughter called *The Runaway Bunny*, by Margaret Wise Brown. It begins this way: "Once there was a little bunny who wanted to run away. So he said to his mother, 'I am running away.' 'If you run away,' said his mother, 'I will run after you. For you are my little bunny.'" I thought to myself, now there's a rabbit who knows what she's doing! After many years of talking with parents, I have come to the conclusion that often *we* don't. Too frequently we misinterpret what children are really saying to us when they threaten to leave home.

Many of us can remember the times when as children we felt angry enough at others and sorry enough for ourselves to think of "hitting the road." As parents we have learned that this is a normal part of growing up, and unless running away becomes chronic and suggests some deeper problem, we are apt to feel we should treat it lightly. One of the ways in which parents try to seem nonchalant under such circumstances is in agreeing with their child that perhaps he does need a change. One mother reported that when her 8-year-old entered the living room carrying a packed suitcase, she offered to provide a picnic lunch and set about doing so. But while she was busy wrapping hard-boiled eggs in waxed paper, her small daughter burst into tears.

Another mother told of an experience with her 10-year-old son who was very angry at her for not getting him a dog. She said it seemed as if he just couldn't find a place in the house where he could get far enough away from her. One night after supper he came downstairs in his pajamas and announced that he was leaving home. (It was snowing too!) Caught unprepared, his mother told him to go right ahead. When he did she had to run after him and was so confused, angry, and frightened that it ended with her spanking him, which didn't solve anything.

One mother of an adopted boy who had previously lived in many homes and received little love described how much she and her husband had wanted to show Fred that they really cared about him. Once when he ran away from their home in anger, they were afraid to be too severe with him. In their uncertainty, they asked Fred what he thought they should do. Without a moment's hesitation he said, "If you love me, you better not let me do that again!"

In other words, children want to know someone will set limits to what they may do. A story told by a New York policeman is a case in point. He was standing on a street corner and noticed that a small boy passed him at regular ten-minutes intervals, so he was obviously walking around and around the same block. The officer finally asked the child what he was doing. "I'm running away from home," the boy explained. "But why do you keep going 'round and 'round the block?" the policeman inquired. The child replied with serious dignity, "Because I'm not allowed to cross the street alone."

In trying to indicate that they do not take the threat of running away too seriously, many parents play along with their children, helping them pack, saying in effect, "We're sorry to see you go, but if you feel you must, well, there's nothing we can do about it." Some parents try to point out the hazards involved but find that this sometimes makes their children even more determined.

Perhaps we parents misunderstand the challenge presented by the child who threatens to run away. We know that anger—his or ours or both—is usually involved and has probably precipitated his wish to run away. "I'll show you," the child is saying. "I'll go away and never come back, then you'll be sorry." In other words, he hopes that after he is gone we'll find out we really care about him —how much we miss him. But threatening to run away may also be a way of asking, "If I got angry at you and felt like leaving you, would you let me go?" Children want desperately to believe that no unhappy feelings or anger on their part could ever persuade us to let them go. The child wants to feel that even though his own sense of reality is distorted by his feelings, his parents, wiser than he and always loving, will set realistic limits to what he is allowed to do and let him know in no uncertain terms that while he may be angry, they will never let him go away from them until he is grown and ready.

Children are sometimes overcome by their own impulses, and at such times they want to be able to count on us to help them control themselves. Children who are permitted to do just as they please become frightened and insecure. Perhaps when they threaten to run away they are really saying, "I feel like doing something I don't really want to do, so somebody please stop me!"

Looked at in this way, the running-away threat has much to say to parents. Besides representing anger and a wish for independence there is present, too, an equally strong wish to be loved and protected and to know for sure that these momentary feelings and impulses cannot really prove dangerous because one has parents who will see that things don't get out of hand.

How, then, should parents handle the situation? They must first try to understand and accept the child's anger or hurt feelings or wish to escape authority, or whatever else may have led to the crisis. They must try to make it quite clear to the child that these are natural feelings that can be comfortably handled within the family. Running away is not the answer, and the child must be given the assurance that under no circumstances will his parents let him go away and stay away. Instead, they must answer the unasked but present question, "Would you let me go?" with a firm and absolute "NO!" This is really what the child wants to hear.

When a Child
Nags All the Time

❋ I was sitting next to the pool at a motel trying to relax and enjoy the sun. But I found my head beginning to pound and realized that I was clenching my teeth so hard that my jaws were beginning to hurt. Near me was a father holding a pretty little girl on his lap. Next to him was an older boy—probably 6 or 7—who kept up a constant whining and nagging. He was nagging to go back into the water, although he was shivering; he nagged his father to buy him a ball for sale in the coffee shop. His whining voice grated on my nerves, and I finally got up and moved away. But as I did so, I saw the little boy's eyes; even as he kept up the whining and the nagging, his eyes were fixed on his father's lap.

There's the "hidden agenda," I said to myself. It isn't going in the pool he wants, or the ball from the coffee shop, or the candy bar from the poolside machine, or to go watch television in the room—it's that place on his father's lap. When children nag endlessly in a whining, petulant tone of voice, they can drive their parents right up the wall; there is little that wears us down more or faster. Unfortunately it is one of those vicious circles; the more annoyed we become, the more it is likely to increase—for behind all nagging and whining is a hidden request for something that usually has nothing at all to do with what the child is asking for at the moment.

When a child begins to nag and whine excessively—when it

seems to become a fixed pattern in daily events—you will get absolutely nowhere by the frontal attack that every parent tries. We are usually so annoyed by the nagging that our spontaneous reaction is impatience and anger; we threaten to punish, refuse to listen, or just yell a lot. I know because I've been there myself. In fact, what brought it to mind recently was the visit of two little girls, sisters aged 8 and 10, to my summer home. The younger, Linda, was driving me crazy. She whined constantly at her sister Andrea's every word or action.

"Andrea is looking at me cross-eyed," she would wail, or, "Andrea has more banana than I do." Such horrendous occurrences would bring on a flood of crocodile tears, and I could feel myself getting more and more impatient. If an event were planned for the afternoon, Linda would nag me forty times during the morning about where, when, and how, until I would threaten to forget the whole thing—and her lower lip would tremble, her eyes fill, and I would feel an irrational, helpless fury.

On the third day of the visit, there was some minor altercation —I think Andrea boasted that she'd found a frog but hadn't called Linda—and the wheepy wailing started again. I heard myself shouting, "Linda, that's enough! Just cut out all the dramatics! I don't want to hear another word!" Linda looked stricken and ran to her room. And I stood at the sink feeling a lot guiltier than most parents do at such moments, because I'm supposed to know better!

Since I'm no longer confronted with childraising on a regular basis, it was easier for me to regain my patience and perspective more quickly. That one dramatic moment brought me to my senses, and I realized that what I was doing was the exact opposite of what I have tried to encourage other parents to do—look for causes instead of treating symptoms.

I knew instantly what was behind Linda's unusually high nagging and whining quotient. I guess I'd know all along but hadn't felt ready to do anything about it. I followed Linda, found her curled up on the bed, sat down next to her, and said, "I'm sorry, darling. The truth is we both feel like crying about Big Things— and that's what we ought to do." Linda's mother had died almost a year earlier. Linda and I hadn't seen each other since the funeral.

When we met again there was the hidden agenda of our terrible sorrow and pain. Until we dealt with that, head-on, Linda would whine and I would yell. Instead we sat on the bed together, holding each other tight, and bawling our heads off. During the rest of the visit we talked—all of us—about what we were feeling and we cried often. Real tears in exchange for crocodile tears. Real feelings to bring us together rather than separate us from each other.

I know full well that there are times when children just wear us down and blowing off some steam won't destroy their little psyches but just may save ours! But when a child becomes a perpetual whiner and nagger, we really need to take a hard look at what the underlying meaning may be. Otherwise we are trapped together in a pattern of behavior that becomes harder and harder to stop.

The most frequent cause of whining and nagging is the sort of thing I've described in these first two instances, when there's an underlying need to face some real problem and we're just not seeing it. The daddy at the pool not getting the message of jealousy; my not getting the message of grief. The child doesn't know the source of his or her own discomfort, and nagging becomes a way of relieving inner tensions. If we want to help a child to stop nagging, we need to ask ourselves, Where could this be coming from? Is Jenny upset because we moved and she hasn't made any new friends? Is Donald trying to take my attention away from the baby? Is Suzy afraid of her teacher?

We can't always hit it right—and we shouldn't expect to. A child needs a parent, not a live-in psychiatrist. If we try to think as sensitively and imaginatively as we can we may at least get close, and the very act of trying is helpful to the child. If we really haven't a clue about the source of steady whining, we can begin to home in on the cause by saying, for example, "You know, that voice you're using is making me angry, so let's see if we can figure out what's *really* bothering you. I don't think it's just the bubble gum you want me to buy; you're probably upset about something."

The most obvious cause of nagging is a plea for attention. From the child's point of view (and this is mostly on an unconscious level), it is sometimes better to have a parent yelling at him than ignoring him. Maybe the reason he's whining so much is because he's scared to death; he hears Mommy and Daddy fighting a lot at night after they think he's asleep. Suppose they get so mad that they leave? Who will take care of him? Is it his fault that they get so mad? These thoughts are painful and terrifying, and there is just no way the child can ask for answers. But his anxiety expresses itself in endless whining and pleading. Even getting a slap or being banned from television aren't really upsetting because he's being noticed. And while the excitement continues, he can forget those real terrors. The trouble is that if nobody helps to answer those questions, the whining and the nagging become a steady, continuing defense against the fears.

When such a pattern seems to be developing, we need to ask ourselves what's happening to the family in general. Children have a very sensitive readar system. If Mommy and Daddy are considering a separation . . . a parent is about to lose a job . . . a grandparent is dying—they know something is wrong. Maybe it's time to sit down and face the issue together so that the child feels he is a part of the family, even if painful events are occurring. There is less need to nag for attention if someone is giving you a little.

One of the most common causes of nagging among children is that a child senses a basic uncertainty or ambivalence in a parent. This is the easiest kind to cure. One mother told me, "I was going bananas every time I had to take the kids with me to a supermarket or a department store. It was like Pavlov's dogs—the sight of a counter full of *anything* and the nagging would start: "I want this, I want that!' I'd get so mad, I'd scream myself hoarse. One day my sister was with me. By the time we left the store, I was in a rage. She pointed out to me that in spite of how mad I was, I'd bought half the things they'd asked for. She reminded me of how poor we were when our dad died. We were just little kids and our mother went back to work and we never felt we had enough of anything. My sister showed me what I was doing. While I got mad about the nagging about buying everything, I really behaved like a kid myself—still wanting what I couldn't have. It was a good shock treatment. Now I say to myself, "Act like a grown-up; if it isn't any good and I don't want to buy it that's it; no fooling around."

When we have mixed feelings ourselves, children sense it immediately. When you are little it is quite natural to want everything you see. And if a parent seems to waver and often give in, no child worth his salt is going to stop asking. Is a child nagging about something you may once have wanted yourself? Is he acting out a drama you once felt you lost with your own parents? It may be time to decide what you want for your child and what you wanted for yourself. A father told me, "When I realized I was overindulging the children because no one had ever spoiled me, I decided it would be much better for the children if I gave myself a present once in a while. Now that I do this, they've become more selective about what they ask for."

Another common cause of whining is our inappropriate expectations of a child. Sometimes we're not even aware of this; sometimes a child has misinterpreted our expectations. In any case, if a child feels that he or she is not measuring up—not learning to read quickly enough . . . not being responsible about taking the garbage out . . . not being nice enough when the relatives visit . . . not giving up the night-light soon enough—it can lead to fear. There is that uncomfortable feeling in the pit of his or her stomach—"I need to grow up faster"—and since that's impossible, the fear grows and the child regresses. Whining may be nature's way of saying, "Don't rush me." This theory is quite easy to prove. Just keep telling a whiner that he's acting like a baby, and the whining will get worse and worse! It would be preferable, however, to do one's "research" in a more positive way. Just keep telling a whiner that you know he feels like being a baby again sometimes and that it's okay. You might even rock him a little or "play baby" or talk baby talk once in a while. You'll be amazed how the whining decreases!

Whining and nagging are signals that attention is not being paid to some genuine need. Nobody can ever meet all of a child's needs, so this kind of behavior is inevitable to some degree. We need only become concerned when it is excessive and seems to be a cry for help. The problem is that nobody loves a nagger, which is tough, since what a nagger needs is love.

When a Child Is Rude

✳ When my daughter was a child we lived on a quiet street where there were many children. At least once a week a certain neighbor would appear on my doorstep to complain bitterly about the rudeness of my child and her playmates. Her usual complaint was that my daughter stuck out her tongue when passing her house and that groups of children, including mine, shouted obscenities at her.

My first reaction was to feel very angry at my daughter. My second thoughts, sometime later, were more candid and impartial. Like so many other parents, I tended to side with the adults in any dispute with my daughter. When I heard an accusation by a teacher or a school crossing guard, I almost invariably felt guilty and angry at my child. Yet if someone accused my husband or a close friend of being mean or nasty, my instinct would be to check it out first before reacting.

What I realized after reflecting over the neighbor's accusation was that the kind of behavior she described was not at all characteristic of my daughter. Even at that age she was a tender, sensitive human being. The truth of the matter was that the lady down the street had a paranoid hatred of children and was sure they had been put on earth to torture her. She was consistently unpleasant to the children and they reacted accordingly. Good manners are reciprocal, and unless children are severely disturbed emotionally, most of them give as good as they get.

Sometimes we don't realize how rudely we treat children. This was amusingly illustrated by a skit on *The Carol Burnett Show* many years ago. It involved four adults having dinner together with conversation imitative of that typically addressed to children. The hostess told her guests to wash their hands before coming to the table, and a guest expressed shock at the "terrible table manners" of the host when he put his elbows on the table. The dinner party was not only a disaster, it was also a cogent reminder of the lack of respect with which we tend to treat our children.

In a similar vein is the poignant story one mother told me about her son, aged 4, who seemed especially grumpy at breakfast one day. When she asked him what was wrong, he replied in a world-weary tone of voice, "Nobody ever says, 'Good morning, Allen, how do you feel today? All you ever say is, 'Have you been to the toilet yet?' "

We are also inclined to be inattentive to our children—to ignore or slough off a young child's wishes or ideas. A charming example of this was provided by a 5-year-old who was taken to an elegant restaurant for dinner. The waiter handed the child an enormous menu and with great dignity asked, "And what would you like to be served, young man?" The child looked up at his parents with wide-eyed wonder and whispered, "He thinks I'm *real!*" This unexpected display of attention brought forth a spontaneous reaction that tells us a great deal about how our children feel about themselves: much less "real" than adults.

It's not surprising that they feel that way either. A friend told me about a recent conversation with her mother that was interrupted by a young nephew. She told him that it was rude to interrupt when other people were talking and that he could have his turn as soon as they were finished. Her mother tends to be long-winded and this was a very long story, but David waited patiently, showing remarkable control over his restlessness and boredom. When her mother finished, my friend said, "Okay, David, now it's your turn." Halfway through David's story, however, her mother interrupted. "I made David wait for you to finish," my friend reminded her, "and I think you can wait for David to finish." Grandma was surprised and hurt, clearly indicating her own double standard about manners for adults and children. Most of us object when a child tries to interrupt a conversation with an adult but are careless about his right to equal treatment.

Another reason children are often rude is that sometimes we unwittingly encourage it. Early one morning when I was having a cup of coffee with a neighbor at her kitchen table, her 4-year-old son suddenly leaned over the table, took the ashtray, and emptied its contents into my coffee cup. "I'm putting sugar in your coffee," he said. I was furious but even more surprised by his mother's reaction. She laughed and said, "He's got such a good imagination." Then she proceeded to play "tea party" with him, as if we were all in the sandbox together. I found myself feeling very unfriendly toward the child, who was being allowed to make a pest of himself.

Although I don't think this sort of thing happens as often as many people believe, some parents do allow a kind of rude behavior that does not help children learn to respect the rights of others. It is a cruel way to treat a child because it makes him unlovable. The permission to do things that make others angry or uncomfortable is certainly poor parenting. The mature and caring parent tries to teach his or her child that good manners are good human relations —that you don't do or say some things simply because you will hurt other people's feelings and they, in turn, will feel unfriendly toward you. It's a simple lesson for civilized living with others.

Another kind of rudeness in children is really just a symptom of difficult or awkward periods of growth. It is normal to behave childishly when one is a child, and some rudeness seems to be just an inevitable function of immaturity. We can show disapproval and try to control the behavior, but we need to have some tolerance and a sense of perspective. We should let the child know that he is just immature and not a bad person, for guilt impedes the growing that needs to take place. For example, you shouldn't be surprised if a 3-year-old gets so overstimulated at a large family gathering that he loses what little social controls he has learned, starts kicking Uncle John in the shins, and then begins to shout all the new four-letter words he's learned in nursery school. Obviously overtired and out of control, he needs to be alone for a while or to take a nap.

A similar situation is created when a teenager comes home in the middle of a dinner party, grunts an unintelligible greeting while looking at the floor, then slumps off to his room while you bravely try to excuse his rudeness with some bright comment about the generation gap. Your guests are all probably people this young man has known (and even liked!) for many years, so why this sudden fall from social grace? Adolescent shyness and self-consciousness—a passing phase. You don't have to condone it; you may even suggest that a slightly more friendly greeting would have been appreciated; but it's not worth any great commotion. This kind of social discomfort is excruciating for many adolescents—far worse for them than for us.

Rudeness that seems clearly related to passing periods of immaturity should be handled with tolerance; making a federal case out of these episodes only increases the youngster's painful self-consciousness. The best cure for such behavior is to let the child know that the adults who love him have faith in his ability to go on growing. I saw an example of this when my father, an excellent chess player, visited friends and played chess with their 14-year-old son, Jason, who was just learning. My father told Jason he would play very well someday, but thinking the boy would enjoy a real challenge, he played a hard game. Jason held up well for a while, but being no match for my father, he was beaten badly. My father wanted to use the game as a lesson in how to play chess, but Jason jumped up from the table on the verge of tears and ran out of the house.

Now one might say this was poor sportsmanship and very bad manners on the part of a young man who should have known better. Many parents would have reacted with outrage and shame, but Jason's mother apologized for him and explained. "Jason is going through a stage," she said, "where he finds his own inadequacies unbearable. He's oversensitive about any kind of failure. I know he feels terrible about what he did, but he's working very hard to conquer this problem."

Nothing would have been gained by punishing or lecturing Jason. Normally a kind and sensitive person, he's wrestling with a problem in growing up. Adults who can understand and tolerate such lapses show respect for a child's struggles—and that teaches more about manners (sensitive caring about others) than any other treatment.

Sometimes behavior that we interpret as rudeness is really just a reflection of changing standards. Although contrary to our own upbringing, the message may be a caring one. If you give your grandson a gift, for example, he may not say "Thank you," but his "That's cool!" means the same thing. The long-haired barefoot young people singing in the park may seem very rude and disruptive at first glance, but you may discover on closer attention that as they sing and dance about, they are picking up the garbage others have left behind. Being concerned with the problems of ecology is one of the most important kinds of good manners anyone can have these days.

It's important to understand that things that represented good manners to us don't always have the same meaning for today's young people. They may not send birthday or Mother's Day cards or come home for Christmas, because they think that the greeting-card business is pure commercialism, that loving feelings ought to be expressed all year, and that they'd rather visit spontaneously than follow a prescribed ritual. You may not agree with them, but to simply dismiss their ideas and behavior as a lack of good manners is to deny the reality of change and the emergence of new ways of showing concern for human relationships.

As far as I'm concerned, the most important reason for the breakdown of good manners among the young is the lack of something I call social parenting—being concerned not only with the human relationships within our own homes but with the lives of *all* children now and in the future.

Good manners arise out of a sense of well-being. When people are in general kind and caring, when the climate of life is full of hope and purpose, children instinctively react with their own joyful acceptance of the necessary rules for living harmoniously with others. If we cared, as a nation, for all our children, we could not tolerate the pollution of our air and water, the intolerable destruction of natural resources, the nightmarish decaying of our cities, the hunger, unemployment, lack of training and job opportunities that influence the daily lives of millions of children. I find it irrelevant —even obscene—to talk of good manners among children when funds for day centers and medical research and education are being cut.

If we want children to show concern for their fellowman, we have to begin by showing concern for them. Any nation that does not look upon its children as its greatest national resource can have no future. None of us is personally responsible for the problems of modern life; we are as much victims as our children. But what will defeat us most of all is discouragement, the feeling that we as individuals can do nothing to improve the world in which our children are growing up. I think we can make a difference—and we must.

In the early days of America, there was a sense of community; people felt involved in each other's lives. I think our children suffer from a lack of watchful, caring adults within the community who care enough to interfere—who show that the way they grow is important to us all. In writing about his experiences on a trip to Russia several years ago, psychologist Urie Bronfenbrenner of Cornell University described how bystanders interfered with his discipline of his own children. When his son misbehaved on a bus, two or three women chastised him gently but firmly. When his children got into an argument with some other children in a park, adult onlookers immediately moved in and scolded the children soundly. At first Dr. Bronfenbrenner was resentful at the interference, but as he observed the Russian people he discovered that everyone felt a deep personal responsibility for seeing to it that the nation's children grew up properly. While I think this can be overdone— and that the right to raise one's children in one's own way has high priority—there is much to be said for an atmosphere of community concern for children.

I'm afraid that many of us have a tendency to look for simple answers to very complex questions. If children scrawl obscenities on a statue in the park, we sometimes scream, "Send their parents to jail; that will make them control their children!" When children start a fire in a school, we sometimes say, "What they need is a good whipping!" The problems of parents and children are not so easily solved. The trouble is not those difficult children so much as it is our own inclination to use them as scapegoats for the larger problems we don't want to face—the sordid, terrible inadequacies of the places and conditions under which they are trying to grow. Painful as it may be to accept, extremely dangerous and frightening misbehavior in children is a symptom of grown-up failure to truly nurture the young. Until all of our children believe that they are our most precious treasure, we may not see much evidence of good manners. That is earned by caring enough to give our children the very best.

Accident Proneness
in Children

❋ A young mother rushes over to her 4-year-old son on the playground; he has just fallen off the jungle gym. At first she is just frightened and concerned, but when she feels reassured that all bones are in their proper location and only a small scratch on the knee bears testament to this latest crisis, she comments wryly to her park-bench companion, "That's the third time today Jeff's fallen; accidentally on purpose, if you ask me. He's still mad at me for going to the hospital and coming home with this noisy, demanding baby sister, so he keeps me hopping."

It all sounds perfectly casual, and most of us understand this idea of "accidentally on purpose." Actually, this is a profound idea, and while similar observations have been made throughout human history, it is only recently that such concepts have come under scientific scrutiny.

When she was 9, our daughter sprained her ankle quite severely. She was overjoyed, once the initial pain and fear were over, to learn that she would have to use crutches for several weeks. She couldn't wait to go to school with them, and she wasn't disappointed by the reactions of her classmates; this event was just as glamorous, as attention-getting, as she had anticipated it would be. Everyone wanted to try the crutches and our young "Camille" gloried in her opportunity to upstage everyone else. One little girl in her class didn't like it a bit; two days before, she had jumped from a stone wall onto a concrete playground and had hurt her foot. She had been limping slightly ever since, but several days later she was hopping on one foot and insisted that her wounded foot was getting worse and worse. We commiserated with her mother and the teacher, and joked about crutches being a contagious disease. We were all being very psychologically sophisticated as we concluded that one 9-year-old's glamour could be another 9-year-old's poison. Fortunately children have a way of insisting that we grown-ups look at reality occasionally, and when things continued to go from bad to worse, a doctor was consulted. The second casualty was a bona fide sprain of the arch of the foot, which doesn't always show up right away but gets worse as time goes by. The sprain had become aggravated by delayed treatment, and much to our daughter's chagrin, her schoolmate had to use crutches for *four* weeks.

We could say, "So much for new theories," but that isn't quite the end of the story. The fourth-grade teacher told us several weeks later that he was now keeping a daily log of accidents in his class. While they were fortunately of a minor nature, his class was averaging three to four crises a day! And it had all started with that first sprained ankle. Were these "accidentaly on purpose?" How can we tell? When does a child get secondary gains from an accident that will give him special attention and recognition? Do children unconsciously bring about accidents? When a series of accidents occur, is it always a matter of chance?

Scientific research is helping us find some of the answers. It is clear that if there is such a thing as accident proneness we need to learn all we can about it in order to take preventive measures. The World Health Organization reports that in the age group from 1 to 19 years, accidents are the leading cause of death and the highest percentage occurs in the preschool age group.

The concept of accident proneness in adults has proved statistically valid and practically workable. There has been consistent agreement in almost all such studies that most accident-prone adults have some or all of the following general qualities:

1. A marked resentment of authority.
2. Considerable difficulty expressing resentment or hostility openly; it tends to stay "bottled-up."
3. A tendency toward somewhat superficial, shifting relationships with other people.
4. They are usually impulsive people who often act quickly, without thinking, and tend to have short-range goals.

Studies of accident proneness in children are fewer, more recent, and somewhat less definitive. The very nature of childhood creates special problems in studying accident proneness in youngsters. Children are naturally more curious, more adventurous than adults. In order to grow and learn, they must experiment and explore, while at the same time they have only limited experience and maturity of judgment. Children do have less inner control over their impulses than adults, and at the same time they have boundless energy, wider opportunities, and more varied experiences. Technological advance has also placed many new hazards in their way—more cars, more traffic, crowded urban living, more potentially dangerous electrical equipment in the home. In addition, conflict with authority, the struggle for increasing independence, and resentment of adult controls are everyday realities with growing children.

Several recent studies suggest some general concepts that may prove helpful to parents and teachers. They report that in studying accident proneness in children it may be important to differentiate between temporary accident proneness, which occurs during special periods in a child's life and is short-lived, and accident proneness that is intense and continuous over a long period of time. It appears that shifting relationships with authority and episodes of intense striving for greater independence may produce temporary periods of accident proneness in children. This may explain why some children have many more accidents than others. It is also possible that the problems of growing up may provoke some accident proneness. If, for example, a child has a series of accidents within a year but up till then had been fairly accident-free, this could be your child's way of dealing with some of the problems of growing up. You can watch carefully, but without undue alarm.

There are some children, however, who have a long history of more serious accidents, and where such a pattern seems to be developing, special help and professional guidance may be necessary. Many adults who have high accident rates were also accident-prone during childhood, and it seems quite likely that such people have used accidents as an unconscious way of solving psychological problems. Some researchers suggest that children who continue to be accident-prone are unconsciously seeking punishment for the relief of guilt feelings: "I'll punish myself so Mommy won't punish me."

Repeated accidents are sometimes a way for a child to relate to others, and get needed attention. They may also be a way of meeting the dependency needs of a child who wants to be babied, comforted, and cared for, and does not know any other way of having this need fulfilled. While appearing to be debonair, treating dangerous situations lightly, without needed caution, such children may really be, like Tom Sawyer, hoping, "They will be sorry when I'm dead!" Feeling unfairly treated, they unconsciously hope that accidents will make parents feel sorry for them.

Serious accident proneness can also reflect deep fears about bodily injury; sometimes a real accident is less painful than childish fantasies about more serious body damage, and may relieve such fears, at least temporarily. Anger and hostility that are too rigidly controlled, without any avenues for acceptable expression, may also play a part in a high accident rate. Some of these feelings may be a response to overcontrolling adults who do not provide the young-ster with enough opportunity for independent self-expression and autonomy; "clipped wings" can cause pent-up feelings of resent-ment that find expression through accidents. These are all complex and serious problems that would perplex and trouble any parent and which require expert consultation. It is fortunate that at the same time that we are learning more about the emotional problems of childhood, resources for help and guidance are also becoming increasingly available through child guidance clinics and commu-nity counseling services.

We need to remember, however, that marked accident proneness is uncommon in childhood and that most of us are going to be more concerned with the temporary varieties of accident proneness. It is also important for us to be aware of the fact that some of the qualities that may lead to a certain degree of accident proneness in our children are really positive qualities. Implicit in all the research reports is a subtle suggestion that some of the most interesting children may be inclined to have accidents! If we reflect a little about some descriptions of accident-prone children—"emotional, lively, daring, responsive, impulsive"—we can see that these are far from negative characteristics, in reasonable doses! Even a certain amount of defiance to adult authority gives flavor and color to an emerging personality! Before we attach a universal label of "signs of disturbance" to all accident-prone behavior, we may want to pause a moment and reflect on the fact that while placid, cautious, submissive children may live safer lives, curiosity and adventurousness, at least in reasonable quantities, are the basis for human progress.

As adults we all share the responsibility for creating a reasonably safe environment for our children. One interesting sidelight of some of the recent research is that there appear to be some children who, while they never have accidents themselves, somehow manage to get other children to have them! This fact points up the general need for some watchful observance of children at play. We want our children to learn through their own experiences, but it would be foolish to stand by if one child is being taunted into danger by another or being picked on by older, stronger, children. We know that children cannot control immediate and strong impulses, and that inner controls develop slowly as they grow up. We are responsible for setting up reasonable safety precautions both at home and in the larger community where our children learn and play. We have every right to demand traffic supervision on busy streets, safe and supervised playgrounds, schools and homes that are constructed under stringent safety regulations, household and other appliances that have built-in safety devices.

The National Safety Council provides excellent literature on some of the most flagrant household dangers that can be eliminated by a little care and caution. Plastic bags still cause totally unnecessary accidents, despite a very intensive nationwide educational program warning parents about this hazard. We have to make some choices, too. Is it more important when we have young children to have lamps, vases, and art objects on display in precarious and tippable places, or to live with a certain amount of aesthetic starkness, at least until our children are older?

When weighing realistic dangers and potential accidents, we are faced with the same dilemma we confront in so many other aspects of living with children: How can we set sensible limits and at the same time not stifle our children's healthy pursuit of independence? Some childhood accidents are provoked by too many "don'ts"; some are caused by a child's sensing too many anxieties and fears on the part of the adults around him.

Each of us, out of our own life experiences and in terms of our temperamental differences, will have to decide on a balanced approach to preventing accident proneness in our children. We can make every effort to see that children who have repeated accidents get help with their underlying emotional difficulties. We can see to it that children who tend to be accident-prone live in a reasonably safe environment in which there are sensible limits and controls. For example, active, impulsive, energetic children should have opportunities for supervised professional training in the physical skills they care so much about. Most important of all, perhaps, we can make a conscious effort to increase our understanding of the children we live and work with so that their real needs for support, attention, and encouragement from interested and loving adults can be met in happier and more constructive ways.

Part V

*

THERE ARE NO GOOD AND BAD HABITS

*

Sense and Nonsensense
About Habits

❋ When little Amy, a 20-month-old charmer with enormous brown eyes and a radiant smile, came to visit her grandmother, it was the start of a month-long celebration. I found her utterly enchanting—and absolutely wallowing in tons of unconditional love.

At least five doting and adoring neighbors, friends, and relatives dropped in every day to marvel at Amy. On a sunny Sunday afternoon, the number sometimes went up to ten or twelve. And of course, no one came empty-handed; by the end of the second week there were nine stuffed animals, two music boxes, and seven pull-toys covering the living-room floor. In the midst of all this, Amy held court, the complete center of everyone's attention, batting her eyes and blowing kisses, teasing and flirting and offering her soggy pretzel to everyone.

How marvelous, I thought; all this nourishing love to stand her in good stead all of her life. But when I stopped watching Amy just long enough to look at her mother and share our mutual delight, I found her looking agitated and troubled. "It's all just fine, right now," she said. "But what's going to happen when we go back home? She's gotten into the habit of being the center of attention all the time and of expecting that everyone who comes through the door will have a new toy for her. How will I break her of the habit of expecting so much attention all the time? It's going to be terrible!

There speaks the average American parent. If there is one universal fiction believed by most parents it is this nonsense about habits:

- Don't pick the baby up at night when he cries; he'll get into the habit.

- Make her taste new foods or she'll get into the habit of never trying anything new.

- If I don't smack him when he tries it, he's going get into the habit of hitting the baby.

I have often tried to figure out where this kind of thinking comes from. It seems to me that life experience ought to have proven to us that things don't work out that way at all. But I suppose the fear that things won't change is so deep-rooted that it blocks out all rational evidence.

I was certainly a victim of this rationale myself as a young mother. Like so many others, I had to be constantly reassured by my pediatrician that my daughter would not wet the bed, eat only strained foods, or need a night-light when she got married! And I had every reason to know better, for I was a psychology student long before she was born and had carefully examined much of the research done on the subject of habits. What we ordinarily call a habit is simply a kind of behavior (which we usually aren't crazy about!) that we give up when we don't need it anymore. When the need behind a habit is met, it gradually disappears.

- The crying baby *does* stop crying when it is finally comforted.

- Children *do* become interested in having variety in foods when the need for familiarity and sameness has been satisfied.

- Brothers and sisters *do* stop hitting the younger child when their own needs for attention and reassurance have been met.

In spite of my own nervousness on the subject, I did try hard to overcome the simplistic kind of thinking that seems to take over in this connection. And there was one research study in the 1940s that greatly helped me to keep my perspective. There were many others of a similar nature, but this one always struck me as especially ingenious and dramatic.

At that time a psychologist working with children being transferred from institutions to foster homes came to the conclusion that their inability to adjust to family life stemmed from very early emotional deprivation. These were children who had been abandoned in early infancy and had rarely experienced any kind of intense or continuing love relationship with an adult. Transferring them to foster homes was often difficult and discouraging because their behavior was so unacceptable. Many were constantly shifted from one foster home to another, and the professional people who felt so strongly that institutional care must be discontinued felt their faith in this newer approach shaken. These were children who had developed such "habits" as stealing, cursing, setting fires, poor school work, and running away.

The psychologist decided that all of these children had missed an important part of human growth—love and care during the early months of life. He got a research grant, rented a brownstone in New York City, hired a staff of social workers, nurses, teachers, and psychologists, and furnished the house with individual rooms containing large cribs, rocking chairs, and preschool toys. Then he selected two groups of boys, aged about 7 to 11. All of them had been in two or three foster homes within a short period of time and had been transferred because of their behavior problems. Half of the group continued to live in their current foster placement with the normal amount of supervision. The second half were taken to the brownstone, where each met his personal counselor, someone who would be devoting full-time attention to him for an indeterminate period of time. Each boy was told, in effect, "When you were a little baby you had a very hard time. There was no one to give you all the love and attention you needed, no one who had the time to play with you. We are going to pretend that you are a baby again. This time things will be different. You can sleep in the crib, be rocked in the rocking chair, have milk from a bottle —even sleep in diapers if you want to. You don't have to go to school, but you can play with the other children, and there's a sandbox and a jungle gym in the basement. You can paint, play with clay, or build with blocks, and you can have your own special doll or stuffed animal. You can make believe you are a baby for as long as you want to, and when you don't want to anymore, that will be fine."

At first the children thought it was some kind of terrible joke. They became even more unmanageable, and some would have nothing to do with their counselors. But within a week or so they were soaking up the attention like dry sponges, and to varying degrees (including simulated baby talk) they returned to a much earlier stage of development. Within a few months all had "graduated" of their own choice; they had had enough of being babies. They were then placed in a new foster home. A year later it was found that the children who had not had this experience were still being transferred as frequently as before. Of those boys who had experienced the regression to infancy, over 80 percent were doing well and had not been transferred.

This kind of research did not teach us that all unhappy children have to have a similar experience. What it did was demonstrate an important fact about childhood, and through the continued development and refinement of play therapy for children in trouble, we have found better and better ways of filling in the missing pieces in a child's life. The essential lesson we learned from this and many other studies was that an unmet need doesn't just go away; until it is met it hangs on with unbelievable tenacity. If a child is deprived of any needs at any stage of his development, it becomes difficult—sometimes impossible—for him to go on growing and maturing. Infantile habits reflect unmet needs, and if we want to eliminate the habit, we must satisfy the underlying need.

An everyday example of this is Andrew the whiner. At age 7, he whined constantly when he was at home, driving his parents up the wall. Every request, every complaint, was a whine. Andrew seemed always to be on the verge of tears. His father decided that the only way to break him of this habit was to ignore him until he stopped.

"Until you can talk to me in a normal voice, I am not going to listen to one word you say," his father said. He was operating on the fairly universal idea that you have to break a habit before it gets too firmly established. But it didn't work. The whining got worse, not better. Finally, in desperation, Andrew's parents accepted their family doctor's suggestion that they turn to a child guidance clinic for help. There they began to look at Andrew in a new light and learned some very interesting things about him.

Andrew was 14 months old when his brother arrived. The second pregnancy had been a difficult one, and his mother had spent a good deal of time in bed from the time Andrew was about 8 months old. A second brother was born when Andrew was less than 3 years old, so by the time he was 7, all but the first few months of his life had been overshadowed by the needs of others. He'd managed fairly well to survive with only a few minor signs of immaturity until second grade, when he happened upon a teacher who probably should have been an instructor at West Point. In her classroom, there was no talking in class, silent double lines in all halls, special permission to go to the bathroom, no help allowed with stubborn boots, and demerits posted on the blackboard for forgetting to say "Please" and "Thank you" on the appropriate occasions.

This seems to have been the final straw. So much was expected of this little boy, and there was so much emotional malnutrition beneath the surface. Without the strength or the resources to handle any more challenges, he simply lapsed into more infantile behavior because his own infancy had been abrupty curtailed many years before.

Andrew gradually stopped whining when he got some babying. Sitting on his mother's lap . . . having Daddy read to him (alone!) at bedtime even though he could read to himself . . . a special trip to the puppet show with the two younger brothers left at home with a baby-sitter . . . a chance to stay with Grandma and Grandpa for a weekend by himself . . . being allowed to play quietly in his own room with paints and clay and blocks, instead of having to mind the younger children in the backyard. . . . All of this and a long, long talk with the principal of the school resulting in his transfer to a classroom run by a motherly lady of 60 who still thought 7-year-olds ought to be kissed, even in school, helped Andrew to kick the habit.

Lynn, aged 12, had "gotten into the habit" of taking things that didn't belong to her. Whenever her parents found items they knew she had taken from a store or a friend's house, they gave her a good beating—"Got to break that habit quick," they said. But it didn't get better, so beatings were reinforced by taking away many pleasurable activities. No luck—only new "bad habits": lying, staying out late, truancy. . . .

Stealing, when it becomes a habit, expresses important unmet needs. Every child has an overwhelming impulse to take something that doesn't belong to him occasionally, but when it becomes habitual it is a message, a cry for help. Twelve-year-olds are perhaps most susceptible to feelings of uncertainty about themselves, terrible feelings of self-loathing. They are changing so quickly and dramatically, and all kinds of frightening feelings inevitably accompany the signs of emerging adulthood. Beatings and other kinds of severe punishment increase the sense of deprivation, of uncertainty and unworthiness, which reinforces the habit that expresses those very feelings. The removal of the habit depends entirely on the degree to which Lynn can begin to feel hopeful and good about herself and her future as a valuable person. There should never be permission to steal, but help with hurting feelings. Punishing a habit rarely succeeds because it doesn't address the underlying need. The whiner may give up whining but start to suck his thumb; the liar may become too afraid to lie but may develop a stutter instead. As parents we need to accept our natural fears and tendencies to get hysterical about habits Then we must take a second look and find intelligent and creative ways of discovering the message behind the habit, responding to that need as effectively as we can.

To return to happy, adorable, loving little Amy—is she being spoiled by so much loving attention? What will happen to the habit of being star of the show when the play closes? Well, chances are that for a while, she will be pretty surprised and even very angry. But having had all that loving, she will have the inner resources, the strength, to move on to new challenges and experiences. She will feel confident enough to move toward other children, to feel safe with a baby-sitter, to play alone when mother is busy.

What I finally told Amy's mother was this: Suppose we knew that in the near future there was going to be a great famine and Amy would suffer from malnutrition. Would it make sense to prepare her for that eventuality by limiting her food intake, her vitamins and minerals, now so she would be accustomed to starvation? Obviously that's an idiotic idea. But experiences in feeling loved are as much a form of nourishment as food, and if a child has that emotional strength it will last him in good stead throughout the inevitable adversities that come with growing up. The well-nourished child has a better chance of survival in a famine than the malnourished one—whether one is talking about food or feelings.

Amy's mother and grandmother seemed quite impressed with my analogy, and I was feeling very satisfied with myself until Grandma said, "And how do *I* adjust to giving up the habit of seeing this wonderful child every morning for breakfast, and all day long? I think I'll die when she leaves." That one stopped me. I thought of such absurdities as, "All those wonderful memories to sustain you," and "Fill the need by loving other people's children." But while they are true and valid thoughts, some habits are too good to give up without a fight.

It Does No Good:
Biting the Hand
That Needs You

❋ There is probably no phase of childhood that baffles and enrages parents more than when Junior gives convincing evidence that Darwin was right, and we are descended from the monkeys. This is the "biting stage," which enters the lives of many parents when a child is about 2 to 3 years old.

We are shocked, first of all, because this biting maniac seems to appear, full blown, overnight; just yesterday he was that adorable baby, full of hugs and smiles, and loving everybody. We are frightened because we know that biting is dangerous and enraged because it seems so unnecessary and so bestial. The combination of warm, soft, cuddly baby and those wolfish teeth gives us the feeling that we are caught in a real Jekyll and Hyde nightmare.

Because biting arouses such strong feelings in us, we tend not to do very intelligent things about it. The typical reaction is exemplified by the mother I saw carefully examining her son's arm, where he had been bitten by his younger brother. After locating the exact spot between elbow and wrist, she bit the same spot on the biter's arm, shouting furiously, "That's exactly how it feels!"

What most parents who use the "tooth-for-a-tooth" approach discover is that such retaliation doesn't seem to have any significant effect on the aggressor's behavior. My neighbor has two children, Greta, 4, and Kenny, 2. When I dropped in to return something a few days ago, Grandma met me at the door. She showed me several ugly welts on Greta's face and arms where Kenny had bitten her. Grandma was beside herself. "We're going crazy—we don't know what to do," she said. "We washed his mouth out with soap and then with pepper, and we've beaten the living daylights out of him, but it just doesn't get through his head."

Having already gained a reputation as a busybody, I saw no reason to change my image at this point. "Oh, you're wrong," I said. "Something got through his head very well. But what got through was this: 'Grown-ups can be just as stupid and bad as children. I'm young—what's *their* excuse?' "

Grandma knows that my heart is in the right place, even if I get nasty sometimes! "I never thought of that," she said, very reasonably. "So what's *your* advice?"

Sooner or later biters stop biting, so that much of the time the punishment has little to do with the matter. However, biting *is* dangerous, and to the degree that it can be prevented or alleviated, we must do what we can. It seems to me that it helps one to decide what punishment is appropriate if we know in the first place why it is happening.

For a 2-year-old, social relations, especially with other children, can be a tumultuous experience. Up to now, if there have been any battles for survival, they have mostly been with grown-ups—and crying has succeeded very well as a technique for getting that extra cookie or not going right to bed when Daddy comes home. But many young children are forced to the conclusion that other children are another story altogether. They can be tough and unsympathetic to one's wishes; they can hit or yell for Mama; and they really couldn't care less about someone else wanting to play with that toy duck or sand pail. There's the young child, practically a baby, for heaven's sake, wanting things, needing things, having these overwhelming impulses to get what he wants when he wants it. What can he do in such a bind? His legs are still a little uncoordinated for kicking, and he's not at all sure his arms are long enough for hitting. But, by God, he does have one piece of equipment that has served him well in the pleasant act of chewing, and there is little doubt about their strength—those lovely white teeth in his mouth. When you are seized with a fear or an overwhelming desire, nothing could be more natural than using the best weapon at your disposal.

So begins the biter's nightmare. His mother, his father, all of the relatives, the clerk in the supermarket, the bus driver—everybody in the world, in fact—shrieks maniacal threats at him, indicating that what he has done is the most terrible thing one person can do to another, and nobody, except a monster, would do such a thing. Then, often as not, they bite back, leaving the child's mind in a whirl. He's faint with surprise and horror. Not only is he a rotten, awful kid, but the person he loves best in all the world is just as rotten as he is!

My advice to parents is: Don't bite the hand that needs you, for a biter needs a grown-up's love and understanding desperately. He's still that nice baby you knew last week, but now he finds that when he's scared or angry some strange and powerful urge comes over him to defend himself, and some deep, primordial instinct has told him, "Teeth Help." He doesn't want to be unlovable or monstrous; he wants to know how he can stop himself. If that is what he wants and needs to learn, then biting back, putting soap in his mouth, or beating him only relays one terrifying message: Even grown-ups, who are supposed to be wise and good, have no solution to this awful problem. They are as much victims of instinctive drives as children.

What a biter desperately needs is someone who is so mature and so sensible that he or she won't be overwhelmed by their own fury, and will be able to find some reasonable way out of this mess. Such wisdom takes the form, most often, of strong and steady arms that lift a child out of wherever he is when he bites, removes him immediately to solitude with a firm and absolute, "NO, YOU MAY NOT BITE." In the quiet of such isolation, the wise and sensible adult uses his mouth for talking—not biting—and this is what he says: "Biting can hurt very badly. I won't let anyone bite you. I won't let you bite anyone. You are very little, and sometimes you can't stop yourself, so that's why there are mommies and daddies. In a little while you will be able to remember, but until you can remember, you will have to stay by yourself and think about it for a while, when you bite someone."

There are several advantages to this procedure. One is that it lessens the amount of social contact between the young child and others. It may well be that the biting stems from a kind of hysteria at being exposed to too many social contacts too much of the time. It also helps a young child to recognize that despite the hazards of social intercourse, it really *is* something he wants very much and misses when it is taken away.

Because it always lessens anxiety and tension when grown-ups behave like grown-ups when children behave like children, it seems to me that biters are reformed far more quickly with isolation than with bites, soap, or spankings. But the actual number of days or weeks that may be needed for rehabilitation is not the only issue. An equally important factor is that this is a glorious opportunity to teach children that growing up is a fine thing—that it can lead to having a level head, being kind and understanding, and knowing what to do in an emergency. When you're 2 or 3, very immature in your ways, and often frightened by your own childishness, it is a great comfort to know that someday even *you* might grow up to be the kind of person who will see one child bite another and have the wisdom and compassion to take that pariah in your arms and out of the battle and say, "I know how to help you."

To Sleep,
Perchance to Dream

❊ Johnny is 9 months old and wakes up crying five to six times every night. It takes his mother or father fifteen to twenty minutes to rock him back to sleep.

Katie is 2½. She comes into her parents' room four to five times a night and wants to sleep with them.

Marian and Kenneth are so exhausted, so much at their wits' end, that they now lock their bedroom door but get no real sleep since they know that 3-year-old Joey is lying right outside their door, refusing to stay in his bed.

Not one of these events is very unusual; these and many other forms of sleeping problems usually drive parents crazy sooner or later. But what has piqued my curiosity in the past several years is an *epidemic* of sleeping problems. It's almost impossible to start a conversation with a young parent without getting into the subject of sleeping problems. I've also noted, listening on the radio to Dr. Lawrence Balter, a very popular child psychologist, that in a total of about four hours on the air, 50 percent or more of the questions he is asked have to do with sleep.

I started meeting with parent discussion groups in the 1940s, and continued into the 1970s. Although the sleeping problems of young children were certainly raised, the proportion was nothing at all like the current concerns. This change has been so marked that I've been doing a lot of thinking about what might have caused it. Over the past year, I think I have developed a theory about what might be happening and what might be done about it.

During the years I worked with parents, life was relatively quiet and easygoing for infants and preschoolers. There were a few "crib gyms" and mobiles, but all they had on them was a ring or two, some cardboard or plastic animals, some large beads, maybe a brightly colored ball. When I was a nursery school teacher in the 1940s and 1950s, we thought a half day at nursery school provided more than enough stimulation for young children. We didn't accept any children in nursery school until they were 3, or very close to it. In those days, most middle-class parents had household help or regular baby-sitters, who were then available in abundance. Children were taken to see grandparents and other relatives but were left at home with baby-sitters when parents went out to dinner or a movie. Children under 4 or 5 were not taken to movies, puppet shows, concerts, plays, or circuses. They almost never ate in restaurants and there were no fast-food restaurants. Two- and three-year-old children ate Italian or Mexican or Chinese food only if their parents happened to be Italian or Spanish or Chinese, and that's what kind of food they ate every day. Most foods were home-cooked, without additives, whatever the ethnic origin.

Thirty years ago there *were* a few people urging parents to stimulate their babies intellectually, but it certainly wasn't yet in high gear. Any kid born today can count on being bombarded by external stimulation from his first moment in a crib or a playpen. There will be a variety of cradle gyms with mirrors and bangles, horns and whistles, an abacus or two (he or she shouldn't waste time getting to arithmetic), and it is very often hard to find room for the child in the playpen because of the array of dolls, trucks, balls, drums, and other assorted equipment to stimulate the mind.

Whether or not mothers work, the idea of a 2-year-old spending a full day (7:00 A.M. to 6:00 P.M. very often) in a nursery or day-care center seems quite acceptable. One hundred years ago most children didn't start school until they were 7. Kindergarten was a novelty and did not include reading readiness unless it was a Montessori school.

In spite of this shocking lack of early stimulation, there were just as many geniuses, just as many smart and not-so-smart kids, in those days as there are today. It seems to me that the early infant stimulation theories created more sleeping problems (among other indications of emotional disturbance) than anything else.

Some babies, given special opportunities to become geniuses, such as being shown flash cards at 4 months, are smart enough to do what a 4-month-old is supposed to do with anything—they try to eat them! But most children who get the impression that Mom and Dad think time is being wasted if their children can't quote Shakespeare or speak Japanese or play the violin by age 2 or 3 or 4 are more than likely to get pretty nervous about these preposterous expectations, which have nothing whatever to do with natural developmental sequences. Insomnia is a very possible consequence.

In talking with a number of pediatricians over the past few years, I've been told they now practice internal medicine because so many young children have ulcers, colitis, falling hair, migraine headaches, and other diseases previously associated with adult stress. But let's stick with sleeping, although it is really part of a larger picture. What other differences are there between the lives of today's little children and those of children who lived a half century ago? For one thing, about half of them will experience the separation and divorce of their parents. A parent is likely to disappear or be seen only once in a while. Because young children have no way of knowing how these things come about, they blame themselves. If they had been beautiful-smart-perfect, this would never have happened.

Young babies today are part of a more hectic, noisy, and rapidly changing life-style than babies of any other age. Washing machines rumble; enormous trucks sound like wartime tanks; you don't go to a nice quiet grocery store on the corner, you go to a supermarket; you don't take a walk around the block, you go to a mall covering 30 acres and 200 stores. Few young children follow a simple, steady daily routine. Instead, they go where their parents go in a new informality that also makes life far more unstable.

Most of all, there is the television set, continually blasting stimulation at a little, tiny, unfinished brain eight to ten hours a day.

And, of course, there are all the new junk foods full of preservatives and other chemicals that give kids a high.

Life for grown-ups has also changed. The planet is getting unbearably crowded; insane amounts of glass, concrete, and traffic dehumanize our cities. The lovely woods, fields, and small quiet towns of an earlier time have turned into superhighways and skyscrapers. It has increasingly become an economic necessity for both parents to work, and many more women want to work in order to fulfill their own needs. Children get shuttled around: wake up fast at 7:00, get dressed, eat breakfast, get driven to the day-care center or some lady's house—maybe to be picked up at 3:00 by a neighbor, who takes them home, gives them supper—then maybe a baby-sitter arrives. A very far cry from the extended family of a century ago, where surely there were family problems, but there was a quieter, less frenetic pattern to daily life for young children.

Perhaps we will never regain the tranquillity of the past, but there are things we can do to alleviate the bedlam. First of all, remove about 50 percent of all the "stimulating" toys in the crib and playpen. A couple of cloth books, a rattle, a rag doll, a ball—these are quite enough for an infant's mind to cope with. Opportunities to kick and squirm and reach and be hugged and talked to are far more important for mental and emotional growth.

Think twice about the casual informality of life. It's great for adults but very hard on children under 5. If you really want to change the sleep picture, you may need to give your baby or preschooler a routine he or she can count on. Young children like to know, "This is when we eat breakfast; this is when we take a nap; this is when we go to the park; this is when we go to sleep."

You may think you can't control your child's schedule if you work. You can. Choose a sitter, day-care center, or nursery where quiet, time alone, lots of free play, paints, clay, sand, and water play are in the program. Choose a place that is not trying to be a second-grade classroom, full of teaching skills that are not natural to most children at least until kindergarten age. Choose a place that has teachers who seem relaxed, don't mind disorder or messiness, know how to help children get along without making them feel guilty or frightened. Choose a place where children aren't herded into crowds.

Choose a baby-sitter who understands that she is not the disciplinarian, doesn't try to "mold" your child but leaves this to you. And for heaven's sake, control that television set! One hour a day for toddlers, *never* more than two hours on any day; and choose the programs—no violence! no news!

If life is hectic and exhausting during the week, try to plan quiet weekends: a walk in the fall to collect brightly colored leaves; a whole afternoon playing in the sand at the beach; a visit to a children's zoo instead of some noisy, crowded amusement park or museum. Take time for cuddling, for reading a story. Be as consistent as possible about definite times for definite routines. "It's my bath time now!" a 2-year-old proudly announces. "I always take a bear, a rabbit, my best doll, and my teddy to bed," another says with great confidence. Rome was not built in a day—or a night! Sleep problems don't go away easily or quickly. But a less pressured, more consistent life will help.

Try to quiet the quality of your child's life. Of *course* children need stimulation to grow, but not frenetic, bombarding stimulation. Bedtime should be very ritualistic. It's the one time of day you really can control the environment. A warm bath first, the same time every day. Each stuffed animal kissed good night and tucked into the crib or bed. A terrific sleep-inducer is to mention all the people who love the child and say good night to them! Sit in a rocking chair, lights low, reading two books every night; not one or three but two! If a child's life is very hectic and unsettled, if there has been a divorce, if the hours at day care are long, if there's been too much shopping and visiting and eating out, if Mom and Dad just may have happened to scream at each other at breakfast, bedtime should also be a discussion of these events, asking the child to talk about his feelings. Even children under two can at least nod in agreement and *feel* what you are trying to do. If a child of three or four can't articulate feelings, you can help by saying "I guess you missed me a lot today," or "I guess you got scared when I got angry at Mommy," or "I know how much you miss Daddy." All these comments open the door to telling a child that all his or her feelings are normal, and that no child is ever responsible for adult problems.

Now, when your child wakes up, you have to do something you are going to hate doing! But if done consistently for several weeks, this rarely fails to work. Mommy or Daddy needs to go into Junior's room, give a calming pat on the back or a kiss, and sit down in a chair (or lie down if a cot or bed is available) and say you will stay until the child goes to sleep. This may have to be repeated two to five times a night for a while, but the number of times will gradually decrease.

Finally, because it is a natural instinct to want to cuddle up against other people you love, there should be special times for being in bed together, such as weekend mornings. Actually, I don't believe there is any harm in a lot of family bedtimes, but I also believe that children need to be taught at an early age to understand that parents have a need for and a right to privacy. I asked my 88-year-old father if he could remember whether or not I or my brother had sleeping problems. I couldn't remember and neither could he. Not exactly a scientific sampling! So I asked a great many of my contemporaries— all infants in the 1920s—and not one could remember getting out of bed at night. They may have cried over a bad dream, but that was all. I asked them about their own children. We all agreed there had been some rough times. We also agreed that our children were having a much harder time with our grandchildren.

One friend said, "We weren't rich but we had a sleep-in maid for ten years. We always stayed with her when our parents went out." Another said, "I stayed home with my mother until I was five, playing mostly with one little girl on my block." One father said, "I never went to a restaurant until I was twelve. And I remember an aunt taking me to my first movie when I was eight."

I believe that the increase in parental frustrations and anxieties about their young children's sleeping problems reflects the worst changes that have taken place in our society over the past few decades—those that have created an antichild, unchildlike life-style. Anything we can do to create a more soothing, natural, quiet, and slow daily routine ought to create more silent nights.

Part VI

*

DISCIPLINE

*

Consistency in Childraising Is Ridiculous!

❋ The first time I had hamburgers for breakfast I was 12 years old. It was a memorable occasion and had a profound impact on my life. Some friends of my parents invited me to accompany them on a trip to visit their three children at a camp in Maine, and on the second day of our trip we got a very early start, without first having breakfast. At about 9:30 we passed a hamburger stand and Henry said, "Hey, how about a hamburger for breakfast?"

My life has never been the same since that lovely question. To me it had the ring of the Emancipation Proclamation! It epitomized all the freedom and spontaneity that characterized the entire trip. I have remembered Henry and Ann with a sense of wonder and delight, and whenever I find myself behaving in rigid ways, becoming inflexible and unquestioning about rules and regulations—whenever I say no to doing something different or unusual without really thinking about it—I whisper to myself, "Hamburgers for breakfast."

The best thing about being human is our capacity to be creative and spontaneous—to change our minds, to be adventurers. But caught as we are in the routines of daily living, we often forget our capacity to make choices. I recently read an article by a child psychologist that really made me angry. It offered parents rules for discipline that started as follows:

1. Be consistent. Don't ever change rules and/or punishments from day to day.
2. Set limits; have only a few rules—and then don't budge an inch from them. Elastic limits lead to insecurity.
3. Make sure the child knows exactly what to expect of you.

It is natural to thirst for simple answers to difficult problems—and the disciplining of children grows more complex all the time—but simple answers don't really help. Telling us to "be consistent" assumes that we are all thoroughly predictable and exactly alike. What nonsense! It's a nice idea to be a consistently serene and understanding mother, but that goal isn't so easily attained on the fifth rainy day in a row when you're trapped indoors with two wild kids who have bad colds.

It seems to me that instead of trying to turn themselves into machines, parents ought to set reasonable goals, try to live up to them—and then allow for the times when they can't measure up. It is good to have standards, but they must be temporized by a sprinkling of human fallibility.

One year I began to have the feeling that the children in our family were becoming satiated with too many *things* at Christmas. Rather than a time of renewal of love, it was becoming a boring ritual. So instead of spending money on too many gifts, we decided to surprise my parents by bringing one of their oldest and best friends to New York from California. All of us had been missing her greatly—she was the Mary Poppins of our family, the Pied Piper of two generations of children. The day before Christmas, my daughter and I went to meet her at the airport. The secrecy and anticipation of the next day's surprise are something neither of us will ever forget. The next morning, when the whole family had assembled in the living room, Aunt Lilly, dressed from head to foot in white tissue paper and a red bow, swept down the stairs. We had recaptured, in that marvelous moment, what Christmas is really all about.

Every family needs to break its rules once in a while. The children need to stay up outrageously late, long after their regular bedtime; they need to stuff themselves on junk at the baseball game or the amusement park. All of us need to run out in a warm summer rain with our clothes on and dance across the yard. I don't mean to suggest that parents should be consistently inconsistent. But love is all we have going for us in any relationship, and love is fed by humanity—being real. We need to struggle to be better people, but to be consistent all of the time is to be a robot.

Along with flexibility parents need the courage to admit when they have made a mistake or done something thoughtless and unkind. When I was a young mother with a master's degree in child psychology one of my more consistent ideas was that adults shouldn't throw things at children. But when my daughter was about 5, I threw a shoe at her. I wasn't really aiming at her—and fortunately it didn't hit her—but I was instantly paralyzed with guilt. Some friends with a noisy, obstreperous 7-year-old were visiting us at the time, and we were all caught in a hurricane that lasted for three days. In the process of feeding everyone and listening to the steady screams of fighting and hilarity emanating from Wendy's room, I lost my cool.

It was a great experience for all of us. I was shocked into realizing that I was losing control and immediately regained it; the children realized I was coming apart at the seams and shaped up; and my guests retired to their room for several hours and then cooked our supper that night. I apologized. The Day Mommy Threw the Shoe has lived in memory, while the days when I was charming, reasonable, and consistent have faded into forgotten history.

A mother once told me that when she scolded her 8-year-old for not making his bed while they were at the seashore, he said, "What you don't understand is that sloppiness is a part of me. You'll have to put up with it *somewhere*." She thought it over, and it seemed a reasonable idea: Away from home is a good place to let down the standards that seem necessary at home.

Spontaneity in life isn't just doing the unexpected. It means getting rid of the *shoulds* in life. It may mean *not* doing something. Thursday may be the night we usually go bowling, partly because we *should* have family togetherness. Sometimes nobody is in the mood and it's time to say, "Thanks—but no thanks" to this week's family outing. As soon as we say, "We should do this," we diminish the pleasure of an event and make it almost impossible for joy to come through loud and clear.

We want our children to be sensitive, compassionate, and flexible. There is only one way they can learn these virtues—from grown-ups acting that way. If we want to teach children that the goal of human relationships is that we become predictable machines, then we must strive to be absolutely consistent. But if we want them to become lively, exciting, spontaneous, creative individuals, then we will have to put up with our human inconsistencies. You cannot, in that case, "make sure your child knows exactly what to expect of you." Only computers can promise that—and lately it has given me the greatest joy to hear that even those teaching machines we have dared to substitute for human attention are getting neurotic and unpredictable!

What we know about children is that they are different, and no rule, no form of discipline is suitable for all of them. Jane may dissolve in a pool of tears if chastened with a harsh word, while John may be so thick-skinned that it takes repeated deprivations to make an impression on his slow-blooming conscience. When she is healthy, Betty may respond only to angry shouts, but right after the flu she might suffer torments of guilt from the gentlest criticism.

One thing is certain: All we can prepare our children for these days is change. We do not have any idea what their future lives will be like. The rapidity of social change is such that our crystal balls are not merely clouded, they are shattered. We need to help our children deal with change without terror, without rigidities that interfere with necessary adaptation. One element of this is to help our children feel secure in the midst of change, not dependent on certainties we simply cannot guarantee.

I think that one of the reasons I became a writer was because once, when I was driving home with my parents, they let me keep a date with a rainbow. There had been a heavy storm when suddenly I screamed out, "Stop the car! I must write a poem about that beautiful rainbow!" My father pulled up at the side of the road and I went off into the drizzle and the sunshine while they waited. It was one of those special moments that change you, make you more than you've been. It is an experience in saying "Yes!" to life —and that's really what spontaneity and joy are all about.

I knew for sure that I had searched for this openness and flexibility when our 6-year-old daughter returned from a week's visit at a friend's house. She complained bitterly that she'd had to eat hot cereal every morning for breakfast. She asked me to heat up a can of chili, and while she ate it, purring contentedly, she said, "Gee, it's wonderful to be back to normal!"

The Pros and Cons
of Spanking

❊ My experience has been that if you ask a group of young parents what subject concerns them most, very high on their list will be the matter of spanking. I see no point in discussing whether or not we *ought* to spank our children; it is an irrelevant question. It seems to me we have to assume that almost every parent who ever lived hit his kid one time or another. Being human, we get mad and lose our patience, and the swift swat is the result. Let's accept that as a basic premise of our discussion.

A more legitimate question is: Is spanking a helpful, constructive form of discipline? No, it is not. Unequivocally! It may relieve our anger and clear the air when the atmosphere has gotten pretty tense and wound up, but it does not teach any constructive lessons about human relations, and after all, that's what discipline is all about: the ways in which we try to teach our children to live in a civilized fashion with themselves and others.

A classic example of the negative teaching involved in spanking is a scene that took place when as I sat in a park playground with my 3-year-old daughter. A little boy of about 5 came over, took a swat at her, and ran off with her pail and shovel. In the midst of trying to comfort my child, wounded in soul as well as body, I saw Mama descending upon the little boy like a wrathful god, slapping hard and howling, "This will teach you not to hit someone smaller than you!" It occurred to me that logic was sorely missing in that all-too-familiar scene between parent and child. There seems to be a natural tendency among us parents to teach by negative example. It hardly seems likely that Junior is going to learn very much about not hitting if that is the technique he himself experiences as a parental solution to all problems.

Even when we think we are being most rational about spanking, we're still not teaching any terribly valuable lessons. We say, for example, "I have to give you a spanking in order to make you remember how dangerous it is to run across the road." The lesson there is: "Here I am, a grown-up—a college graduate, even—and the only resource I have at my disposal to teach you the dangers of traffic is physical violence!" What a discouraging picture of human potential!

I believe there is only one appropriate reason for spanking, and that is when one is so frightened or so angry or so impatient that one spanks without trying to justify it at all; it just happens because you can't help it. You and your child know that you are resorting to the lowest possible level of human interaction and that you don't approve of it, but that sometimes things just get to be too much. If, after such an episode, you are so awash with guilt that you cannot even talk to your child about it, he learns that one should feel very guilty about being human and therefore imperfect. If, out of guilt, you try to find a justification, such as "I had to do that to make you understand," you are still in trouble, because you did *not* do it with premeditation, so you are just plain lying to salve your own conscience. If, on the other hand, you feel a normal amount of guilt for a fall from grace and can apologize quite honestly and straightforwardly, both you and your child can pick up the pieces and move on to some better way of communicating with each other.

Parents sometimes underestimate the importance of being able to say "I'm sorry" to a child. It is one of the best lessons in discipline, for its message is simply this: "People sometimes lose control. If they are decent, sensible, grown-up people, they try hard to be reasonable, but they don't always succeed because living with kids can be pretty trying sometimes. But the great thing about human beings is that they can always strive to improve." That's an important lesson: it is an example to our children. It suggests that they, too, being human, will falter and that it will not necessarily be fatal; they too, will be able to make amends and continue growing. It is essentially a decent and hopeful view of human beings as people with weaknesses for which we are sorry but also strengths that we keep trying to bring to higher levels of development.

The aim of being a grown-up parent is, of course, to try to increase our sensitivity, our responsibility, so that we resort to primitive behavior as infrequently as possible. We certainly don't try to justify brutal or harshly punitive actions as being worthy of the label "sound discipline." At the same time, it is not necessary to get out the sackcloth and ashes or give ourselves thirty lashes when we spank. Children are great forgivers; they know when we are scared or when we have reached the end of our endurance, and they do not see our momentary loss of control as a terrible threat to their well-being. Quite the contrary; when you're little and weak and very much in the grip of impulses you often cannot control, it is very comforting to discover that those giants of strength, your parents, have their imperfections, too.

Spanking has no great lessons to teach about wisdom and self-control, but until some sort of mutant—a new species of superior man—arrives on this planet, we are stuck with it.

Healthy and Irritating Signs of Independence

❋ I was talking with a friend on the phone the other day, offering my sympathy and compassion. She was the distraught mother of two boys, ages 7 and 9, both of whom had been home from school with the flu for two weeks. In addition to reporting on the usual lack of sleep and resulting exhaustion that attend a mother's role as Florence Nightingale, she was full of anecdotes about the boys' hair-raising escapades. After describing some of their more colorful and nerve-shattering activities, she sighed and said, "This much 'togetherness' tries a mother's soul. They haven't enough to challenge and stimulate their seething little minds, so they are giving me the works. They're just as defiant and argumentative as they can be." She paused, then added more cheerfully, "Of course, the nice thing about fresh kids is that they are so *smart.*"

That comment stuck in my mind. I remember a mother in a parents' discussion group who became very much upset when the other members complained about children who defied what their parents felt to be the most reasonable of controls. She interrupted these tales of woe with a story no one in the group will ever forget. "You know," she said, "it's very hard for me to listen to you complain. You should be glad your children have such spirit. I have two children, an 8-year-old boy and a 4-year-old girl. Paul was a devilish one from the day he was born. He was always getting into things. He was hard to discipline. He wore me out. When my little girl was born, she was entirely different—quiet, passive, uncomplaining. She was so undemanding and easy to handle that I thought to myself, 'Well, thank goodness. At least I've got one child who isn't going to be a lot of trouble.' But Carol didn't seem to develop right. She didn't try to sit up, she didn't crawl, she didn't play. To make a long story short, she is a retarded child. Now every time Paul gets hard to handle, my husband and I thank God that he's a normal child."

Though this is an extreme situation, it does illustrate dramatically and clearly that we parents and teachers can't have our cake and eat it, too.

What do we want our children to be like when they grow up? Most of the parents and teachers I've met seem to agree that they want their children to be responsible, independent adults. They want them to be able to make mature decisions about work, marriage, and parenthood. They want them to be discriminating in their judgment of people and ideas, and to live fully with a sense of adventure, unafraid to explore the world (even the universe) around them. They want their children to be flexible enough to accept change, courageous enough to meet new challenges, loving and sensitive enough to care deeply about life and people.

The catch is that there is no way to achieve these goals except through the innate human struggle to grow. We applaud this force when it gives our children the impetus to learn to walk, speak, eat without help, tie shoelaces, make friends, read and write, add and subtract. But we are often somewhat less enthusiastic about the natural impulse to grow when it shows itself in the form of defiance, stubbornness, toughness toward ourselves, indifference to the rules of cleanliness, and irresponsibility about chores that are important to us but not to them.

Not long ago I asked a group of parents and teachers to give me quickly a list of one-word descriptions of school-age youngsters. The first words offered were "noisy," "jumpy," "sloppy," "fresh," "wild," and "rebellious." As the list grew, somewhere way down toward the bottom they got around to some other kinds of words: "curious," "adventurous," "eager to learn," "full of questions," "very emotional," "bright."

That mixture of words represents the "package deal" we get with a school-age child. How, we ask ourselves, can we help our children become civilized beings yet still allow for the wonderful richness of individual difference and the development of mature independence? Probably the first thing to do is accept the fact that children have to test themselves against adult authority. How do you know what you can do until you try it? Can you always take your parents' word for it that you are not ready for some new experience? Maybe you are and they don't know it.

Most parents and teachers recognize that when a child insists on getting his own way and goes through the "emancipation acrobatics" typical of children his age, this is evidence of growth. Many of us have a sense of proportion about trial-and-error experiments with independence such as bad table manners, indifference to neatness, or occasional lying, fighting, tantrums, and defiance.

Certainly the healthy struggle for independence doesn't always take the form of fighting against adult authority. It shows itself in an eagerness for learning, in rapture over opportunities to increase physical skills, in a valiant struggle for acceptance among one's own friends. When experiences at school and at home encourage self-confidence and pride in real accomplishments, children find many avenues for self-development.

Intense and continuous rebellion is something else again. When the irritating signs of independence outweigh the positive ones, we may need to ask a few questions. Are we getting an inordinate amount of defiance because our controls are too stiff? Are we giving 8-year-old Johnny no more freedom that we gave him at 5? Or have we gone so far to the other extreme that 10-year-old Judy's constant rebellious behavior is really a plea for more limits, because she isn't ready to handle the choices we are giving her? Is Fred just being ornery in his stubborn refusal to wear that pair of slacks or will he really lose face with his friends if he does?

As adults we have the right to set limits for our children. We are responsible for their safety and well-being; we must safeguard them from real dangers when they are too young and inexperienced to protect themselves or one another. Most important of all, we are responsible for serving as living examples of what we believe. Yet we also need to allow children to be children. We can tell them what we believe and expect of them, but we must give them time in which to measure up to adult standards.

Assuming that the unlovely behavior we see in most growing children is natural, do we have to resign ourselves to living with it? Most seasoned parents will say, "Yes, at least some of the time." But this is not the whole story. There are lots of things we can do to make life reasonably pleasant for ourselves as well as our children, permitting growth and at the same time maintaining sound and satisfying human relationships.

First of all we can *choose our battles.* (It takes two to tangle!). We can decide what is most important and not fight all the windmills at once. Teachers constantly make such choices. If they concentrate their efforts on quiet, neatness, and orderliness, they will probably get it. But they will have very little time left for teaching, for encouraging the wonder and enjoyment of learning, for giving children enough freedom to work out their feelings about one another. If they try for a certain minimum amount of quiet, and see that childish exuberance has opportunities for expression, they and their pupils will have much more fun, like each other better, and learn much more.

Another thing we can do is *respect our children's work.* They will feel less need to prove they are growing up if the people around them seem to know it. When the family sits down to dinner, how often do the children get a chance to tell about their day? As a charter member of the guilty club, I can remember many conversations centered on the trials, tribulations, challenges, and successes of my husband's day or mine, but not very many about our daughter's. Do we let our children know that growing up, learning new skills, working at becoming an accepted member of one's group is *really* a hard job? And that we respect and admire this task enough to realize that children, too, are often discouraged and tired as well as excited and triumphant at the end of the day?

"Accentuating the positive" is another attitude that can be helpful. Our children would have to be deaf, dumb, and blind not to know what we dislike about their behavior, but how often do we tell them how proud we are of their successes? Do we praise the

signs of growth that impress us so enormously? And above all, when they are behaving in the most exasperating or impossible ways, are they aware that we *know* they really want to be liked, to behave well? Children can feel pretty awful about what they do or say. They know when they're being childish, silly, or naughty but can't seem to help it. Why not reassure them by pointing out that childishness is pretty logical when you are a child, that we realize they are constantly struggling to become more grown-up and that it takes a lot of practice and hard work.

Humor is another asset in living with the irritating aspects of growth. When Ronnie comes home mimicking his tough pals by answering our requests with "So what? You can't make me," "You wanna bet?" and other, more unprintable declarations of emancipation, we can get huffy and stern, moralize and punish—or we can joke about it. "Boy, aren't *we* getting tough!" said with a wry smile carries as much of a message as a lot of parental sermons—perhaps more.

Sometimes we are so fearful of losing control over our children that we get too serious and intent about superficial and insignificant evidences of their struggle for independence. We can often make it clear to children that we "get the message" with a laugh or a joke or a game of words instead of a scowl and a command. No child that I know ever saw this as either an abdication of adult authority or a wishy-washy permissiveness to do whatever he pleased. Quite the contrary. Our children know very well that they are children and that we grown-ups hold the reins. That's why they defy us.

Most of the children we live and work with admire and respect us. They want, eventually, to be like us. They know perfectly well what we stand for, what we believe to be the essentials for decent human relationships. They are nice, normal, healthy, wonderful— though annoying and provoking—children who have to test us and themselves, who have to feel and act like children, who have to learn, slowly but steadily, inner controls and acceptable forms of self-expression. They drive us crazy, but they are also enchanting. In spite of the torn sock, the unbrushed teeth, the forgotten chore, the restless feet that keep our shins black and blue at the dining-room table, they will surprise us by rallying to an emergency, showing tact and sensitivity in a complicated relationship, working out a difficult and original science-club project, getting sentimental and slushy about last summer's family camping trip.

Concern about the apparent increase in antisocial behavior among youngsters is clearly warranted; hysterical, undocumented warnings of doom for all lively children are not. When Junior talks back, and the next-door neighbor's eyebrows go up, keep a sense of proportion. Junior is not a deprived, hurt child who is hungry for recognition and affection, for the stability and security of a loving family. He is your child, someone who knows you love and respect him, who has a deep sense of the interdependence of mutual need and love. This sometimes rebellious, often sloppy and forgetful, occasionally naughty boy will someday be a mature, responsible, and *independent* adult—I promise.

Making the Punishment Fit the Need

✽ Cathy was 7 years old and we were teasing each other. "Suppose I hit you on the nose," she said. "What would you do?" I had to think up some outrageous punishment, such as, "I'd pack a picnic lunch and send you to the moon." Cathy was becoming increasingly giddy and overexcited. I could feel the tension building and was wondering how to end the game when she said, "What would you do if I yelled so loud in your ear that it busted?"

Without thinking I replied, "I think I'd send you to your room for an hour and make you rest."

Cathy's face fell. "Now you're not playing the game," she said, "because that's a *good* punishment."

"You're right," I answered. "That's not a funny one because that's the one you need."

"You're a silly dumb-dumb," said Cathy. Then, shyly and with obvious relief, she added, "I guess I'll pretend I'm a baby and take a little nap."

I was visiting Cathy's family because her older brother had just died. It was Cathy's first experience with death, and it was just as awful as it could be. Sixteen-year-old John had been her idol, and in the time it takes to wrap a car around a tree he was gone. The series of events that followed had left Cathy utterly exhausted. She needed an adult who could help her do what she needed most—to escape for a while into sleep.

I was startled by how clearly Cathy had stated the basic premise of good discipline. It's the "good punishments" that help you to grow. These days we parents tend to complicate the meaning of discipline until we become confused and hung up on the subject. We go around in circles in our attitudes about how to discipline children. Having watched this for many years, I become impatient with people who are quick to blame the not-inconsiderable sufferings of some of our teenagers on the fact that they were "raised too permissively." Disturbed by our young people's reaction to the terrible problems of our times, we search for some simple answer, some scapegoat to blame. Rather than face the issues that shake up our children, we attribute their attitudes to the fact that Dr. Spock had us spoiling them irresponsibly.

That's a cop-out. Neither Dr. Spock nor any other bona fide authority on child development ever suggested that children needed or could handle complete freedom. Our aim was to find the best way to help children grow to maturity. We didn't find any simple panaceas, but we had some very sensible goals. Although some parents made mistakes and went to extremes, it seems to me that we succeeded more often than we failed. The kind of discipline we were searching for then is just as valid today.

All the anxiety about discipline that today's younger parents seem to experience has led me again and again to Cathy's notion of "good punishment." An understanding of what she was really saying might help to clarify what discipline is all about.

Put in its simplest terms, discipline helps a child to grow when it fits his real needs. What are the real needs of childhood? That, of course, is the heart of the matter. Beyond the obvious physical needs, the most crucial, perhaps, is the need of each child to feel "It's wonderful to be me! I'm lovable!" In addition, all children need to know there are external controls (such as mother's firm hand when you get to near a hot stove) that can keep them from harm until they are able to control their own impulses. They also need help in handling their feelings of guilt when they inevitably transgress in the process of growing up.

Children need a chance to develop some inner controls through life experiences—a chance to make some gorgeous mistakes! If we are honest about our own murky past, we will probably admit we learned more from our mistakes than from anything else. Perhaps the hardest task for all parents is to have the faith to allow a child this necessary experimentation.

Children need our help in finding a balance between personal needs and group life. They need our help in understanding their own motives as well as those of others. Children also need parents who are capable of some perspective and sensitive to what is special and different about each child's personality. The same kind of discipline can have totally different effects on different children of the same age, and on the same child at other ages.

All this may sound like a terribly big order, but broken down into component parts, it's not so overwhelming.

1. The Promise of External Controls

Too emotionally exhausted to manage herself at all, Cathy wanted an adult to tell her to take a nap. Likewise, the 2-year-old who cannot control the impulse to bite when he wants someone else's toy needs to know that someone older and wiser will intervene. He needs someone to keep him from getting into the kind of trouble his impulses can get him into.

We sometimes become confused about the difference between understanding a feeling and allowing an action. They are not the same thing at all, and the failure to understand this causes many of the problems that relate to permissiveness. One dramatic example of this misinterpretation was the mother I saw allowing her 3-year-old son to hit his baby sister on the head. She turned to me and said, "What can I do? You educators are always telling us about sibling rivalry." What she could do was remove her son from the range of his sister's head! No one would be more relieved than the brother, who wants desperately to be stopped from doing naughty things when he cannot stop himself. It is one thing to understand jealousy and allow a child to express feelings about it in acceptable ways; it is quite another to allow dangerous behavior.

Parental control shifts and changes as children grow. At 7 it may mean not leaving money around where it is too enticing; at 17 it may mean arranging for your daughter to stay in a girls' dormitory and not at a motel when she goes to a college prom. With experience and gradual maturation, young people gain control over drives and needs that cannot always be gratified. In the course of this growing, however, they must have some help.

2. The Feeling of Being Lovable

Some limits and controls can cause children to end up hating themselves—especially if "goodness and badness" are used as clear alternatives. If we say, for example, "I have to punish you because you are a bad boy," we damage the child's self-esteem. But if we say, "I have to punish you to help you grow. What you did was wrong, but you are young and obviously couldn't help yourself," the message is far different. Children should never be made to feel they are bad. It is as inaccurate as it is damaging.

If we have learned anything at all in the past half century of psychological research and discovery, it's that all human beings have the same lovely and unlovely potential, and it's what we do with this equipment that counts. When you are a child it ought to be legitimate to be childish! When a 5-year-old hits another child in order to get a wagon he wants, he needs to be stopped, of course. But even more than that, he needs to be reassured that what he did was childlike and human, and not a final judgment of his character. He should know that some things cannot be allowed but are still understandable.

If your 11-year-old brings home a leather jacket that he says a friend gave him, but that you later find out he took from an open locker, you can read him the riot act, spank him, and isolate him —or you can try to figure out how this reflects his needs. What *does* he need? Above all he must have self-esteem—and this incident has undoubtedly shaken his view of himself. Why did he take the jacket? He probably won't be able to explain it to himself, much less to you, but it might have something to do with feeling masculine. Perhaps having the jacket fulfilled some much-wished-for desire to look more manly. Whatever the reason, it was an infringement on another person's rights, and restitution must be made. It's important, however, that this be done in a way that does not sabotage the young person's need for dignity. Maybe he can return the jacket and apologize, saying he took it by mistake. That's certainly true; it *was* a mistake. Or perhaps he'll just have to admit he took it on purpose and apologize. If the jacket is damaged, he may have to work to earn the money to replace it. He must face the fact that he made a serious error—but that does not mean he is headed for a life of crime!

Too often when we stop a child, or punish him, we attack his good opinion of himself and lose more than we gain. The strong-willed youngster who is by nature dramatic, high-strung, and easily overstimulated begins to see himself as a "fresh, impossible troublemaker." The shy, self-conscious child who doesn't need much socializing or organized play finds himself feeling clumsy, inept, stupid. Discipline must respect the personality of the child. It must convey the message that we recognize and accept his unique qualities and love him despite his misbehavior.

3. Understanding a Well-Hidden Need

A child needs help in recognizing that human beings sometimes behave in very strange ways. When you are being most unlovable, for instance, you may be searching for love. As David's birthday party came to an end, his younger brother, Peter, began to behave like a monster. The fact that his mother and father had been centering their attention on David was just too tough for a 4-year-old to handle. When his father handed him a glass of milk, Peter pushed it out of his hand and said, "I hate you—go away and leave me alone!" His father could have given him a sound thrashing, told him he was a very naughty boy, and sent him to bed without his supper. I witnessed this incident, however, and will never forget what Peter's father really did. He looked at Peter gravely—and Peter looked back, wide-eyed and shaken by the awful thing he had done—then picked him up, rocked him in his arms, and said, "Poor Peter—you're feeling sad and mad. Let's go to your room and take a rest."

If this be permissiveness or "spoiling" a child, then I say we can't get too much of it! Meeting needs is far more important in child-raising than punishing crimes. In the long run, Peter will have learned a most valuable lesson—that people have problems and need help, especially when they feel bad and do things they shouldn't. Such help does not indicate parental approval of spilling milk. Peter had no doubts about the unacceptability of what he had done. It seems to me that such insightful, compassionate discipline has given us a generation of compassionate young people. Peter is now 22, and I suspect his current concern for the problems of the human race is related to the understanding he received as a child.

4. Getting Rid of Guilt

Sometimes a child needs to be punished just so he can go on living without drowning in his own guilt! Six-year-old Sarah had been mean to her friend Janey and refused to let her play with one of her dolls. Sarah's mother, who was busy with household chores, lost her temper and told Sarah she was "mean and selfish." Later Sarah's mother realized she'd been a little unreasonable. After all, at 6 it is still hard to be generous about some things (even adults don't want to share everything!) As the day wore on, Sarah became more upset and cranky until she finally had a terrific temper tantrum. Her mother told me, "I had the feeling I'd made Sarah feel doubly bad about being selfish when she was really feeling guilty all by herself. It seemed as if she wanted to be punished so she could stop feeling guilty. I really didn't think it was that important, but I finally told her she couldn't have a bedtime story. She grumbled but appeared relieved. That was a fair 'penance,' and the subject was closed."

5. A Chance to Gain Experience With Decision-Making

Parental example and reasonable external controls help a child to develop his own internal controls, but neither does as much as the sometimes painful opportunity for *practice*. Parents must have enough faith in a child to allow him to make some discoveries through direct experience. This may range from such ordinary issues as a son who foolishly spends a week's allowance on a junky toy advertised on TV, to a daughter discovering for herself that she feels awful by noon if she doesn't have breakfast. The right to make mistakes is an essential part of discipline, for mistakes—even serious ones—are often the best source of learning. We all want to protect our children from painful experiences, of course, but we need to remember that even serious problems can be solved, sometimes resulting in remarkable maturation. We cannot keep our children in cotton batting forever; sooner or later they must seek their own strengths.

Choosing a summer camp only because a friend goes there, cheating on a test instead of studying the subject, lying to a teacher —these experiences all have their natural consequences, and all the talk in the world doesn't match living through them. Letting go is an important part of parenthood. We must permit a child to take more and more steps alone while remaining available to help pick up the pieces when the going gets rough.

6. Balancing Personal Needs and Group Life

One of the great age-old problems of mankind has been how to realize the marvelous uniqueness of each person without permitting anyone to exploit others for his own ends. When it comes right down to it, that is really what parenthood is all about—helping a child become the most he can be, but not at the cost of others.

These goals are more compatible than they may seem. The late humanistic psychologist Dr. Abraham Maslow suggested that self-actualization is the most important aspect of human growth, and that the deepest fulfillment of each individual enriches the community as a whole. In other words, *the more meaning anyone finds in his own life, the more he can be in harmony with others.*

In disciplining children, it is not enough to teach prohibitions, to tell a child, "You can't hurt others because they will hurt you back." If we set as our goal a better life for everyone, then discipline must go beyond teaching the do's and don'ts of social living. The needs of the individual child are paramount. We are not spoiling him but helping him grow toward a selfhood in which he attains all that he wants to be and can be.

Connie, a brilliant youngster, was bored to death in the first grade. She had a very sweet, slow-moving teacher who was fearful of allowing children to go off on their own. Forced to wait for the others to catch up, Connie became defiant and devious. She would sneak off to the library instead of going to music class and whisper and giggle while other children were trying to concentrate.

Finally, Connie's parents were called in for a conference. They suggested that Connie be moved to another class or allowed to do special work at a more advanced level. Connie was tested and found capable of doing second-grade work. She was moved up on an experimental basis, and three months later she was blooming. Given a special assignment to study water pollution at home, Connie went with her father to look at some badly polluted rivers over the weekend and later gave a report to the rest of the class. She was getting along beautifully with the other children and had no further behavioral problems. The self-actualized child "doing his own thing" feels good enough about himself to feel good about everybody else.

The main difference between discipline today and a hundred or more years ago is an underlying assumption about the nature of man. Our ancestors assumed that badness had to be whipped out of a child, and the only way you could make a child behave in a civilized manner was through fear. Today we take the view that human beings have primitive instincts that may lead to destructive behavior, but they also have the capacity for compassion, tenderness, courage, generosity, and selflessness. What's more, we've learned that the best way to emphasize these positive qualities is by encouraging a person to fulfill himself.

The more a parent does to meet the genuine growing needs of a child through sensitive and tender concern, the more he will encourage the very best to develop in his child. There are no formulas for this kind of discipline; each situation has its own special qualities. You have to play it by ear and trust in yourself as a human being. The more you can respect your own life, the more you can find lovable in yourself, the better equipped you'll be to give this valuable gift of selfhood to your child.

Saying "No" to Children: Loudly and Clearly

✱ In the supermarket the other day I was standing at the checkout counter behind a woman with two children. Her cart was loaded to the brim with what I had watched her children pick out as we went up and down the aisles: Sugar Frosted Flakes, TV dinners, potato chips, Twinkies, several loaves of soft white bread, and the economy package of Cracker Jacks. Mother had at one point started to add some canned grapefruit juice, but the two boys howled and she quickly changed to an artificial fruit punch. She had, of course, added a few items herself—some hamburger, hot dogs, and milk, but it was clear that her central goal was to please her children and to entice them to eat.

These days we are exposed to the ever-mounting evidence that in spite of eating a great deal, we and our children may well be suffering from malnutrition. On all sides we hear that we "are what we eat," that processed sugar is being eaten in such quantities by children that they may be toothless by the age of 35. And yet most of us are too easily seduced into allowing our children to eat junk foods. Why do we do it? Why is it so hard for us to say no, loudly and clearly?

Too many of us have trouble acting like responsible, knowledgeable adults and turn into lily-livered weaklings. Are we *afraid* of children these days? That may be so—and understandably, for there is bound to be a sense of uncertainty in such troubled and confusing times. But as I watch parents retreating from what seem to be clear areas of responsibility, I have the feeling it's because they cannot bear their children's disapproval. Is it possible that parents now want to be loved more unconditionally than their children?

As we have come to understand the real and genuine needs of our children, we have gotten confused about the way to satisfy these needs. Instead of responding with love, understanding, and genuine communication, we go to any lengths to avoid their anger and rebellion. It has always seemed to me that the reason there are grown-ups around for children is to keep them from doing things they ought not to be doing, and since no child in his or her right mind willingly gives up any momentary gratification, parents have to be the heavies and put up with a lot of anger.

There is no subject about which this is more true than television. It has become our favorite national scapegoat—responsible for everything from violence in the streets to hyperactivity and boredom in the classroom. Television may in truth have the potential for causing us to make foolish decisions and develop bad habits, but what I'm afraid we're inclined to overlook far too often is that it is a machine that can be turned off with a slight twist of the wrist; children can be forbidden to watch programs that parents find tasteless, overstimulating, or a thorough waste of valuable time. Parents can refuse to spend their frighteningly inflated dollars on advertised products that are useless at best and truly harmful at worst.

The simple truth is that what families buy influences whether or not children arrive at school overstimulated or exhausted, and, to some degree, which television programs get high ratings depend on what adults permit or do not permit. As much as I have been an advocate of less authoritarianism on the part of parents, I now find myself longing for the sight and sound of parents being loud and clear in saying "No" to children when it is appropriate to do so.

I think the inability to take strong, responsible action in the care and feeding of the young probably stems from two central issues. The first is the fact that we have lived through a major revolution in parent-child relationships during the twentieth century, and there is bound to be a great deal of confusion about what it means to be a reasonable and understanding parent. I applaud the desire to treat children of all ages with sensitivity and concern for their feelings and needs. But I'm afraid that in the pursuit of that noble ideal we may have gone overboard too often—leaning so far toward a desire to be our children's friends and companions that we forfeit the inevitable responsibility to set firm limits and demand that children accept some of the fundamental rules and regulations they desperately need for healthy growth both physically and psychologically.

The second challenge to today's parents is the issue of how to handle what no earlier generations ever had to deal with, and this is the constant, never-ending bombardment of useless products that none of us need to live comfortably or sensibly: Television advertisements, supermarkets, and shopping malls tend, I fear, to break down the good intentions and high resolve of even the most inner-directed adults. It becomes ever more clear that we have become a culture that wants what it wants when it wants it—and that parents have been swept up in the tide, without much clear thinking about consequences.

We need to do some careful soul-searching at this point. It is wonderful that today's children are for the most part less afraid of parents and teachers than children have ever been before. But it is not so wonderful that adults now seem afraid of children—afraid to say "No," afraid to deal with a child's natural reactions to being thwarted and frustrated. What we need to become more aware of is that children *want* us to act like grown-ups who know how to take care of them even when they pout or stamp their feet or yell at us. Children cannot learn inner controls without direction and guidance and most especially not without the example adults set by their own behavior.

This does not mean returning to an equally unfortunate relationship in which children are to be seen and not heard, or one in which parents are arbitrary and insensitive to children as human beings. It does not mean saying "No" without discussion, explanation, and genuine sympathy for a child's frustrations and anger. It does not mean a quick swat on the behind when children nag, plead, exhort, and threaten that they "will just *die*" if they can't watch television for thirty hours a week or eat all the enticing garbage they love. We need not be victims of extremes—either totally abandoning the prerogatives of parenthood or being mean and hardhearted. What we can do is live with a child's annoyance—even fury—without overreacting, spend all the time that may be necessary in explaining why we withold certain permissions, and discuss reasonable compromises. "I know you are mad at me right now, but I cannot let you do that because I think it is bad for you" is one necessary approach in raising children. Another equally valid response may sometimes be, "I think that television program is a pretty disgusting way of looking at human beings, but I will let you watch it (and I will watch it with you), and we'll talk about what makes me so upset about it." Or, "Yes, you may buy those crazy blue and red sneakers with the money Grandma sent you for Christmas, since you say your entire class is wearing them, but you may not wear them all the time and they are absolutely out of bounds when the temperature goes below thirty degrees, when you will wear your winter boots."

A friend of mine, a single parent who has two teenage daughters, seems to have managed this balance between the "Yesses" and the "No's" of parenthood with great intelligence and spirit. Junk foods are never purchased, never kept on the pantry shelves—but once a week she and her daughters go out for dinner and the girls can choose the restaurant and eat whatever they please. They are given total freedom in the use of a reasonable weekly allowance but are expected to save at least half of what they earn as baby-sitters. On important occasions, Mom shows great flexibility about the time they are allowed to return from weekend parties. However, when one daughter stayed out until 3:00 A.M. without calling, she was grounded for the next three weeks. What her daughters know, beyond a shadow of a doubt, is that she is in charge, that she loves them a lot, and that she is aware they need and must have opportunities for increasing amounts of self-determination as they get older—but that this depends on the degree to which they show good judgment and self-controls. Most of all, she makes every effort to be an excellent role model—a person who is thoughtful, disciplined, unwilling to allow her life to be ruled by television, advertising, the availability of things she does not need, or the pressure of what other people believe or do. She is available for discussion of all issues and makes a genuine effort to be reasonable and fair, but she never loses sight of who she is—a parent. Her daughters seem to thrive on her carefully thought-out balance between loving kindness and strong discipline.

Many years a go a friend of mine, a social worker, was assigned to work with a teenage girls' gang in a tough and severely deprived neighborhood. It was a period of great social unrest and justifiable anger on the part of the young people, caught in a world of poor or absent parenting, slum living, lack of decent recreational facilities, and educational services that were irrelevant to their problems. She tried very hard to gain the trust and confidence of the girls, and at first she thought it necessary to change her own behavior, to try to be one of the gang. She learned to use their often foul and colorful language; she went along with their attitudes toward their "enemies"; she accepted without comment their street ethics about stealing, fighting, and sexual promiscuity. But as the weeks and months passed, she felt more and more helpless and hopeless. She was getting nowhere.

One afternoon she asked the leader of the gang to walk with her to the subway on her way home. She asked for help, admitting her sense of failure. She said, "I really have tried to understand how you all feel, and I hoped so much I could become a friend, that you would get to like me and trust me. But I feel I have failed—can you tell me why?" The girl became very thoughtful and quiet, and finally she said, "The trouble is, you're trying to get more like us instead of helping us get more like you."

She got the message. What these girls needed was the kind of caring that indicated she was a grown-up person and could help them develop new attitudes and behavior. They needed to know that she was not afraid of them. Slowly but surely over the next few months she began to make demands and set limits. She said what she thought and invited the group to see the alternatives that were open to them. She gave loving approval and encouragement when that was appropriate and expressed anger and disappointment when that seemed to be what was needed. At the end of two years of hard work the level of truancy went down about seventy-five percent and half of the group had part-time jobs. What these young people were hungry for was parenting, not palship.

It's wonderful to have fun with children—to break rules sometimes, to share a spree, to indulge in pleasures of all kinds. But that can never be a substitute for using our most important asset in childraising—our greater maturity.

If You Want Your Child to Be Responsible

❋ "I wish you would write something about teaching children responsibility," a mother wrote me. "Somehow my children always manage to find an excuse when it's time to dry the dishes or make their beds."

This comment made me nostalgic for "the good old days" in my own life when I, too, thought that responsibility had to do with simply making children do their chores. The past few years have changed my thinking a great deal. Teaching children responsibility now seems to involve communicating some of our deepest and most important values; it has to do with human survival itself.

All I have to do to see responsibility in its broadest perspective is take a walk or read a newspaper. I did both today. On my walk my eyes were assaulted by the ugliness around me. I passed a McDonald's and on the street, in clear view of a large refuse can, were six empty "Big Mac" boxes, four discarded drinking cups, and some French fries squashed underfoot. In the gutter on the next block were some empty beer cans and broken bottles. Every few feet there were little mounds of cigarettes where car ashtrays had been emptied on the streets. A statue in the park had been defaced by expletives painted in red. I saw an old man lying in the street, muttering to himself as we passersby ignored him. Whenever and wherever I walk these days, I feel assaulted by our collective indifference to the environment we share as well as to the people around us.

Reading the newspaper reinforced my sense of despair. Defects had been discovered in a nuclear reactor; scientists were uncertain of just where our "Sky Lab" would crash to earth; the weather report concluded with the unsettling information "Air—Unsatisfactory."

The dimensions of the word *responsibility* have changed dramatically in my lifetime. It is surely something I want to teach children, for it is clearly necessary for their survival. In that light, teaching responsibility to children takes on monumental proportions. It may seem at first that arguing about who mows the lawn or getting into a power struggle over whether the garbage is taken out or the beds made is insignificant, but it is not. The bigger issues of imminent social disaster may well be decided around just such routine daily matters—but with a difference. Becoming a responsible person is no longer a matter of whether or not a child hangs up his pajamas or puts a dirty towel into the hamper but whether or not he *cares* about himself and other people, and sees these everyday chores as being related to how we treat and share this planet. We may face the same routine tasks, but we must help our children to understand the sacredness of human life and the necessity for caring about ourselves and each other.

How do we begin? It seems to me it starts during the first years of life, when we let our children know how much they matter to us; when they begin to sense that each human being is precious and beautiful and different. It is extremely difficult to grow up caring about others unless you have experienced being cared for yourself. That is the first step in becoming responsible.

The second step has to do with encouraging young children to see themselves as being capable of action, of participating in family life and making a difference. It is a bore sometimes to let a 3-year-old vacuum the living-room rug or help bake a pie or make a bed —but it is not a waste of time. Whenever a child feels a sense of accomplishment the roots of responsibility are growing strong, for next to caring, the belief in one's own capacity to make a contribution is essential. If there is one idea we desperately need to believe in, it is that each individual counts and can make a difference.

Inevitably, participation must allow for the right to fail. It takes a lot of experimenting to learn to do anything well, and failing is a necessary ingredient along the road to successful achievement. Failure is a built-in necessity during childhood, the very nature of growth itself. It is normal to spill flour on the floor when you're learning to cook; it is normal to spend your allowance on foolish things when you're learning to handle money; it is normal to hate most of the results the first time you redecorate your own room; it is normal to be so preoccupied with whether or not that bully is going to beat you up on the way to school that you forget to take out the garbage. When adults are sensitive to the natural limitations of a child's techniques and powers of concentration, he feels respected for what he can do rather than ashamed and anxious about what he cannot yet do. As one wise youngster put it to her father, "I'm too young to always remember to feed Prince, but I'm old enough to hug him and let him know we love him!"

If we set up arbitrary rules and regulations and demand enforcement, we are missing a great opportunity. A sense of responsibility never evolves from angry coercion but rather from feeling respected as a person and discovering how much people need each other. If we demand too much, too soon all that our children learn is that we are more powerful. If we expect too little, we rob our children of the opportunity to feel that they have a contribution to make.

I know of no better way to work out a balance between expecting too much or too little than family conferences. By the time a child is 6 or 7 years old he is articulate enough to express his opinions and sufficiently aware to understand the need for cooperation. What most youngsters complain about is that parents dole out chores arbitrarily. "We get the boring jobs," one 9-year-old girl told me, "the things everybody knows I can do. I'd like to do new things, harder things." A 12-year-old asked, "Why should kids get all the lousy jobs? I think a family should all do some of the interesting things and some of the dumb things." One 10-year-old boy commented, "My mother thinks I can't do anything but take out the garbage. She won't let me use the washing machine and she won't let me go to the supermarket on my bicycle. I could do those things. My parents act as if I'm always staying the same age."

What children need and want is challenge—a feeling that parents see them as growing and changing and capable of taking on new responsibilities. A mother told me, "When we were deciding who would do what, one week Kenny wanted to paint the kitchen. I had a fit—I knew he couldn't do it as well as I could. But it seemed terribly important to him, so I taught him how to use a roller and how to clean up, and we covered everything we could with newspaper. There are some places on the wall that are a little lumpy, but the kitchen certainly looked better. Every time I notice one of the defects, I remember how proud he was. His feeling of making a real contribution—of having taken on a difficult job—is worth a few lumps."

Another mother reported: "When Liz insisted she was perfectly capable of baby-sitting our two-year-old after school, I was nervous about the idea. When she said, 'How do you *know* I can't do it until you let me try?' we decided that was a fair question. One Saturday morning we left them alone while we went shopping. When we came home, Peter was sitting on the kitchen floor happily banging pots and pans together and Liz was sitting at the table doing her homework *without being nagged!* Giving her a big new responsibility seemed to make her more responsible in general."

A father told me: "At first I resented the idea of discussing the assignment of obligations. After all, I go to work every day and earn the money—why should I do anything else? I was shocked to discover that my children feel that *they* go to work every day too, and that school is as much of a 'job' to them as my work is to me. It made sense. We learned a lot about each other! We decided to have a meeting every week and take turns doing all the household jobs. We feel closer; it's as if we are learning how much we need each other."

We need to understand that order means different things at different stages of growing up and for different personalities. Susie's parents may think they're doing a wonderful job when she lines up her shoes in military formation, puts her dirty clothes into the hamper, and folds her underwear. This may well be, but it is also possible that (a) Susie is the kind of person who will always feel more comfortable in an orderly atmosphere or (b) she's going through a period of inner turmoil and is comforted by being a little compulsive about the external world. Jeff's parents are likely to feel they have completely failed to teach him a sense of responsibility when they walk into his room; it seems utterly chaotic—but not to Jeff. He knows that the most important things—his Frisbee, his baseball card collection, and his frog bones—are all in the top drawer of his dresser, where he can find them easily. Having his sneakers and his baseball bat under the bed suits him fine because he likes to look at them when he's sitting on the floor.

A child who is preoccupied with his proficiency in throwing a ball or whether his best friend is turning to someone else isn't highly motivated to pick up a wet towel. The crucial question is, Will the child become more responsible if he and his father get into a fight about the towel or will he learn more about responsibility if his father says, "I know you're worried about some things, especially that math test you have tomorrow, so I put your towel in the hamper." When adults behave responsibly toward each other and their children—caring about people's needs and feelings —children have an opportunity to experience the kind of attention and caring we hope they will express toward others.

One of the most important things we need to strive for is a balance in which *things* never become more important than *relationships*. People must always matter more than the objects with which they surround themselves. A mother told me this story: "One day I yelled at David to make his bed and clean up his room before he left for school. I told him not to go out the door until it was done, but when I finished the breakfast dishes he was gone and the mess was still there. I was furious. I felt he had taken advantage of me, that I was nothing but a servant around the house. I kept thinking about it all day long, becoming more and more sorry for myself and madder at him. By the time he came home, I was boiling; I began screaming at him. I told him he wasn't going anywhere until he did his chores and that from then on there would be a daily inspection after breakfast. He had looked happy and eager to tell me something when he came in, but I never gave him a chance to say a word. He got very quiet, did what he was supposed to, and went out without a word. An hour later his sister came home and said, 'Isn't it wonderful about David?' I didn't know what she was talking about. It seems he was chosen as the only representative from his school to be on a radio program having to do with a city-wide contest for the best composition on 'Why the United Nations Is Important to Me.' The only child in a school of eight hundred children! I realized that was what he wanted to tell me when he walked in. I lost a precious moment of excitement and happiness with my child for a lousy unmade bed!"

One of the most serious mistakes we make with children is equating success and achievement with a sense of responsibility. We need to remember that some of the people who are polluting our environment are considered to be very successful because they have money and power. Is a father most responsible when he earns a great deal of money and in the process almost never sees his children? Is a child a successful achiever because he gets excellent marks in school without having to study? Is a child a successful achiever because she becomes captain of the baseball team only to please her mother? We are fooling ourselves if we think that a child's willingness to keep his room neat or do homework assignments perfectly means that he is necessarily learning to be responsible in the deeper sense in which I have been discussing the subject. Pride in accomplishment is vital, but only if it represents the development of one's unique and special gifts and is in the service of something larger than competitiveness.

Nowhere is this more true than in our schools, where we often celebrate competition at the direct expense of cooperation. Often it seems to me that we need to add a fourth "R" to "Reading, 'Riting, and 'Rithmetic": Responsibility. Children surely need to develop the necessary skills that can lead to intellectual and vocational proficiency, but if we are to learn anything from the state of the world, it ought to be that this kind of achievement is hollow and meaningless without a deep concern for life itself.

"I believe that I teach responsibility," a teacher told me. "But some of the parents don't agree with me. We take a lot of nature walks and we do a lot of studying about the changing seasons; we can spend a day looking at the patterns of veins in different leaves, or at a snowflake under a microscope. We watched baby chicks hatch, and I have all kinds of growing things in the classroom. I want the children to have a sense of wonder and awe about the natural world of living things. I also try to help each child feel proud of his or her own work; we have exhibits to which we invite other classes and parents. When a child sees her painting well placed on a mat on a clean wall, I think she senses the importance of space and order. We do a lot of voting about such things as who will clean the blackboard and erasers, because I want the children to feel responsible to each other, not just to me, and to understand that their happiness depends on others."

We tend to do the same thing at school that we do at home— conceive of responsibility as something a child learns from fulfilling our expectations: doing homework, learning the multiplication table, or passing the milk and cookies. There is much more to it than that. How responsibly do teachers work at understanding individual needs and different rates of growth? Do we encourage children to search for their own unique gifts and potentialities or do we force them to compete with each other in unrealistic ways? Do we create school environments in which children can feel pride in their surroundings or are too many of our schools cold and forbidding places with classrooms that are too crowded? Do we take responsibility for really getting to know each child or do we spend too much time on administrative details?

A child's sense of responsibility to others grows in direct proportion to how responsible he feels others are toward him. If he feels lonely and frightened, if he feels he is failing to measure up to arbitrary adult expectations, he has little time or energy to worry about others or to care what happens to them. What seems shocking to me is that a child can go through school—all the way through high school and college—without ever being asked to help someone who needs him. How often do we ask older children to help younger ones learn to read? How often do we allow children to be useful to others in a hospital or an old-age home? In one school the kindergarten children bake cookies to take to a tea party at a senior citizens' club. I know a grade school teacher who gave homework credit to youngsters who spent a weekend helping to clean out a neighborhood pond. Some high schools now give credit to young people who work in a hospital one afternoon a week.

A high school was closed some time ago because it had been built on the dumping ground for chemical waste from a nearby factory. Over a ten-year period it was discovered that an abnormal increase in childhood leukemia and other diseases was occurring because of the seepage of decaying containers buried underground. A number of parents and teachers were interviewed on a television news program and one teacher commented, "The closing of the school and the delay in moving is going to interfere with the academic achievement of the students. This is especially serious for our seniors who plan to go to college." No statement could have more sharply defined our priorities.

If we want our children to become responsible citizens, we need to share with them our profound concern for human well-being in every part of our environment. We need to encourage young people to participate in necessary social change, to feel a sense of commitment and power to make a difference. It is hopelessness and despair that make us behave in irresponsible and uncaring ways.

Ultimately, what it all comes down to is that the opposite of responsibility is *carelessness*—indifference to other people's needs and feelings, indifference to the environment we all share. We become uncaring in an atmosphere in which human life and human relations seem to be devalued. A mother recently told me, "One day I was in the park with my five-year-old daughter. An old woman was sitting on a bench not far from us, and she was crying quietly. My daughter ran over to her and began to ask why she was crying. Without thinking, I jumped up, rushed over, and said, 'Leave the lady alone—it's none of our business,' and started to drag my daughter away. Suddenly I realized I'd made a terrible mistake. My daughter had a greater sense of social responsibility than I. I asked the woman what was the matter and she said she could not remember her name or her address. I thought that perhaps she had had a slight stroke, so I went to a public phone nearby and called the police. My daughter and I stayed with the woman, trying to comfort her, until the ambulance came. Afterwards I realized that my beautiful child had taught *me* the real meaning of responsibility—*caring.*"

"Cheer up," I replied. "You're better than you think you are. Your five-year-old wouldn't have been able to care if you weren't doing something right!"

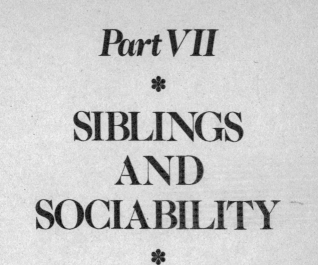

Part VII

*

SIBLINGS AND SOCIABILITY

*

Are You Fair
With Your Children?

❋ A father had some very mixed feelings one day when he wanted to bring his little girl a special present. She had been ill and was wonderfully cooperative about taking her medicine, and he felt a gift would cheer her up. He went into a store to buy a toy for her and then began to wonder what to do about the two younger children. If he just brought a present for their sister, he thought they would be jealous and feel he was playing favorites. He decided to bring each of them a present, with the result that the present brought to the sick child missed its purpose and didn't represent anything special because all three children got presents.

This makes me think of the mother who told me recently that her little 3-year-old girl felt that she wasn't being treated fairly because she had to go to bed before her 5- and 8-year-old brothers. So every night the boys played at going to bed when their little sister went and after she was asleep they came back downstairs and played a little longer. Their little sister isn't going to be satisfied with this solution to the problem for very long, and neither are her two brothers.

These are examples of parents trying to treat all of their children alike in order to be fair. But how do children interpret this kind of equality and so-called fairness? Usually as an indication that they are not treated like the young individuals they want to be but are lumped together in their parents' thinking and feeling. Mommy isn't really looking at 3-year-old Suzy and saying, "I don't care about what anybody else does, but *you* are three years old and you need more sleep!"

Well, what is the best way to handle such situations? Many parents are puzzled and our children seem to sense the fact. Especially when we are sensitive about our even-handedness and on the defensive our darlings have been known to take advantage of our indecision. When they shout we are unfair, what are they really saying?

It seems probable that the taunt of "You're being unfair" is really a challenge to the parent. What the youngster is asking is, *"Am I special and do you see me as a separate person?"* Individuality is more important to all human beings than absolute equality. It is actually very reassuring to the child when Mother or Father can agree completely and say in effect, "Yes, you're absolutely right; I don't treat you and Jack the same way and I don't even give you the same things, because what may be good for one of you may not be for the other."

If children find us constantly trying to be fair in unrealistic ways, they are likely to continue to accuse us of the opposite—because our way of handling such situations is basically unsatisfactory. We are trying too hard. We become suspect in spite of ourselves—maybe, our children reason, we *do* have a favorite, or why else should we go to such lengths to disprove it?

To go back to the little girl who had been ill, she deserved a special relationship with her parents at a special moment in her life. She needed, for that moment, a one-hundred-percent relationship of approval and encouragement. The other children would have their moments of needing something special at other times. Each child wants to feel that at certain times in his life one or both parents are fully focused on his particular need. There can and should be times when the whole family creates a party atmosphere, and at such times parents should plan little gifts for each child in the family. The point is to strike a balance, to know when to treat all of our children alike and when this is actually unfair.

Take the 3-year-old who didn't want to go to bed before her older brothers. This is a situation in which parents need to be matter-of-fact and firm. Three-year-olds go to bed earlier than 5- and 8-year-olds. And that's that. When the 3-year-old is older she will go to bed later, too. But not now. On the other hand, because she is 3 she can take several cuddly toys to bed and her older brothers don't do that anymore.

As it was, the two older brothers were playing a kind of trick on their little sister when they pretended to go to bed at the same time she did. Little sister is apt to catch on to this before too long. Surely we don't want to bring our children up to think that even such well-meant subterfuge is perfectly acceptable. In the long run we don't want them to rely on these methods to gain their ends. It may be hard to be frank and firm, and make it plain that children of different ages just naturally need to have different bedtimes, but it is the only practical way to handle it.

The basic fact is, of course, that what may be right for one child may be wrong for another. Big brother has been given a "neat" football. That doesn't mean that small Bobby needs one, too. He is perfectly happy with a new set of crayons. Yes, of course you spent more for the football than for the crayons. But that isn't the point. Bobby needed them and he is happy to have his parents know what he needs and get it for him.

This whole matter of fairness needs careful scrutiny. For instance, a young teacher described her experience in teaching a class of twenty children. During the first year she wanted to be fair and show no favoritism. She decided never to do anything for one child if she could not do it for all of them. At the end of the year she reported that she felt she didn't have a warm, close relationship with any child in the class. The fact was, of course, that all she had ever given any child was one-twentieth of herself, and that was never enough. The next year she relaxed. When a child needed her attention, he got it, even to the exclusion of others. Each child got the attention that suited his own needs and interests. At the end of the year each child had had one hundred percent of his teacher at one time or another, and she had made twenty enthusiastic friends.

Everyone benefits when children are *not* lumped together and when our sense of justice is based on individual needs. We should not become confused or worried if our children sometimes shout, "You're an old meany. It's not fair." Just be sure of the basic principle that every child is an individual with individual needs and that treating them accordingly is fairer than trying to treat all of them alike.

Love and Hate:
The Sibling Condition

✽ My younger brother is a very witty man. He was the master of ceremonies some years ago at our parents' fiftieth anniversary party, and when he introduced me he said, "My sister and I had a very normal sibling relationship—she just wanted to kill me!"

It got a big laugh. Everybody understands sibling rivalry; it's been the "in thing" for many years. But it occurred to me later that behind the humor (and the undoubted sometime-truth of what he said) was one small undeclared detail—that I laugh harder at his humor than anyone else, that I am his favorite audience, and that (I'm almost embarrassed to say it!) we love each other.

When I ask people what word comes to mind when I say "sibling," more than half reply "rivalry." Most of the rest say, "brother" or "sister." In my nonscientific but provocative survey, no one has responded with the word "love." I have become quite fascinated with this for it hits me where I live. As a teacher and parent educator for more than forty years, I've done a lot of talking with parents about sibling relationships. It has suddenly occurred to me that ninety percent of these discussions have dealt with jealousy, rivalry, and hostility between siblings, with only a few passing comments on the fact that they often enjoy each other's company and may end up liking each other quite a lot!

There is a logic to this pattern. In the old days people believed that brothers and sisters loved each other because they were supposed to. Then along came Sigmund Freud and a lot of new psychological insights. Freud and others taught us that in sibling relations, as well as in all others, every human being experiences the full range of feelings. No one is good or bad, tender or mean, compassionate or competitive, loving or hateful, but *all* of these. (This was beautifully expressed by the very contemporary child who, writing to her brother from camp, signed her letter, "Love and Hate, Karen.")

In that light it is small wonder we focused our attention on the rivalry rather than the love; we were merely redressing a balance. But now that the negative feelings that normally arise between brothers and sisters have been so thoroughly examined, it's time to look at sibling relations with the more balanced perspective available to us.

To begin with, we should understand the perfectly natural reasons for sibling rivalry. Siblings don't choose each other, yet they have to share the two people they want most for themselves. They are frequently different sexes, are almost always different ages, and have different temperaments. Siblings also have perfectly natural reasons for loving each other. As children caught in the inevitable struggle against their parents for autonomy, they have a common enemy! They can entertain each other on a rainy day at the seashore; they can giggle in the dark together over a dirty joke; they can share the noisiness and messiness their parents object to. They remember the same funny, sad, happy events—the trip to the circus when Jonathan threw up all over the clown; Thanksgiving at Grandma's when the turkey slid across the table; that horrible cousin from Chicago who was such a tattletale. There is nothing like a big brother when there's a bully on the block, and nothing like a younger sister who shares your fear of the dark. It was simpleminded of us to think that siblings could love each other all of the time, but just as simpleminded to behave as if they hated each other all of the time.

With this in mind, let's take a new look at some of the things that influence the way brothers and sisters feel about each other. To begin with, we are born with different temperaments that don't always mix well. In some relationships, simple toleration may be the highest goal one can seek. A man told me, "My brother and I were like oil and water from the first moment we laid eyes on each other. I was shy, introverted, inarticulate—a worrier and a dreamer. He was sociable, physically active, an optimist. We never liked the same people, books, movies, school subjects, or hobbies. Our parents made us feel guilty as hell because we couldn't play well together. Now that we're adults and can understand how utterly different we are, we respect each other. But we still don't force a relationship that just isn't right for us."

Finances can influence sibling relationships. As one man explains, "I envy my older sisters because we had money when they were growing up and Pop could send them to college; when my time came we were too poor and I had to go to work." A woman recalls, "When I was young we lived in the country. I had a great deal of freedom, loved being outdoors, and became very independent. My parents thought I was a great kid! Then we moved to a small city apartment where my younger sisters and I had to share a room. They had much less freedom and no privacy and were thus less contented, more selfish, and more dependent than I. They sensed that our parents were more satisfied with me and they resented me, but circumstances were really responsible."

The simple reality of position in the family can also influence sibling relations. An oldest child says, "My parents expected me to be responsible and take care of the younger children; it made me hate them." A youngest child says, "I had a brother twelve years older, and I thought he was God. I spent my whole childhood trying to live up to my image of him; that's not very good grounds for loving feelings."

Sex can affect such relationships, too. A son may hate his sister because Daddy is partial to little girls. Or something quite different may happen. One woman told me, "My sister and I really didn't have too much in common, but we got along well. I think it was because we both knew our father wanted us to be boys and we comforted each other for having the feeling that it was a misfortune to be born female!"

Age is another factor that can cause siblings to either relate warmly or grow apart. A 5-year-old and an 8-year-old can play many games together, but when the same pair become 10 and 13 they may have nothing at all in common. A brother and sister who are eight years apart may have little interest in each other until they both become adults. In all of these situations the more subtle emotional aspects of the relationship seem to be secondary to the circumstances of life itself.

There can be little question in any careful observer's mind, however, that parental attitudes play a crucial part in the love-hate ratio among brothers and sisters. In the nursery school where I worked as a consultant, we were very concerned about a most unhappy and angry little boy. When we asked his mother to come in for a conference she sounded quite exasperated over the telephone. She arrived at the appointed hour in her son's classroom holding a pretty 2-year-old girl by the hand. In front of her son, and pointing at her daughter, she said, *"This one suits me fine."* The teacher whispered to me, "Well, we have the diagnosis—but what's the cure?"

The "cure" is surely not trying to love our children "equally." In our sensible concern for this destructive kind of favoritism, we are sometimes inclined to go to the other extreme and hide the perfectly natural differences in feeling that all human beings must have for each other. One mother told me she was upstairs when she heard the kitchen door slam. "I called, 'Is that you, darling?' and one of my sons answered, 'No, it's John.' When I realized what he had said, I was stunned. He was right; he wasn't my 'darling'! How I cried that night when I told my husband about it. My younger son, Jerry, is more like my husband—very easygoing and affectionate. John is like me—solemn, shy, and undemonstrative— things I can't stand in myself. That night my husband made me list all the good things about myself and John, and to try to see that differences between the two boys could be pleasurable, not upsetting. It's been a struggle, but I hope someday I'll say, 'Is that you, darling?' and John will answer, 'Yes.' "

In worrying about showing partiality we sometimes overlook the inevitability of feeling differently about children who are different persons with different needs and possibilities. It is impossible to love any two people equally or in exactly the same way. When we try, the message the child gets is, "She's so guilty about how she feels she's covering it all up by trying to be fair." The message our children want to hear is the exact opposite: "You're darn right I'm not fair; you're two different people." When a child says, "It's not fair; why should I go to bed earlier when I'm older?" he wants to hear, "Because you don't take a nap and you wake up earlier." Or if a youngster says, "It's not fair—you took Sharon to a puppet show and you didn't take me," he wants to hear, "Well, she's the right age for puppet shows and you're not. She felt just as left out when you went to that baseball game with Daddy."

Giving children an even chance of liking each other seems to depend heavily on *not* trying to be fair in the expenditure of time and attention. When we begin to weigh and measure these we dehumanize the relationships we have with all of our children. One mother told me, "Every time I hugged the baby I could feel Joel's accusing eyes on me, so I'd stop hugging the baby. Then I realized that was making me mad at Joel; I like to hug babies! So I did, whenever I felt like it—and that made me feel good. Then I felt like taking Joel off by himself for a story. No more watching and measuring; that cheats both of them."

When a child is sick or scared he needs *all* of our attention. When it's his birthday, it should be *his* friends, *his* presents, *his* day. He shouldn't have to "be fair" and share it with his siblings. When children tell us we're unfair, what they're really saying is, "Do you see me as a separate, special person?" If we react by getting flustered and wondering if we *are* being fair, their worst fears—that we see our children collectively, not individually—are realized.

The best thing we can do to enhance relations between our children is to *stop making comparisons*. Children can tolerate almost anything if they feel they are seen in the fullness of their own unique variety. What cripples their growing is the feeling that they are seen and judged only in relation to others. An important aid in seeing each child as a distinct person is the ability to look at ourselves and determine what makes us react positively or negatively to certain qualities in our children. If we had a good experience growing up and have developed a positive self-image, it may please us to see some of our own qualities in a child. But if what we see emerging are qualities we have always rejected in ourselves, we may need to do some mature soul-searching before we can begin to appreciate these qualities in our child.

A friend once told me she was sure her mother hated her when she was little. "I felt there was nothing I could do to please her," she said. "No matter how I tried. When I was about twelve we had a terrible fight and she suddenly blurted out, 'You and I fight the way I used to fight with Aunt Martha because you're just like her. We were awful to each other. Sometimes I think I act more like your sister than your mother. I'm sorry.' I didn't really understand at the time, but after that I'd watch her with her sister whenever they were together. I finally saw what she meant; I *was* like my aunt, and they fought the same way my mother and I did. But I could see that they loved each other too, and it made me feel better."

Sometimes a parent is so protective of a child who is less able and successful that the more competent child begins to see his successes as a handicap to being loved. The fact that a parent has special feelings for one particular child doesn't mean that the other children in the family need feel rejected and unloved. I remember the story one man told me about his family. "We all knew how Dad felt about Willy," he said. "Ken and I were okay—Dad loved us and was proud of us—but Willy was the apple of his eye. Strangely enough I don't remember feeling envious, because Willy really *was* something! Dad and Ken and I are stocky and sort of clumsy. Then along comes Willy—like a young God! Blond, tall, athletic, full of life—the kind of boy whom teachers, girls, and kids on the block all get crushes on. Dad just couldn't get over this miracle; *he'd* created this beautiful creature! When he says Willy's name to this day, he gets such a look on his face!" There are such children, and they do evoke such responses. But when other children in the family are able to share in their parents' pleasure without resentment, it means their parents have given them a deep sense of their own worth as well.

One of the most difficult challenges parents face in fostering good feelings between brothers and sisters is how to avoid making them feel guilty. Ever since we discovered sibling rivalry and decided it's normal, we've had a terrible time figuring out what to do with it! First we must understand that feelings and actions are not synonymous. It may be normal to *want* to hit the baby on the head, but parents must stop a child from doing it. The guilt about acting so mean is a lot worse than the guilt that goes with feeling mean, not to mention that poor baby's head. What seems to make sense in such situations is the response "I know you feel angry; lots of boys and girls feel that way, but I cannot let you hurt her. If you are too little to stop yourself, then I will have to stop you."

Permitting brothers and sisters to settle their own differences may be sound in theory, but it can be terribly unfair in practice. In a contest of unequals (age, strength, vulnerability) the weak usually lose. When it's not just horsing around but gets to be near the brink of war, it is time for parents to step in and mediate. Some of the most long-lasting grudges among grown siblings reflect memories of not being protected in their minority rights. A mother of two children given to verbal fighting told me, "My attitude was that as long as it was pretty equal and nobody was getting too badly bruised, I wouldn't interfere. But one day I heard Paul call Nancy 'A dumb, stupid girl,' and then I interfered—but fast. He's a brilliant student; she's four years younger, adores him, and is doing poorly in school. He was hitting below the belt and that I wouldn't allow."

However sensitive and perceptive parents may be in such matters, it is a mistake to assume that all siblings can be close all their lives. The important thing in any relationship is to *allow it to happen*—without claims and preconceptions of what it ought to be. This is especially true in sibling relationships.

My brother and I had a not uncommon relationship between an older sister and a younger brother; I tried to make him my slave! I even succeeded for a while. When I studied the medieval period —all about knights and squires and lords—I decided to dub my brother my knight. I insisted that he kneel in front of me while I tapped his shoulder with a wooden sword. I told him that he would have to obey my every command and the poor, foolish boy believed me. He caught on after a while, but it was fun while it lasted.

I did have all sorts of guilt feelings when I grew up and began to realize how much advantage I'd taken of him—the times he took the blame for naughty things I did, the times I dared him to show his courage and he got hurt, the way I cheated him at Monopoly. But the memory that is most distinct of all was the day I came home from school and found my brother weeping on his bed. He'd been badly bitten by a dog, and there was no one at home. I became Florence Nightingale: I called the doctor, found enough money for a cab, got him there, and brought him home. But most of all I showed how awful I felt, and how I shared his pain and fear. I felt good because I'd taken care of him. This was just as real as the exploitation, the teasing, and the fighting. And if each child is encouraged to become most truly himself, this is what lasts.

What we seem to be saying about relationships—sibling or otherwise—is that, being human, we will falter. We are sometimes cruel and thoughtless, sometimes lacking in compassion, sometimes driven by our jealousies—but we are trying to be what is best in us. What we seek from each other is that unconditional love that says, "Yes, I can love you—vulnerable, weak, beautiful you—and I hope you can see me whole, too." Such loving has to be the most civilizing influence the world has ever known. It is surely the essence of what has always been meant by "brotherly love," and it remains the only hope for man's salvation on earth.

Getting Mad Is Quite Okay

❋ My husband and I were visiting friends who have two children —a 3-year-old boy and a 1-year-old girl. Josh was pounding pegs with a wooden hammer while little Kim was in a playpen in the middle of the living room. As we sat talking, Josh sidled up to the playpen and bopped Kim on the head. She cried, her parents comforted her, and we resumed our conversation. After the third or fourth such episode it was obvious that my husband and I were uncomfortable and completely distracted by what was happening. Finally the embarrassed mother said in a defensive tone of voice, "Well, what can we do? You psychologists keep telling us jealousy is normal!"

"What you can do," said my husband quietly, "is take that hammer away from Josh and tell him he can't have it until he learns to stop hitting Kim." We then tried to explain that the fact that a child's feelings are normal does not give him license to behave in cruel and dangerous ways. Instead of permitting such behavior, the parents might have said, "Josh, many little boys feel angry when their baby sister gets a lot of attention. In fact, everybody feels jealous sometimes. But we cannot allow you to hurt Kim— any more than we'd let some big person hurt you."

When we tell a child, "You are a great kid and your feelings are normal, but you just can't hurt people," we acknowledge that he or she is a perfectly nice person who just needs help with a universal problem. Josh's parents were right to recognize that the boy's anger was normal and needed someplace to go; their mistake was in thinking that it had to go into harmful action. The guilt and anxiety Josh must have felt after he was allowed to hurt the baby is surely as serious as telling him he is a bad person just because he feels mean.

Many parents would have done that. They'd have said, "Joshua! Stop that this minute and go to your room! You are a very bad boy to hit your little sister. God will punish you if you don't get over that mean streak of yours!" In that case we can be sure that Josh, who needs love and approval as all children do, would find ways to repress his angry feelings. He probably wouldn't hit his little sister anymore, but he might become asthmatic, develop chronic bronchitis, or begin having terrifying nightmares about being killed by wild animals.

Contrary to what many people think, anger is not something we should try to avoid at all costs. It is an entirely normal part of human experience. Its power to be harmful and destructive is completely dependent on our ability to face angry feelings and learn how to deal with them.

Once we help a child to understand his or her angry feelings and make it clear that hostile actions are not allowed as an outlet, many other alternatives can be offered. It usually helps to talk to a sympathetic listener about our angry feelings, for instance. It may help a child to pound some clay or punch a pillow, pretending it's the person he's mad at. Sometimes it helps a child to get into the bathtub and smear fingerprints all over or to yell at the top of his lungs. Giving children acceptable outlets for anger makes it possible for them to be in touch with their feelings. Such guidance can help a child grow up to be an adult who can have an unpleasant experience with a nasty boss or a manipulative relative, recognize that it has made him angry, then arrange to take a long walk, go fishing, or smack a tennis ball around until the anger subsides.

The capacity for anger—even rage—seems to be at least partly instinctive. One look at an infant who is wet, hungry, or lonesome confirms this. But during the first years of life, when a child has no language and thus no conscious awareness of anger, the feeling tends to be a generalized, physiological sensation. A baby arches his back, yells, gets red all over, waves his arms.

Somewhere around the age of 2 a child begins to be conscious of the way he feels. Pleasant feelings become associated with language: "I *love* this wonderful lady who sings to me and gives me cookies and milk . . . Oh, how happy I feel because Grandma is coming and will tell me stories." Loving, happy fellings—which lead to loving, compassionate, charming behavior—never get anyone into trouble. Everyone is delighted with this side of being human. The troubles begin with less lovely thoughts: "When Momma yells at me, I hate her; I wish she'd go away and never come back . . . When Daddy says I can't go to the store with him, I feel like throwing my books . . . Oh, how I wish they'd take that terrible noisy baby to the hospital . . . If Grandma doesn't stop asking me for kisses, I'm going to smack her!"

Now life gets very scary for a child. Everybody loves him when he's "good," but he keeps having "bad" thoughts and sometimes he can't seem to stop himself from doing "bad" things. He doesn't want to share his wagon, so he hits the girl who tries to take it away; he doesn't want to wear those ugly yellow socks, so he stuffs them down the toilet; it makes him mad to be told to eat that awful cereal, so he pushes the bowl off the table. Most confusing of all for the child is the recognition that grown-ups seem to be allowed to get angry. They "have a good reason" for yelling and spanking; they say it's "the only way to make you good."

To a young child, words seem very powerful—even magical. Just look at what happens the first time he or she says "No!" It causes unbelievable panic and havoc! Adults are shocked, angry, confused, hurt—all because of a one-syllable word! And many words also evoke sharp reactions. A girl says "kiss, kiss," and Grandma melts; a boy says "penis" or "dammit" and Grandma washes his mouth out with soap or smacks him. Imagine! All because of a certain sound made with the voice. It's no wonder children begin to believe that thoughts can make things happen.

The belief in magical words makes a child's hostile thoughts even more terrifying than "bad" behavior. For example, suppose a little boy thinks, "I hate that baby; nothing around here is any fun since she came," and then the baby gets very sick. He may well think his thoughts made that happen. Or suppose a girl gets mad at Grandpa because he keeps telling her to sit still and be quiet, and she wishes he'd go away and never come back—and then he goes to the hospital and dies. Angry thoughts become so frightening that most children—unless they get direct guidance—begin to repress their anger. They fear that angry thoughts can hurt people; they know that angry behavior makes people dislike them and they really need to be loved and cared for.

At this period in a child's life—when he is afraid of angry thoughts and feelings, and begins to believe anger means you are a bad, dangerous, unlovable person—it's essential for parents to intervene. They must make it clear to the child that bad thoughts cannot hurt another person, that all human beings get angry, that children need adults to help them control angry impulses. It's important to point out that nobody can control his feelings all of the time; mommies and daddies lose their tempers, too. Part of being human is getting angry, and part of being little is being unable to deal with anger all or even most of the time.

There is no subject connected with childraising about which I am more passionate because I've seen what happens when children feel guilty and unlovable and repress their anger. It never just goes away; sooner or later it finds an outlet. Here are some of the consequences:

1. All emotion gets repressed.

If a child becomes frightened and guilty about angry feelings, he may unconsciously begin repressing all kinds of thoughts and feelings. Curiosity, wonder, and creativity are severely damaged by such a generalized block. The child draws inward, experiencing a loss of all emotions—including positive ones.

2. Anger is turned against the self.

When anger has no place to go, it turns against the self on a profound physiological level. This leads to psychosomatic disorders such as migraine headaches, intestinal problems, ulcers, asthma, or various allergies. Anger is not the whole cause of such disorders, of course, but it's a strong contributing factor. Self-hatred and unconscious anger are also major factors in neurotic disturbances—compulsions, obsessions, difficulties in all kinds of relationships. We punish ourselves for our anger, which can lead to serious depression —even suicide.

One woman was so seriously depressed that she was unable to work or even leave her apartment for many months. After successful psychotherapy she said, "It now seems impossible that I could have been so afraid of showing how angry I felt that I nearly destroyed my life rather than face it. Where do people get such a terror of being angry?" They get it early in life from their parents and other adults who indicate that open anger leads to severe punishment and withdrawal of love.

3. Anger is turned toward "socially acceptable" targets.

People who hate "all Jews" or "all blacks" or "all Russians" or "all intellectuals" or "all rich people" have found an outlet for their repressed anger. Taught to believe that they must never have angry feelings for their own loved ones, they rationalize that it is right and necessary to attack groups of "troublemakers." The Nazis who kept the gas chambers going would undoubtedly have denied that they ever had violently angry thoughts about their own mothers, wives, or children. They had been taught that God will punish you if you do not love and honor your family. But when society offers a scapegoat on which to focus anger, then it is appropriate to fight —even to kill. Few people speak more righteously of the virtues of motherhood, God, and country than those who form secret societies to take the law into their own hands—to lynch, burn churches, and threaten the lives of those on whom they vent their repressed anger. No one is more vulnerable to irrational racial, religious, and ethnic prejudices than someone raised to deny all anger. Nothing scares me more than a child who "yes ma'am's" me constantly and behaves like a polite automaton, for such a child may be a potential bigot.

4. Repressed anger suddenly explodes into violence.

Some people manage to keep their anger so deeply repressed that they are totally out of touch with this part of their nature. If you have feelings you don't know about, you can't handle them—and they remain a powder keg that could go off unexpectedly, at any moment. Whenever a violent, senseless crime is committed, it's usually a terrible shock to everyone who knows the person who did it. A neighbor says, "I can't believe it—he was always the best behaved, most polite child on the block." His aunt reports, "I never ever heard that boy talk back." A storekeeper says, "He always treated his mother with more respect than any child around."

For a number of years I have been meeting with groups of ex-convicts at the Fortune Society, a rehabilitation center in New York City. Many of them are afraid that their children will turn out to be criminals too, so much of our talk is about how they got involved in crime. Most of them were victims of terrible deprivation in every aspect of their lives—rejection by both parents and society. The majority had suffered severe physical abuse—being whipped with straps, belts, switches, and whips for the smallest childish "crime." They were told, "Your soul will burn in hell if you go on being so bad" by the very adults who abused them. The typical reaction in our discussion was, "I knew I was an evil child who needed to be punished. If I was angry, I was *bad.*"

These ex-convicts were shocked when I told them it was normal to hate a brother or sister, a parent, or even their own child. And when I confessed that I sometimes felt like throwing my own baby across the room when she cried for hours on end, they looked at me in wide-eyed horror. They'd been taught that anyone who had such feelings was not really human. I was a terrible shock to them —"a nice, respectable lady" who got mad!

One former convict, who'd been left on the doorstep of a church as a baby and had lived in fifteen foster homes before being placed in an industrial school at the age of 13, was involved in an armed robbery during which a man was killed. He spent twenty-eight years in prison.

I met him five years after parole, when he was married, working, and the father of a darling little girl. "I've been so scared Marcia would turn out rotten like me," he said. "But I keep remembering what that psychologist who helped me in prison said—that if she feels like a really good person, she'll act like one. The other day she broke my pipe; she was furious at me for keeping her indoors because she had a cold. I wanted to smack her, but I didn't. I said, "Marcia, you can't do that. Daddy wants his pipe. But you're just a little girl and sometimes when you get angry you make mistakes. You are too little to stop yourself, so it's my job to help you." His eyes were shining as he told about this episode in parenting. "I didn't make Marcia feel like a bad person," he said. "Maybe the rage can end with me."

The most dangerous acts of violence come from those who are least aware of their own feelings of anger. By the time it explodes, it's usually too late. Everyone feels angry from time to time, but some people seem to get much angrier than others. Reactions vary with individual temperaments. One person gets steamed up about the most trivial frustration, while another seems hardly rattled by constant irritants. Some people need a great many outlets for their angry feelings; others don't. It is important for everyone to have an opportunity to talk about such feelings. Parents can often help a child get in touch with his anger by expressing their own feelings. "You made me very angry when you told me to shut up; it hurt my feelings and I don't like it" is a good beginning. It might be followed by "If you're angry with me, let's talk about it."

We need to be honest with children about our anger toward them. We yell and threaten and punish children when they are angry, but how often do we stop ourselves when we're angry? A girl hits a playmate in anger and we spank her for being so bad. A boy bites a cousin who tries to take a toy away and we bite him "just to show you how it feels." We stoop to the very techniques that make us angry with children. Logic is surely absent, but we, too, are human and we behave quite irrationally at times. Children should understand that we don't admire such outbursts wherever they come from; that there are far better ways of dealing with each other. We all should strive to improve, without wallowing in guilt when we fail. "I'm sorry I got so mad. That was a dumb thing I did, and I'll try not to do it again—but sometimes you really bug me" is a perfectly appropriate and civilized apology for being human!

Occasional explosions need not be damaging unless we over-react. Brothers and sisters will hit each other; husbands and wives may throw a plate or two. Volatility is usually not so serious as an atmosphere heavy with fury in which everyone is controlled and very polite. A friend told me she was never afraid of her mother. "She'd yell and carry on," she said, "but when it was over, the air was clear. My father, on the other hand, spoke quietly and was always in control. His anger was much more frightening because it was always beneath the surface where I couldn't connect to it or respond in any way."

We are all born with a capacity for loving and hating, for compassion and selfishness. We need to experience both love and anger, to learn how close they sometimes are, and to learn to deal with this complexity. Anger seems to be a necessary instinct for survival, a response to being attacked or in danger. It mobilizes the individual in one direction when his very "selfhood" is blocked, his growth frustrated. Whether it's a baby crying furiously because a pin is sticking him, a 4-year-old angry because too many people are telling her how to behave, a young adult enraged by being mugged and beaten, or a sick old woman who is bitter about being treated like a "thing" in a nursing home, anger is a way of expressing the life force when a person's safety and identity are threatened. Anger is a reaction to dangers both within and without. If we treat it with respect, honor its fundamental integrity, and deal with it openly and courageously, we might begin to alleviate the inner anger that is so dangerous and focus our attention on the fact that consciously directed anger can be useful.

We *should* be angry at human suffering, at social injustice, at inequality, at poverty, at war, at bureaucracies that interfere with human needs and rights. Anger turned toward a fight for liberty and justice is what democracy needs for survival. It is a kind of anger that does not come from people who feel bad or evil or worthless; it comes from those who feel good about themselves, who have forgiven themselves for their human weaknesses and can therefore feel compassion for others.

The Shy Ones

❋ "I *know* Laura is adorable and smart, but why does she have to be shy? That's what drives me crazy!" The mother who made that remark had just been told by both Laura's teacher and me what a joy it was to have Laura in the nursery school where I was working as a parent counselor. I was usually able to keep my cool, but on that particular day I'd had it. It was late afternoon and by some strange coincidence Laura's mother was the third one to complain about her child's shyness.

"What the devil is wrong with being shy?" I heard myself saying stridently. Meeting a shocked silence I explained, "It's just that some of the nicest people in the world are shy, and I get so tired of hearing it discussed as if it were a disease!"

Laura's mother looked me straight in the eye. "I can't say I love you for mentioning it," she said with a smile, "but you're right— that's just the way I feel about shyness. I was terribly shy myself as a child, and I'm doing the same thing to Laura that my parents did to me—letting her know I worry about it. I just can't seem to help it."

She went on to describe one of her most vivid memories: "I was about four or five and so shy that I would practically disappear into the woodwork when told to talk to people. My parents said I could go with them to a convention in Atlantic City, but only if I promised to smile and say hello to my father's friends. I had no idea what Atlantic City was, but a trip with my parents seemed the greatest thing that could happen. For weeks they kept reminding me of my promise to 'be a friendly girl.' By the time we left, the whole thing had been built up to such proportions that I was sick to my stomach with panic. When the time finally came for me to say hello and shake hands with a friend of my father's, I threw up —right there on the boardwalk! To my dying day I will never forget that sense of shame, of utter despair about ever measuring up to my parents' expectations."

After hearing that story I did a lot of thinking about shyness. I have reached the conclusion that there is something wrong with the way most of us think about this very human quality. Why do we see it as a negative trait—something in our children that must be changed, something we try to deny in ourselves? If we gave some thought to the shy people we know, it seems to me we might be forced to admit that they're some of the nicest people of all!

I remember being at a dinner party with a number of people I'd never met before. The two I remember most vividly were exact opposites. One was a middle-aged man who kept embarrassing people by telling what he thought they were thinking or feeling. "I've got extrasensory perception," he told us. "I can read your minds. Now this charming lady is having love troubles . . ." I don't know about his extrasensory powers, but he seemed to hit several nerves in his observations. He was "onstage" all evening—the life of the party—and I found his cruelty and insensitivity detestable.

The other person I remember was a young woman who seemed painfully unhappy at being among so many strangers. She was sitting in a corner of the couch, nestled so deeply in the pillows that it seemed as if she was trying to disappear. Every time the extrovert made another smart-aleck comment, she winced. After a while, I introduced myself and sat down next to her. I was surprised to discover that in a short time my companion not only found out what I was doing with my life but also learned a good deal about my hopes for the future. She was a warm, responsive listener and it was impossible to view her shyness as a fault—especially with that unpleasant clown in the background.

The ability to elicit—to draw people out in quiet conversation

—is a common characteristic of shy people. They also tend to be private people who respect the privacy of others. They're often sensitively tuned in to what people want to reveal or conceal about themselves. The shyest person I ever knew was Emily, a girl in my class in high school. It was torture for her to speak in class. Although she never said very much, she listened and somehow let us know that she really cared. For instance, one day at lunch I mentioned how much I loved homemade Toll House cookies. About a week later I found a box of the most delicious cookies in my desk with no note or anything, but when I started to talk about them, Emily got very red. After class she whispered that her mother made them all the time and she had brought them.

Emily was always doing things like that. When another girl admired a wool cap she'd knitted, Emily made another and just handed it to her one day—stammering that it was an extra one she didn't need. What I remember best is the day I was crying in an empty classroom because I had not been invited to a school dance. Emily came in, hesitated a moment, then sat down quietly, gave me a tissue, and stroked my hand. She didn't say anything, didn't ask me what was the matter, she just stayed there with me while I bawled. It was one of the kindest things that ever happened to me and I've never forgotten it—or Emily.

The more I've thought—and talked—about shyness, the more heartwarming stories I've heard about shy people. One woman told me about a shy friend of hers who always writes notes. "She doesn't say much when you're with her," she explained, "but if anything out of the ordinary happens she'll write you a beautiful letter. I received one, for instance when I got a new job, when I was sick, when I was going on a trip, when my mother died. Her letters are so sensitive and caring they really give you a lift. I've heard many people talk about how much these letters have meant."

Shy people may not be very articulate in speech, but they have other ways of communicating that can be most effective. A member of a school committee charged with recruiting volunteers to help students after school told me that some of the best volunteers are very shy people. "At first," he admitted, "we tended to dismiss those who didn't seem articulate or outgoing; we considered them unqualified. After a while, though, we learned that some of the quietest, least talkative people were absolutely marvelous with the kids. They didn't overwhelm them with verbal directions but encouraged them just by being there—completely.

"One man who must be 80 years old, for instance, speaks very softly, pats the children gently on the head or back, asks one or two questions, and lets the children talk to him. He's a wonderful listener, and I've watched him help a child to read simply by the loving warmth he exudes. The kids call him 'Grandpa,' and they adore him. What's more, they are learning! A year ago I'd have said we couldn't use him because he wasn't able to tell us his ideas for teaching children with learning difficulties. But having seen what some shy teenagers were able to do, I took a chance on him. Now, I find myself seeking out that inner quality of caring. I'm far less impressed with the talkers who know exactly what they want to do and how they're going to do it."

What worries us about shyness is the paralyzing effect it can have when it takes the form of great self-consciousness—the preoccupation with self that makes the individual utterly miserable. For example, consider the misery of the shy adolescent who feels fat, clumsy, or ugly. He's so caught up in his own self-hatred that he cuts himself off from the human relationships he desperately wants and needs. His constant thought is, "Everybody is watching me—and I am awful." In this case, shyness is not necessarily part of the true nature of a person but is rather a distorted self-perception. When you are moving very dramatically from childhood to adulthood, it's natural to feel confused and out of touch with who you really are. A general feeling of unworthiness or self-contempt is common during this period of growing, but it is painful to watch and frequently evokes anxiety in parents.

Shyness is also worrisome when it's used to mask feelings of aggression, of hostility toward others. I remember a time, many years ago, when I was watching the children on a nursery-school playground. The teacher, Lillian Weber, commented to me, "You see that little boy standing on the sidelines looking so woeful? I'm worried about him because he's not a naturally shy child. I think he's really quite aggressive and angry, but he's kept it in for so long

—and he's so afraid of his feelings—he's using shyness as a defense." I had never thought of shyness in that light before, and at first it seemed like a nutty idea.

Two weeks later I met Mrs. Weber in the supermarket. She was beaming. "Remember Allen?" she asked. "This morning I took him by the hand and said 'Allen, you had that wagon and it was your turn. You *should* be mad at Alison for taking it away from you. If you let her know you're angry, it isn't going to kill her. Now let's go and tell her you're angry.' I led him across the room and literally demonstrated how you yell at someone in righteous indignation. He got so caught up in the drama of it all he was soon doing his own yelling. It was marvelous! You see, I'm teaching him that you can express angry feelings without really hurting anyone. That way he won't hide under a cloak of shyness." She was right. Allen's shyness gradually disappeared.

Shyness can also be a way of avoiding reality. Some shy people are so sure they'll fail to make friends or get ahead in their work that they retreat and say, "I can't do that—I'm too shy." A psychiatrist told me that some shyness he sees in patients comes under the heading of "Walter Mittyism." He explained it as "having lovely daydreams about being powerful and successful, but being so sure you won't measure up that you never try. The wallflower says, 'The only reason I'm not popular is because I'm too shy.' What she really feels deep down is that nobody would like her anyway. Or a patient will say, 'I'm just too shy to ask for a raise' when we both suspect that he doesn't really think he deserves it. When shyness is a retreat from challenging the best that is in you, it can certainly be a handicap."

Another situation that creates unreal shyness is being asked to play a role that doesn't suit us. A child having a lovely time taking ballet lessons or learning to play the guitar suddenly becomes shy when asked to perform for company. Her pleasure in the activity itself is corrupted by the demand to play an impossible role. Not all dancers and guitar players want to or can be performers, and the situation floods them with discomfort that manifests itself as shyness.

Complicating the matter still further is the fact that some of the noisiest people may actually be suffering from painful shyness. The clown, the cynic, the dirty-story teller—even that unpleasant man with his game of clairvoyance—may have an innate shyness that they feel obliged to hide from the world at all costs. Not all shy people are shrinking violets; some compensate for such a quality by striving to become the center of attention as a way of reassuring themselves that they are not really shy.

To deal successfully with shyness—in ourselves as well as in others—it helps to understand its origins. While environment can certainly modify our personalities, we seem to be born with many basic traits. An inherent shyness has frequently been observed in the study of children from birth through early adolescence. Despite wide variations in life experiences, some babies get more flustered than others when approached by strangers. Some toddlers seem more prone to run and hide when visitors appear, while some grade-school-age children start off feeling very shy and uneasy with each new teacher—regardless of the teachers' personalities. Some teenagers seem to need a great deal of reassurance before they can feel at home at a sleep-away camp, a club meeting, or a school dance. This pattern shows remarkable consistency. The shy baby becomes the shy toddler, who becomes the shy schoolchild—even though the home and school experiences of such children may be totally dissimilar.

This seems to suggest that some people are "born shy," and that whether it becomes an asset or a drawback depends on how it is treated. The shy child who feels that shyness can be an admirable quality—who is not pushed and shamed into being something he cannot be—can grow up liking himself and feeling hopeful about his life. The mother of a shy child might say, "I know you feel shy when we have company, darling, so why don't you take charge of passing the canapés? That way you'll be too busy to feel uncomfortable." Or a father might say, "Now look, Josh, don't get upset if you feel strange and unhappy at camp the first week. We both know that's just the kind of person you are; it takes a while for you to get warmed up, and there's nothing wrong with that." The shy child who hears a parent say, "Yes, Sara is a shy child—and I'm not a bit sorry! It's a wonderful thing to be gentle and sensitive," can use her shyness as a positive quality in realizing her full potential.

Shyness that is perceived as a handicap, a barrier to a successful life, on the other hand, often becomes distorted and twisted. A mother may say, "These are important guests we're having tonight and I don't want any nonsense about you hiding behind me"; or a father says, "You are really too big to be hanging back this way at camp"; or a parent says, "Yes, I know Harold is shy; it worries me half to death." The shy child treated this way is filled with a hopeless despair about his worth as a human being—and that, not the shyness, is the source of disturbance.

If shyness is not a consistent personality characteristic, it may be viewed as a sign of growth and maturation. During the Korean War my husband was stationed at an army post. When I walked past the parade ground with my 2-year-old daughter in her stroller, Wendy would stand up, wave gleefully, and shout, "Hi, Daddy!" to an entire company of soldiers. Aside from my mortification, I was pleased that she was such a friendly child! A year later, the story was quite different. Greeted by a kindly neighbor, Wendy would freeze; smiled at by a friendly elevator operator, she would retreat behind me, sucking her thumb; asked for a hug by a devoted relative, she'd run to her room.

As a properly brainwashed mother of the 1950s, my immediate reaction was, "What did I do wrong? How did I turn a friendly, outgoing child into this shy mouse?" On further reflection, however, I finally realized that Wendy was simply growing up. At age 2 she knew nothing of social niceties, while at 3 she could begin to perceive the complexities of social relationships. She became more sensitive to the subtleties. She could see that grown-ups talk differently to different people, that you have to learn to behave differently in different situations. Because it was all very puzzling and confusing, she needed to find her own way with people. Shyness in growing is evidence of increasing awareness and sensitivity, not a sign of an insidious pathology.

Acknowledging and accepting shyness as a necessary, respectable, and potentially good human quality is really the heart of the matter. If shyness is your natural way of feeling and being, it can be a source of joy; it can lead to sound choices in friendship, work, and love. The person who chooses a few close friends over a large circle of acquaintances . . . the person who chooses to work in a small laboratory rather than a huge office . . . the person who falls in love with another gentle soul or someone who appreciates gentle souls . . . can all have a full and wonderful life. If the world ever needed gentleness, it surely needs it now.

In its best and most profound sense, shyness can be an expression of compassion, a concern for not hurting others. The shyness that so often accompanies falling in love suggests that shyness can be a longing to be known for what you really are as well as a deep caring for another human being. It is a shyness of discovery—very private and totally without deceit. It is, in fact, a shyness that grows out of caring for another human being with such hope and tenderness that you are quite overwhelmed by the awareness of how beautiful life and love can be.

Most people are shy some of the time. Some are shy most of the time. If seen in its healthiest aspects, this should give us hope for man's survival on this planet!

Part VIII

*

CREATING
GOOD
CITIZENS

*

Nobody Likes a Tattletale

❋ On a visit to a nursery school, I happened to be witness to a common drama. Ted was playing quietly in the sandbox with a dump truck, minding his own business, when Charlie, a bigger and tougher type, commandeered the truck without so much as a by-your-leave. A small and indignant witness to this injustice, Susan went running to tell the teacher on Charlie. The teacher was busy helping some other children put away the outdoor blocks, and without paying much attention, she said, "Nobody likes a tattletale, Susan," and went on with her cleanup activities. Susan looked thoughtful and hurt, and crept into the playhouse, where she sat down and sucked her thumb.

This scene seemed to plague me; I just couldn't seem to shake it from my mind. About a day later I realized why it was bothering me. I recalled that just a few days before I had been watching some important hearings on police corruption that were being televised, and at one point a reporter had asked one of the police informants how he was being treated by his fellow policemen. He had smiled ruefully and said, "Nobody likes a tattletale."

What had bothered me about Susan's dilemma was that it seemed to me that she was reporting a social injustice, just as a most moral and courageous policeman had done, and that this kind of good citizenship is something that I want very much to encourage in young children. I have been watching nursery-age children struggle in their growing for about thirty years, and I have never been especially bothered by the issue of tattling. Now I began to realize that my greater sensitivity to this issue was probably due to the fact that we are living in dangerous and frightening times and that the question of social commitment to good values is something that I think about far more than I ever did before.

What further encouraged my preoccupation with this matter of tattling was that on the day when I returned from my nursery school visit and walked into the kitchen in our apartment, I was appalled by the familiar and acrid smell of smoke. Next door to us is an apartment building that is about four stories below our kitchen window, where there is a chimney from which billows of black smoke always poured. Without a moment's hesitation I went to make a telephone call that I have made many times before to the New York City Pollution Control Board. I had been pestering them for months, and I planned to continue to do so until something was done about that chimney. I am, in fact, a tattletale; I was reporting antisocial behavior to a higher authority of law enforcement. And that is exactly what Susan was trying to do.

Justice did not triumph in either case; I have not yet been successful in my complaints about the polluting of the air I breathe —and as far as I know, Charlie is probably going right on taking what he wants when he wants it, feeling confident that nobody will pay much attention to the female agitator who tells the teacher what he is doing.

In my case there is hope; the Pollution Control Board *wants* me to be a tattletale, and it *has* responded to many other tattletales, for there is less black smoke pouring out of chimneys now than there was five years ago. I have less hope about Susan achieving her goal of social justice because it seems to me that as parents and teachers we have overlooked some of the deeper meanings of tattling, and until we are willing to reexamine this aspect of child-adult relations, injustice may indeed win out.

As I think back over the years of my own teaching as well as training other nursery school teachers, I realize that there were many times in my own experience when I should have been more sensitive and responsive to a child's tattling, which often had a great deal to do with a search for justice. The young child is just beginning to develop a conscience—a system of moral values that he incorporates from the attitudes of the adults in his life. It is a very shaky system when you are very young, and when a child says to a teacher or parent or baby-sitter, "Johnny pushed me off the swing when it was my turn," he is really expressing two feelings. In the first place he is saying that an injustice has been done and he is turning to the only law-enforcement agency at his disposal to redress a wrong. In the second place he is saying, "My conscience is still so new, so confusing, and so uncertain that I need reinforcement; it *is* wrong to do what Johnny did, isn't it?" The young child needs constant confirmation about truth and validity, and the importance of the rules we tell him we believe in. He needs bolstering.

It seems to me that once we have recognized this legitimate—and very constructive—need, it behooves us to respond helpfully by saying to a child like Susan, "Let me look into this, Susan. If Charlie has really been unfair we will have to help him understand that there *is* a rule against taking somebody else's toy. You are right about that being unfair." The tattler is then assured that his or her stirrings of conscience are indeed authentic and valid.

If I see someone stealing someone else's pocketbook, I consider it an obligation of citizenship to call the police; if somebody finds out that some poultry companies are injecting chickens with antibiotics that are dangerous to the health of my family, I want them to tell the Food and Drug Administration about it, and I want such agencies to take action on my behalf. If a group of chemists discover that soap manufacturers are putting phosphates in laundry detergents that will irrevocably destroy the lakes and rivers of my country, I want the government that I helped to elect to stop them. But we seem to have a double standard—one for me as an adult and a different one for our children. I have a right and an obligation to make such reports and to want them made by others, but when children take on a similar responsibility we do not provide them with a similar recourse for seeing that justice is done; we tell them not to be tattletales. Once in a while we become aware of what we are doing, and this gives us a moment's pause. When I discussed this matter with a teacher, she became very thoughtful and then said, "You know, I think you've got a point; a few days ago Jackie came and told me that Bobbie was putting paper towels into the toilet. I responded with our usual line about tattletales—but the next day all the toilets overflowed!"

I think I can understand how we got into this bind with children. There is no question that some tattling—both on the part of children and adults—is petty and vindictive. There are many times when it seems quite clear that the tattletale is nothing more than a cruel gossip at best and a jealous and hostile informant at worst. The older sister who is constantly reporting the most bland and minute infractions on the part of her younger sibling may very well be expressing feelings of rivalry; the child in the classroom who feels he cannot seem to get the attention he craves in any other way may surely become a compulsive tattler; when any child feels unloved, unappreciated, or mistreated, it is a natural recourse to want to get someone else in as much as or more trouble than you feel you are enduring yourself. As one teacher put it, "It may be true that some tattling is a plea for justice, but you know as well as I do that even at 3 or 4, a child can be insufferably self-righteous and drive you crazy with the reports of others' wrongdoing. I have a little girl in my class that nobody can stand. Ellen reports to me about one hundred times a day on such things as, 'Judy's socks are not the same color,' or 'Ronny's wiping his nose on his sleeve,' or 'Janet's only washing one side of her hands before juice time.' I'm in a rage at her at the end of the day."

Why would a child become a compulsive tattler? It seems to me that it is just as important to understand that as to respond more sensitively to the tattler who is just trying to be a good citizen. When we get an unusually persistent pattern of tattling, we need to ask ourselves what *that* child is really expressing. Does Ellen have other ways of getting attention? Does she feel deeply competitive with the other children because she has too little self-esteem? Or might it be that just below the surface of consciousness, she herself has some naughty impulses that frighten her? Is it possible that sometimes she feels like giving someone a shove or a poke in the stomach? Is she scared to death of that impulse to take someone else's toy when she has been taught that she will only be loved if she is good? Such a child may become a tattler as a way of controlling her own impulses; by constantly reporting the wrongdoing of others, she manages to keep control of her own aggressive and angry wishes.

Telling such a child to stop tattling is no more helpful than responding negatively to the tattler with a genuine social conscience. The answer "Nobody likes a tattler" is really equally inappropriate in both cases, so we had better think about finding more helpful approaches, whatever the quality of and the meaning behind the tattling.

With the compulsive tattler we need to have the compassion and understanding to respond to the deeper need the child is expressing for help with his emotional hang-ups. For example, if, after careful observation, we decide that an obsession with tattling is probably an expression of fear on the child's part that he might do something mean or bad, we might say, "Yes, I know that little children often do things they are not supposed to do—it takes a long time to learn and grow. I will remind them. And it's all right if sometimes you do something that's not exactly right, too; you're too young to have to worry all the time about being good. Grown-ups are here to help you."

Tattling, after all, is not the minor issue we may have thought it was. We need to do some thinking about it and observe it more carefully, making more insightful judgments of the various meanings it may have. When tattling is related to unhappy feelings, we must address ourselves to the underlying problem. And when a child is asking us to affirm a sense of right and wrong, when his request for attention seems to be clearly associated with injustices and dangers that we ought to be concerned about, he deserves our respect and cooperation. We *don't* believe that bullies should be allowed to take over; we *don't* approve of children putting toys in their pockets and taking them home when they are visiting a friend; we *don't* believe that bribing a child with a lollypop is the way to get one's turn on the slide, when five other children have been patiently waiting in line ahead of you. When a child reports such events he has a right to know that he will be heard and that adults will try to see that justice is done. A child's use of tattling may very well directly reflect the way the adult responds to this behavior. The tattling will tend to be mean if an adult responds by saying, "Okay, I'll give Freddy a good spanking." The tattling is more likely to be appropriate and helpful if the adult responds, "Thank you for telling me; I guess Freddy needs my help in remembering that we don't finger paint on the walls. Maybe he needs to sit down and think for a while, so he can remember better next time."

Such a response will help a child to feel the same way I do when I hear that not only are Ralph Nader's accusations about the unsafety of the average car getting a hearing, but new rules of safety are going to be imposed on car manufacturers. After all, in our time Mr. Nader is really the biggest tattletale of all—and personally, I am exceedingly grateful to him. Maybe somewhere along the line some parent or teacher told him, "Yes Ralph, I'm glad you told me about that. There *is* an important rule on this playground about people not hurting each other—you were right to let me know." If more adults would encourage this kind of committed good citizenship, we might be able to solve some of our major social problems.

Teaching Children About Evil

❋ It seems to me that today's children experience terrors unknown to any other generation of children because when terrifying things happen anywhere in the world, they see it all right in their own living rooms. The technology of rapid communication means that we all know, immediately, every day, the very worst things that are happening.

Human history is not exactly without blemish! Every child ever born sooner or later—mostly sooner—discovered that there are loving people and hating people, but the scale of knowledge was less global.

I think, for example, of the faces of the children at an airport when the victims of a hijacking are finally released after weeks of unbelievable tension and anxiety. What must happen to both the children who were victims themselves as well as those who may have had a loved relative caught in the crossfire of history? And what happens to the children who watch it all on television?

It seems to me that all of us have a special responsibility to help children survive such horrors. Trying to cover it up, hide it, reassure too much, won't help; the terror must be faced. To some degree all of us are changed by such events—there is a kind of grief from which we cannot escape. Human beings did these terrible things —and we are human. We mourn for humanity at the same time as we are naturally terrified that it might happen to us.

Whether a child is a direct participant or an observer, the first necessary ingredient for recovery is to share the anguish, to experience the fears, to be held close, and to be given permission to cry in pain. Older children need many opportunities to talk about their feelings without shame—no feeling is too silly, too irrational, all feelings are normal and human. Younger children tend to work out their feelings through play—they need to reenact, act out the events in order to gain mastery over the event and themselves.

All through the years of growing up children need constant redefining of the human condition. Most people are kind and caring; most people love little children; most people won't hurt you —but there are a few people who are sick in their feelings, who are crippled in their minds. They are the kinds of people who can assassinate a President, take hostages, hit an old man to take his wallet, steal a bicycle. We need some rules to try to control such people, and we do everything we possibly can to avoid them. We don't go out alone at night; we ride a bicycle in the park only when there are lots of people around; we never go anywhere with anyone we don't know. Still children know that even with all the precautions they have been taught, terror can strike. How can children grow up without feeling that the world is dangerous and terrible?

No one goes unscathed—child or adult. But in addition to being allowed to express one's feelings fully and feeling protected by reasonable rules and adult supervision, what helps children most of all is to become active participants in the fight against the forces of evil, whatever they may be, wherever they appear.

I recall, for example, my own daughter's terror when she was a child and saw pictures of starving Biafran children on the television screen every day. I also recall her pervasive terror of atomic warfare, for she was a member of that benighted generation of children who had to sit under their desks during air raid drills and were exposed to the immoral insanity of atomic bomb shelters to be built in every backyard. We let her ventilate her anxiety, shared ours with her, reassured her of the probabilities—and made very little impression on her! Not until we encouraged her to become a concerned citizen was she able to develop the strength to endure the awful nature of our shared reality. We collected money for food for the Biafran children; we marched in protest against state or federal spending on shelters; we went to Washington to express our opinion of the Vietnam disaster. The most important antidote to helpless anxiety is to feel competent—to know that one can make a difference.

Terrorists play most of all on this profound need; they make their victims feel utterly powerless, and that is the deepest part of the anguish they create. We need to help children to understand that one is not totally helpless even in such circumstances; there are still subtle choices to be made of how to respond to the sick minds that hold one captive. It seems to me that because of the fear and the increasing use of terrorist tactics in so many political and social situations, we ought to be giving courses in how to meet such situations in our high schools if not in our elementary schools—and I'm not sure I wouldn't do it there, too.

The wonderful thing about being human is that when we face the dangers—however awful they may be—when we really look them square in the face, we rarely find ourselves wanting in courage and dignity.

How to Teach Your Child to Be Generous

✻ At the indoor pool where I swim during the winter, a little girl always greets me by saying, "This ball is *mine!*" "This is *my own* towel!" At first I thought it was a charming way for a 4-year-old to make conversation with a stranger. But a few days after Christmas, Jennifer ran over to show me her new beach sandals. "Santa gave them to *me*," she said. "They are *mine!*" Another little girl named Karen was at the pool that day. The two girls had a good time splashing in the water until Karen spotted Jennifer's new shoes. "I want to try on your shoes!" she announced as she climbed out of the water. She put the sandals on and began racing around the pool.

Jennifer let out a howl and went in hot pursuit of her shoes. She pushed Karen down, grabbed the shoes, and ran. Jennifer's father had been watching the whole thing. He caught Jennifer, gave her shoes to Karen, and spanked Jennifer. "I don't know what makes you so selfish!" he exclaimed. "You have to learn to share with other children. Either you let Karen wear your shoes for a while or I'll take them away for good." Jennifer sat huddled at the edge of the pool, sobbing and sucking her thumb.

That gave me a good idea of why Jennifer started every conversation by reporting what belonged to her. The problem was that nothing really *did* belong to her. Like many other parents, Jennifer's father seemed to think that the way to teach a child to be generous is to make her behave generously. *Not true.* Teaching young children to be generous starts with allowing them to be selfish.

When children are very young they do not have a clear perception of where their bodies begin and end. When Nina goes to bed at night and hugs her Teddy bear, the stuffed animal is as vital to her well-being as an arm or a leg. At 3, Stephen was so attached to his special blanket that he asked, "Mommy, when I was in your uterus, I had my special blanket, didn't I?" Most very young children, if they could draw, would probably add several objects as appendages on any self-portrait.

Precious possessions are so meaningful to young children that they cannot comprehend the idea of sharing them. To a 2- or 3-year-old with a special truck, the request to "let Gerald play with your red truck for a little while" is just like being told to "lend your toes to Gerald; he needs them for climbing and you must learn to be generous."

Children become generous only when they are certain that the adults in their lives respect the importance of special possessions. When my daughter was small and young children came to visit, I would take her aside and say, "I know it is very hard for you to let anyone play with Furry or your new train. Choose your most precious things and we will hide them while Judy and Paul are visiting." Once my daughter knew that I cared about her feelings and respected her rights to her own possessions, she was able to relax. Knowing that her special things were hers only and safe, she was positively magnanimous about sharing her blocks, clay, and puppets.

Jennifer is so full of "my" and "mine" because she's never sure that anything is really hers. If her father had told Karen, "Jennifer just got those shoes for Christmas; they are very new and she's not ready to share them yet. But maybe if you ask her, she'll let you play with her rubber duck," Jennifer would have felt protected. She would have known that her father *understood her feelings*—and nothing is more conducive to a generous spirit than that.

Generosity, a wish to share with others for mutual enjoyment, can be nourished only in a climate where a person's needs are understood and respected. When they're not, selfishness is inevitable. The most generous adults are not necessarily those with the most possessions but people who feel good about themselves, who feel loved and respected. The most selfish, on the other hand, may actually have a great many possessions, but if you look behind the fur coats and the fancy cars, you're apt to find someone with a need to hold on to things in the absence of love and respect.

We all have certain possessions we don't want to share with others. I feel that way about my typewriter. A friend can't stand it when someone asks to borrow her tennis racket. "It feels like an invasion of my person," she says. One mother never understood how her daughter felt about a favorite doll until her sister wanted to borrow her cashmere stole to take on a cruise. "It was old and not particularly valuable," she said, "but Jerry gave it to me as a peace offering when our marriage was kind of shaky. The emotional attachment was too important. When my sister said I was being selfish, I suddenly realized how often I'd said that to Janey."

We need not fear that a child whose feelings are respected will never learn to share. Children quickly realize that sharing is often essential to having fun. A 4-year-old quickly discovers that nobody gets to use the playground slide unless everybody takes turns; a 6-year-old realizes he isn't going to get to try that new bicycle unless he lets the owner play with his shiny new truck; an 11-year-old discovers that a shelf full of games is boring if you don't have a friend to play them with. The *pleasure of sharing* is a powerful force in all of our lives.

The best way to teach the rules of the game—the joys and the hazards of being generous—is by example. Parents teach attitudes about possessions when they say, "I'd be happy to let you wear my beads, but not my new watch," or, "I'd never use your hairbrush and you may not use mine." To become warmly giving, children need an opportunity to experience the importance of private things as well as the great pleasure in sharing.

The kind of generous sharing we all wish for our children is illustrated by the story a loving grandmother told me. She tells her six grandchildren, "Sometimes you have to share me, and sometimes you can have me all to yourself." When all six visit during the summer, they go to the beach, have picnics, and play games together. But each morning she has breakfast alone with a different child. She also takes each grandchild on at least one outing alone every year.

One day 6-year-old Johnny called and told Grandma she had to go to school with him the next morning. She was mystified, but Johnny insisted that the teacher had told him to bring her. When Grandma arrived with Johnny the next morning, the teacher looked puzzled; all the other children had brought stuffed animals, seashells, books, and dolls. Then the teacher smiled and said, "Oh, how lovely! I told the children to bring *their greatest treasure* to school—and I guess you're Johnny's!"

When Grandma told me the story, her eyes filled with tears. "It's a wonderful thing to be a grandchild's treasure—and even more wonderful for him to want to share me with the other children. I guess he's gotten enough of me to want to be generous!" That seemed to me like a very profound observation.

Do You Worry About Your Child's Choice of Friends?

❋ When I was in the seventh grade I was a fat, miserable little kid with most of puberty ahead of me. None of the boys ever looked at me, and I expected to live a quiet life of anguished celibacy. I was a studious girl, mortified by poor marks. I gave little thought to clothes because I was sure I looked terrible in everything.

But my best friend in those days was a girl named Jean who talked about clothes constantly. She dragged me on shopping expeditions where she bought dresses I knew must cost as much as my family's monthly food bills. At 13 Jean wore black net stockings and high heels and even bleached her hair. I remember her as having a voluptuous figure and wearing sweaters several sizes too small. She dated "older men" of 18 or 19. That may not sound like much these days, but in my school in 1935, Jean was considered a fallen woman!

My parents were professionals, intellectuals who were feeling the full impact of the Depression. But Jean's father, who'd never gone beyond the third grade, was a millionaire. Jean told me he'd made his fortune during Prohibition. Her parents never asked how she was doing in school and allowed her to stay out on dates as late as she pleased. I never had occasion to test how late I could stay out because I had no place to go. The teachers loved me and hated Jean. In fact, after we'd been best friends for about a year, my English teacher was so concerned that she called my mother in for a conference on what to do about this "most unsuitable friendship."

My mother was a wise woman; she made it clear that nothing would be done. Jean was invited to my house often. My parents made a genuine effort to get beyond the peroxide and false eyelashes. They never said they were crazy about Jean, and it was obvious that they considered some of her behavior inappropriate. But I got the feeling that they were sorry for her and thought she was lucky to have me for a friend.

I learned a great deal from Jean as well as from my parents' attitude toward her. Now I realize that I needed her to help me overcome my fear of boys and begin the process of moving from girl to woman. At the same time, I helped Jean value some of the qualities she saw in me and my family. The best and most important thing about childhood friendships is that we often choose our friends because they meet our needs at a particular time.

At 3, for instance, Billy is a gentle soul who is afraid to hit; his best friend in nursery school is Larry, who isn't afraid of anything. Geraldine, at 9, is extraordinarily shy and studious; her best friend is Marcia, who hates school and plays baseball every afternoon with the boys. Many childhood friendships are based on wish fulfillment. One's best friend is all the things one would *like* to be. This is one reason many friendships are transitory, because a child's goals change as he matures. "Karen and Susan have absolutely nothing in common," a mother says, "except each wishing she were the other!"

Some friendships are also based on the need to find someone who can express feelings the child is not ready to express. If this persists into adulthood it can cause problems, but in childhood it's a necessary technique for growing—a testing ground through which a child discovers what it means to be most truly oneself. Johnny, at 10, is afraid of his father's violent temper. A quiet and reserved boy, he shakes with fear when his father roars. He chooses a friend who's a bully and, by identifying with George's aggressiveness, begins to understand his father. He will never be a bully himself, but he is learning that he can cope with bullies.

These are all positive reasons for the choices children make. The child's unconscious longing for growth and change is most obvious in the case of crushes on older children. As I look back on some of my own school crushes, I find that those children—at least as I remember them—were often quite similar to the kind of person I think I have become. The qualities I have struggled to achieve —independence, creativity, a capacity to love and be loved, sensitivity to the natural world, concern for the needs and rights of others—are all qualities I remember in those I admired most when I was growing up.

It takes a lot of experimentation to reach such goals, and it's important for parents to understand that their children's friendships are exploratory. Some of the most intense end after a few months; they last only as long as they're needed. Friendships are one of the most profound ways in which children test themselves. Critical judgment of others is not easily gained; it requires experimentation and practice. To be most helpful to our children we'd do well not to get uptight about friendships that seem unsuitable or strange. They are meeting some inner need of the child and will persist beyond that point only if we lose our sense of perspective.

"I must admit," one father reported, "that my wife and I were sure David was going to be a no-good bum; all of his friends seemed to be kids who hated school. I guess that's how he felt, too, until he got to high school and took his first course in biology. Then all of a sudden David's best friend was the boy who had the best microscope and whose father was a hospital pathologist who took the boys into his lab on Saturday afternoons!"

One of the most difficult things for parents to tolerate is the misery and heartbreak of childhood friendships. It's especially painful to see a child picked on or dropped by friends. Barbara and Phyllis have been having a marvelous time together for months. One afternoon they bring Janice along to play, and the next thing you know Janice and Phyllis have ganged up on Barbara. It's heartbreak time for Barbara—and often for her parents as well.

In the process of growing up children often feel insecure. When they find someone to pick on, it makes them feel more confident for a time. If we wring our hands in anguish, we do not help the scapegoat to gain perspective—a sense of proportion about how transitory such experiences are. It's better to point out that Janice and Phyllis feel insecure and scared too, and that picking on Barbara makes them feel more successful and well liked. One of these days Barbara will probably do the same thing herself, leaving Janice or Phyllis feeling like the outsider. When we help children to see such situations as a normal part of growing up, they're able to use their inner resources more effectively.

The loss of a much-loved friend may bring on tears and torment, of course, but we need to keep our wits about us. "I really came apart at the seams when Jenny's friend went off to somebody new," one mother told me. "When Jenny cried, I cried too. I remembered how I felt when that happened to me, and I just couldn't bear it. But Jenny got over it within a week, and I realized I'd overreacted. Jenny is *not* the same child I was at all." When we overreact, we seem to confirm the child's belief that this really *is* the end of the world—when it's nothing of the kind. We might say, "I know how awful you feel; I felt the same way when I was your age, but you're a wonderful person and you'll have lots of friends as you grow up."

Certain situations do require a closer look, however. Some intense and prolonged friendships, especially those that exclude all other children most of the time, reveal things we need to know about our children. Twelve-year-old Jed, for example, spends all of his time with a youngster who seems to live in a world of fantasy. Kenneth is full of wild stories; he boasts continually about how much money his parents give him, the dangerous and exciting trips he's been on, the famous people he knows. At the same time he's failing in school and seems totally dependent on Jed.

Jed, on the other hand, is beginning to tell tall tales about his own imagined exploits and seems less and less confident about his schoolwork. When Jed becomes completely preoccupied with Kenneth, it's time for his parents to examine his feelings about himself. It may be that his estimate of himself is very low, that he's so lacking in self-confidence he's clinging to Kenneth because he cannot imagine anyone else caring for him. Or perhaps he feels his father is disappointed in him because he is neither interested in nor adept at team sports. Maybe he's just unbearably uneasy because he's the shortest boy in his class. Under such circumstances it is certainly wise to seek help in strengthening Jed's self-confidence, but it is never a good idea to try to terminate a relationship directly.

In the first place the attempt to break up a friendship may become an unnecessary battle—inappropriate in the child's normal struggle toward independence and autonomy. What's more, letting a child know that you consider his choice of a friend a failure of judgment on his part will only increase whatever feelings of inadequacy already exist.

The most common parental concern about children's friendships seems to be that of the mother who asked, "How can you discourage a child from mimicking the undesirable behavior of a playmate? Must you restrict him from playing with a child whose behavior is not acceptable?" Certainly parents should prohibit behavior that is cruel or dangerous or that goes against the basic values of the family. But it seems to me that we must examine more profound questions than what to do about the friendship. The real issue is what the child is telling us about his or her needs. The child who feels inferior and rejected may compensate by befriending the class bully. The child who is terrified of his own angry feelings may choose a friend who is cruel to animals. Friendship is surely not the problem in such situations. These children are expressing serious emotional problems through their relations with friends.

Children who are under psychological stress can be influenced by the unacceptable behavior of other children, but they're the exceptions—the truly vulnerable children who need help anyway. The reasonably normal, happy child is rarely influenced by another child's antisocial behavior. In fact, research generally shows that disturbed, unhappy children are almost invariably helped by the well-adjusted children. Mental health seems to be far more contagious than emotional disturbance! This is really quite logical when you think about it. Even the most deprived and rejected youngster hungers for love and approval. And contact with children who can offer a way out of despair is often the turning point in such a child's life.

If we have faith in what we are doing in our own homes, we need not fear outside influences. A white father who teaches in a public school in which about eighty percent of the children are black, mostly from poor families, told me, "I love teaching there, but I must admit I was nervous about my own kids' attending the school. I was afraid they'd get into drugs or stealing—our two most serious problems. An interesting thing happened. At first they became victims. My daughter's wallet was stolen, and my son was picked up as a suspect in a theft of some office equipment. They were outraged. I knew they could never be influenced in the wrong direction. On the contrary, they began to have a better influence on the other kids than I have; they communicate more effectively as peers. The best way to get rid of the serious social problems among the most deprived kids is integration—and I don't mean color. Kids from stable, happy families work like antibodies on the less fortunate youngsters."

When a child brings home a friend who seems to encourage unacceptable behavior—such as stealing or lying or hurting others —we need to ask ourselves what hidden problems and needs *both* children are expressing. Our first responsibility is to our own child, but if we care about the world our children will live in, we also have a responsibility toward the friend. The situation gives us an opportunity to let our own child know we're concerned about all children and about unhappiness, and that we're ready with understanding, compassion, and a willingness to help. This does not mean the problems will be easy to solve. At times we may have to insist on confrontations with the other child or his parents. But such an episode will have more meaning for us and the children if we're clear about our motives—if we're not seeking ways to exclude a disturbed and hurting person from our lives but want to find resources to help relieve that hurt.

One such case involved a child who seemed totally preoccupied with sex. "When Stephen was about five or six," his mother told me, "we discovered that his closest friend, Peter, was initiating all kinds of doctor games, mutual undressings and masturbation. It became clear to us that Peter was really very disturbed and that Steve must have needed some part of all this. We had lots of discussions with Steve about sex and read some good books together. Steve began to lose interest in Peter, but we didn't. We talked to his parents, explaining that we were concerned, not angry. At first they were furious and told us to mind our own business. But a day later Peter's mother came over to apologize. She thanked us for forcing them to face a problem they'd been trying to avoid and said they'd made an appointment with the school guidance counselor."

One area of children's friendships in which parents may have to play the heavy is in gang relationships. Groups often take on characteristics of their own. People who would never dream of certain behavior on their own or with one or two others seem to become immune to the cries of inner conscience when they are part of a large group. Michael, ordinarily a well-mannered young man of 13, was one of a group of boys arrested for stealing liquor from a store. "The only time I really felt good—high and happy and excited," he told his court-appointed counselor, "was when I was with those kids. The rest of the time I feel like a nothing." Lee, 16, broke both legs when his gang dared him to jump from the roof of one house to another. He said, "I can't believe I did such a stupid thing. I don't know—the others got me all steamed up."

Adolescence is the period of greatest inner turmoil, uncertainty, and need for peer approval. It's also the time of greatest vulnerability to group pressure. The hazards—including experimentation with dangerous drugs and high-speed driving—are very real. Parents must be on the alert and far more direct and authoritative in their reactions to gang activities. Restrictions and punishments are surely no answer, however. Such methods tend to push a child into the welcome embrace of those who won't sit in judgment upon him. The most important antidote is free and honest discussion of the temptations and the dangers. We need to learn to listen, to encourage our children to talk to us about their feelings. If we merely lecture, our children tune out. If we ask questions, reflecting genuine interest and concern, we help a youngster to think and develop his own critical judgment.

At times young people desperately want to be extricated from situations they can't handle, and they'll ask for help if they don't think they'll be shamed or punished. The more we indicate our love and respect, the more likely a child will be to ask for our help. In other words, we need to create a climate of feeling that allows a child to feel comfortable about saying, "I wish you'd forbid me to go driving with the others. I'm scared of what they do, but I don't want them to think I'm chicken."

No discussion of children's friendships would be complete without mentioning those children who, at various stages of their development, seem to have no friends at all. Many children need to grow at their own rate before they can have more than fleeting friendships. Some children—like some adults—have such a rich inner life that at times they prefer their own company. And some children simply withdraw from friendships that become exploitative. I remember one time when my own daughter was about 7 and playing in the backyard with a group of neighborhood children. Suddenly she kicked them all out. Without thinking, I said, "If you keep doing that, you'll have no friends."

"But I don't like them," she answered. "They were getting too wild and breaking things." I suddenly realized that she had more strength and integrity than I. How much better to be alone than with people we don't like!

There is great variation in children's needs for friends. Most children go through periods of rejecting the overtures of other children or of being rejected themselves. Whether this becomes a serious problem often depends on how the parents react. If we are devastated and frightened, the child sees himself as a failure. If we take it in stride and assert its temporary nature, the child is free to explore new possibilities when the right moment comes.

Sometimes, of course, a child wants and needs friendships but doesn't know what to do. In such cases, parents can help a child move toward new friends and relationships. An only child who has been around adults too much, for example, might be encouraged to go to a sleep-away camp. A shy child can be encouraged to invite a schoolmate along on a family picnic where brothers and sisters with more self-confidence can lead the way. A child in a new neighborhood can be helped to plan a very special birthday party to attract new friends.

The most important help we can give a friendless child, however, is to avoid pushing the panic button. We might do well to remember the transitory periods of pain and loneliness during our own childhood that we managed to survive. In fact, not only do we have some very special friends, but many of us are even married to the best friend we ever found! Which brings us to what childhood friendships are really all about—to prepare us for loving and being loved. The greater the experimentation and the more freedom we have to explore all possibilities, the better we get to know and trust ourselves. And if we really know ourselves, our adult choices will be more sound and meaningful.

When I was halfway through the eighth grade, Jean and I drifted apart and Mildred came into my life. She was more like me—full of dreams, a poetry lover, ready and eager to meet boys but more comfortable in groups with common interests. Our parents were friends. Together we joined various groups where our self-consciousness was neutralized by being with young people who had similar interests. Some of the friendships that bloomed during the next few years have lasted more than forty years. In fact, it was through Mildred's brother that I later met my husband.

But I remember Jean in a very special way. She was the other side of me—the unlived part at 13. That fat, scared little girl longed to be a femme fatale; she wanted desperately to grow into womanhood. Somewhere, lurking deep inside, was a passionate, open, free spirit. And through Jean that part of me began to be. During our friendship she changed too. She later told me that being with my family had helped her realize what she had been missing. She softened while I got a little tougher—more demanding of life.

We hope that by the time we are grown up we will be whole, that all of our potentialities will come to fruition. Along the road to that maturity each of us uses childhood friendships to fill in the missing pieces of ourselves. The nicest thing we can do for our children is allow them to find all the pieces to the puzzle of what it means to be the distinct and beautiful people they can become.

Children, Chores, and Work

❋ At a child-study meeting we had been discussing the importance of play in a child's life. One mother commented, "I agree with you that play is important, but isn't *work* important, too?" It most assuredly is important and I have found myself wrestling with the question of why it seems to be more difficult to articulate the meaning of work in the lives of young children than it is to discuss their need for play. I have come to the conclusion that despite the changing environment in which our children play (the new kinds of toys and recreational resources available to us, and the natural differences between play in an urban rather than rural setting), play itself—what it means, what needs it fulfills—hasn't changed as much as work. The concept of work in a child's life is more difficult to deal with because the nature of work in *all* our lives has changed in many profound and dramatic ways.

Many examples of the new confusion and dilemmas we face in thinking about our children and work began to occur to me. Typical of these was a recent discussion with 10-year-old Eddy's parents, who were feeling pretty frantic about him. He is a vivacious, alert youngster with boundless energy, but despite Herculean efforts on his parents' part to help him develop "good attitudes and habits," he has to be constantly reminded, threatened, and punished to get him to clean up his room, put the garbage cans out on the right days, and do his homework—the only "jobs" his parents expect him to do. Caught up in the immediate problems of two lost left shoes, an expensive bicycle ruined by being left out in the rain, and an infallible ability to forget what he'd been asked to get at the corner grocery, he has left his parents frightened and confused. What did they do wrong? Will he ever become a responsible person able to take care of himself and his own family?

In the course of meeting and talking with parents, I have gotten a strong impression that the frequency of such concerns makes Eddy almost a cliché. High on the list of any discussion about what bothers parents most in their children's behavior is their attitudes toward chores. "How do you get a 9-year-old to put his pajamas away?" one mother asks, while twenty others laugh ruefully with immediate sympathy and understanding. Another mother gets the same response when she says, "Honestly, I think we ask so little of our kids—and no matter how I nag, threaten, or punish, it's a war every time I ask Peter to straighten up his room or put dirty underwear and towels into the hamper." There is immediate and vociferous agreement that our children are spoiled, lazy, irresponsible, and uncooperative about the simplest chores, no matter how intense and forceful our efforts to produce more acceptable behavior.

There have always been rambunctious, lively, rebellious youngsters who have caused their parents anxious moments of self-doubt and serious misgivings. We take what comfort we may from such old notions that "children will be children." But I think we are still more uneasy than parents before us; there is something new and different about our concern. Ruminating about all this one night at the dinner table, I asked our then teenage daughter what she thought about work. Her immediate and unhesitating reply was, "Work should be fun and interesting." She startled me. Would any generation before hers have thought of work primarily in relation to fun? In any previous generation the spontaneous response to any question about work would have been, "Work? Why, that's how we stay alive!" Just that simple and uncomplicated—a matter of survival.

At one time we took our daughter and several of her friends to visit the restoration of the first settlement at Plymouth Rock.

There was a look of wonder and shock on their faces when the guide told them that children as young as 3 had to begin to learn to weave and spin; that 7- and 8-year-old boys worked beside their fathers, plowing the fields, building houses, and making tools; that by the time a pioneer daughter was 12 she could sew all of her own clothes, make soap and candles, grind corn, and bake bread. None of this was for fun or recreation but was the deadly serious business of learning how to survive in a tough and dangerous wilderness.

In such a world nobody really had to teach a child lessons about work; he was born into a world of shared work and he knew, almost before he could walk, that he was a *needed* worker. This is a world that we can barely imagine; it is a world our children never saw, and we are faced with a dilemma never dreamed of by our ancestors —how do you get the children to help with the chores when they know darn well we don't *really need* them?

In addition to our relative affluence today and our nonsurvival orientation to daily activities, our notions about work have also changed under the influence of changing educational expectations of our children. Up until the past fifty years, formal academic schooling was not nearly as important as it is today. Most of the survival skills had to do with learning crafts—learning to *do* more than learning to *know*. A child who could learn to make shoes or build boats or milk cows could have a feeling of worth and a hopeful view of his future; he could do something of value. The 16-year-old girl who went into the garment factory and learned to run a sewing machine didn't feel like a second-class citizen because she had only an eighth-grade education. It is possible that our Eddy's great-grandfather ran away from home at 12, got a job, and with Eddy's drive and intelligence achieved success in life. If this seems a wildly unlikely statement, let me try to document it. Thomas Edison entered public school at 7 and was considered a dunce; he left after three months. His mother became his teacher. At 12 he began to make his own way in the world, peddling newspapers, candy, peanuts, and sandwiches on a train. At 15 he was publisher and editor of a weekly newspaper, while he read and studied avidly on his own. Benjamin Franklin, sent to school at 8, had to leave school at 10 to work in his father's candle-making shop. At 12 he became a printer's apprentice and taught himself arithmetic, navigation, grammar, and logic. At 16, John D. Rockefeller was a clerk in a wholesale produce firm, and Andrew Carnegie was a bobbin boy in a cotton factory when he was 13.

In today's labor market we have no room for early "doers"; we require all of our children, whether or not they are so constituted, to become thinkers and knowers. If some of our children seem lazy and unmotivated, it may be partly because they were born in the wrong century—for them! If we find it difficult if not frequently impossible to interest our progeny in making their beds and putting away their toys and clothes, it may be that we are underestimating the kinds of pressures with which they live. It may be true that our children are lucky that we are enlightened enough not to permit them to work as juvenile slaves in mines and factories, but we are kidding ourselves if we think they are not often enslaved in new ways. How many of our children would prefer to go to work than battle the new math or struggle through examinations until they are 20!

Where do we go from here? Despite changes in our way of life, we know that work—the ability to do the job, to feel the satisfaction of a job well done—is still an essential in human experience. The challenge that confronts parents today is how to give children a new sense of the meaningfulness of work when it lacks the element of survival necessity.

Many people who can afford to retire at an early age are thoroughly miserable; they would prefer to keep working regardless of economic necessity. We know from numerous research studies that in almost every profession, people tend to die at a statistically significant earlier age if they are forced to retire; they die of loneliness, boredom, and a feeling of uselessness. A feeling of accomplishment in work seems to be a necessary ingredient for good mental health, and work as a way of participating in life still gives meaning to people's lives.

We need to take a new look at what we're doing in our homes. Are we helping our children to understand the satisfactions of work? Are we holding on to old and outmoded attitudes that no longer apply in our affluent and automated world?

One of the problems is that the jobs we tend to give children to do are terribly dull and inconsequential. They are the jobs we feel sure they *can* do. We never let them wash the dishes until we're sure they won't break every third one, hence they feel no sense of challenge. We also tend to assign the chores that *we* despise doing, so that we end up teaching the exact opposite of what we want to teach; instead of demonstrating that work today can be a challenge, we show it as an unpleasant duty. One mother solved this problem by having every member of the family share the menial tasks, while at the same time, every child got a chance to take on something more exciting, such as cooking a meal, planning a family picnic, or shopping at the supermarket. "We start when a child reaches his fifth birthday," this mother told me. "And you would be amazed at what a damn fine meal a five-year-old can prepare—if you're crazy about peanut butter and jelly, that is!"

When our children ask "What for?" when we ask them to put away their toys or straighten out the record cabinet in the living room, the answer can be honest and realistic—to give us all a comfortable, attractive place in which to do the things we enjoy doing. However, we need to be clearer in our own minds about what's really necessary. How often do we demand a kind of perfection in orderliness that really has little or nothing to do with the goal of comfort? Aren't there many tasks that could be eliminated or modified? One way to find sensible answers to this question is to think in terms of what will give a child the satisfying feeling that he is really needed. The world will not come to an end if Junior doesn't take out the garbage or mow the lawn or wash the car. Getting him to do these jobs doesn't make him feel needed, so that while we may still see good reasons for demanding his cooperation in these tasks, we might think about dividing them up more equally among all of the family members. We might, on occasion, sit down with our children and talk to them about what *they* think is needed. Maybe they think the dog needs a longer run in the backyard or they need a more spacious shed for outdoor toys; maybe they have some practical ideas for creating more shelf space in the playroom or building a desk top that can be folded up against the wall to save space in their bedroom. We might all discuss together how these important-to-them projects can be carried out. They will learn far more about the real meaning of work by doing what makes sense to *them* than by simply carrying out our orders for things we think are important. Too often the reasons we give for getting a job done seem silly and entirely irrelevant to our children—and sometimes they may be right!

We need to be careful that we don't interfere too much in those jobs that our children do, however imperfectly. Too often we "help out" when a child does something that doesn't live up to our higher standards, with the unhappy result that he can't feel any genuine sense of accomplishment. A 4-year-old dusts the dining-room table, shows it to us with pride, and while we're saying, "That's lovely, darling," we are absentmindedly rubbing at the smudge he missed. Part of learning to enjoy work is to be permitted to execute and complete it to our *own* satisfaction, not someone else's. When 7-year-old Debbie makes you an apron with one fat tie and one skinny tie, that's the way it ought to stay if you want her to go on to other pleasures in sewing all by herself.

A little drudgery falls into the most glamorous of lives; this is a fact about household chores that must be accepted and tolerated. Our children need to understand that you can't love what you're doing all of the time. Some things just have to be done in order to reach a goal. For a 3-year-old this may mean, "If we clean up your toys together, we will have time for a story." For a 5-year-old it may mean, "If you put your bicycle in the garage every night, it won't get rusty." For a 9-year-old it may mean, "If you help me with my chores—save me some time by watering the lawn—I'll be able to drive you down to the high-school football game on Saturday."

We have to communicate to our children that cooperation is good human relations, and we need to be clear in our own minds that no inborn instinct will drive a child to shoulder responsibilities that annoy or bore him. It wasn't strength of character that drove Great-Grandpa to the woodpile after school every day—it was the sure knowledge that there would be cold winter nights if he didn't do his job. We can't pretend with our children that what we ask of them is nearly so vital, but we can make it clear that sharing what has to be done, however unexciting the jobs may be, is an expression of love and a sure road to self-respect. Despite affluence and automation, the family is still a cooperative enterprise. One mother put it succinctly when she said, "When I ask Jeff to do something he thinks is just another of my compulsive stupidities, before he even asks why I say, 'For love, that's all, just for love!' "

One of the complications we face in getting chores done is that a great many of us *could* afford to hire someone to do the jobs we ask our children to do. When I expressed horror that a friend was having trouble finding a new gardener because the lawn hadn't been mowed for three weeks she said, "You're right—we do have three ablebodied sons, and it's disgusting. But they know darn well I can afford to hire someone." We have to make it clear that money has nothing to do with self-respect, and the lack of an economic motive does not make work obsolete. A father told me recently how distressed he was by a conversation he had had with his 16-year-old daughter, who wanted to spend the summer vacation "just loafing around." This father had suggested that Karen at least try to find a part-time job. He agreed that she had worked hard in school all year but did not agree that doing nothing for two months made any sense. Karen argued that it was silly to get a job because she didn't need the money. She said, "It's not costing you anything. You don't even have to give me an allowance if you don't want to —I have enough saved up." Her father replied, "It isn't a question of money, it's what you are doing with your life that matters." Even much younger children can begin to discover that meaningful work has to do with personal fulfillment, not necessarily with monetary considerations.

You can encourage autonomy and self-direction in your children by seeking out work that satisfies them. We are going to have to become more flexible about such things as how a child takes care of his room—or doesn't. If it's really his room and he loves his personal garbage dump, is it really so terrible if he only cleans it up once or twice a month so that the room can be vacuumed and properly aired? Does he learn about the significance of work when we nag him every day to do a job *he* thinks is entirely unnecessary? If we leave him alone, or work out a compromise, we don't have to feel we're destroying his character or moral fiber as long as there are other opportunities that *do* help him to see what work is really all about.

To do this we have to reverse an old pattern. We should nag less about chores but demand more and expect more of our children when it comes to working for their own goals. By that I mean, for example, our too-quick purchase of anything our children want us to buy for them. Whether or not we can afford to buy that tape recorder or the dump truck for the sandbox or the new wading pool for the backyard, we might be helping our children understand a good deal about work if we weren't quite so quick and eager to provide the wherewithal for these special treats. Improvising, inventing, making something oneself, or earning the money to buy it are natural and obvious (and honest) ways to learn about the satisfaction of work.

If I were starting out all over again as a young mother, I know that there is one area of childraising in which I would change my ways drastically. I think about it (painfully!) every time I see the expensive guitar we bought lying on the floor, its strings sprung, or the typewriter, all wound up in its old ribbon, used maybe for a month, or the sewing machine gathering dust on the closet floor, used to make one dress and then never used again. I yelled too much about cleaning up, and I was too permissive and easygoing about satisfying my daughter's every whim. When my daughter became a teenager she began to understand the connection between what one gets and does for oneself and the pleasure derived from this experience. If we had insisted that there had to be some real effort on her part to acquire special things, I think they would have meant more to her. But even more important, the process of acquisition itself would have been such an important experience in learning what work can mean that I don't think I would have felt so angry and frustrated if the things she acquired through her own labor were also set aside or discarded.

Children can begin to feel that their contributions are needed and important at a very young age. In one family a two-dollar contribution is made to UNICEF every time a child mows the lawn. In another, a teenager is relieved of all dishwashing because he gives two afternoons a week to teaching children to read in a special volunteer teaching program in a deprived neighborhood. In still another household, all major household cleaning is done by the whole family on Saturday mornings so that Mother and her two youngsters can have the free time during the week to take ceramics and dancing classes.

There has never been a time when young people had more scope, more variety of opportunities to find work that will be meaningful and fulfilling. Our children can realistically expect to find work that they will enjoy doing; there is nothing sinful or immoral in that! Sometimes it will be the work they do to earn a living, and sometimes it will be the work they do that has nothing to do with earning a living. The important thing will be knowing that to be most truly and joyously alive, one must work. Fun is when you feel challenged to do your best, when somebody needs you, and when you are proud of what you are doing.

Part IX

✳

SPECIAL PEOPLE, SPECIAL TIMES

✳

The Teenager and
the Telephone

❋ The father of a teenage daughter had gone to Detroit on business and wanted to let his wife at home in New Jersey know he'd be able to get home in time for dinner. First he tried to call from the office he'd been visiting. He tried again at the airport before his plane took off. He tried again at Newark Airport, hoping his wife would be able to pick him up. The line remained busy, and after taking a taxi to his home, he discovered his 14-year-old daughter still on the phone. "I have been to Detroit and back, all on one phone call!" he said.

The frustration, annoyance—the mounting fury—experienced by this father is painfully familiar to those of us who have lived—or are trying to live—with teenagers. Any one of us could provide a rich and varied array of "reasons" for that lengthy phone call. Undoubtedly one of the two girls had just gotten a new Michael Jackson record that the other was dying to hear; one of the major functions of the telephone in the adolescent world is to serve as a private radio station playing request numbers! Or there may have been a terrible crisis in school that day. Frequently it is the unexpected test announced for the next day's math class—and it should be obvious to anyone that the only way to face such a ghastly event is by talking about it on the phone until time for class!

It is also possible that the Don Juan of the ninth grade failed to say hello when they passed him in the school cafeteria today. In order to fully explore the fine nuances, the deep and significant causes of this social lapse, a full discussion of the matter is absolutely essential before the next cafeteria encounter. This, roughly speaking, may well take an hour and a half. Or there may have been a far more serious crisis on the rocky road to love—a misunderstanding, an argument, hurt feelings—a crisis involving copious tears, long silences, whispered snatches of conversation barely noted by any attending adult, as the phone is taken into the hall closet for absolute privacy and the world waits breathlessly to know if all is lost.

Parents find themselves going out of their minds—screaming one minute, trying to reason the next, setting up rules and regulations that are immediately broken, and generally wondering if they will ever again be in touch with the outside world between the hours of 3:00 and 10:00 P.M. We joke about it (to keep from crying), we give grateful thanks for the hours our teenagers are in school, and, dizzy with rare power, we can phone a friend who's "got one too" and commiserate with her.

Parents have tried all sorts of arrangements and solutions. Many families have "solved" the telephone problem by letting children have their own phones. This is especially true—and perhaps most easily justified—in homes where constant availability is necessitated by a parent's profession or some other special circumstance. Some families do it simply because they feel they can afford it. Others who could afford it go on struggling with one telephone line, feeling that this is a matter for family cooperation and mutual respect, and that more will be lost than gained by "making it too easy." In some homes, where parents tend to feel bombarded by too many people all day, there is a general acceptance of the teenager's long evening conversations; as one father put it, "It's the best wall of defense against being bothered ever invented!"

We all handle it in different ways, depending on our feelings, needs, and attitudes. But whatever we do, we often feel bothered and bewildered by it. We might feel more comfortable about living with these adolescents who are attached to a long cord so much of the time if we had some idea of what it meant to them and why. Why is the telephone apparently an essential lifeline? And will this attachment go on forever? While it is true that there are now many adults who like to talk endlessly on the telephone, they are still a relatively small group in comparison with the teenage talkers. What is it, then, that makes the telephone so much more meaningful and important to our adolescent children? For all our talk about it, do we have any clues as to why the telephone becomes such a vital factor in teenage social life? Is it simply that our children have grown up in a world where this is a natural and continual means of communication?

There are undoubtedly many reasons, but it is my impression that there is a very special reason the telephone is so important— a reason that makes so much sense that it helped me live more tolerantly and optimistically with this phenomenon!

I happened to listen to a conversation between two psychotherapists who were discussing the fact that each of them, completely independently, had discovered that certain of their patients seemed to do much better with "telephone therapy" rather than a person-to-person confrontation. They had both noticed that several patients who had called them at times of great crisis were greatly helped by the ensuing telephone conversation—and never did as well at such moments in the office. In several cases, patients had moved away, but contact was maintained by telephone and the patients often continued to do better than they had done in regular therapy. Having made this observation, they continued to experiment, to talk to other psychotherapists, and found that this was neither unusual nor uncommon. It seemed best suited to those patients who were unable to establish intense emotional relationships without great anxiety. They were usually adults of intellectual superiority, but with severe defects in their capacity to deal with the emotional side of life and in relating to other people.

As I listened, it occurred to me that while it might be abnormal for adults to have such severe problems in relating emotionally, it was not at all abnormal during adolescence. This is a period of transition from childhood to adulthood, a time of painful self-awareness and terrible uncertainty about how to behave in relation to one's peers, as well as to adults, a time filled with so much change, uncertainty and self-doubt that one wants to hide. The mother of a 15-year-old reflected what we see so clearly when she said, "They run in packs to avoid being seen individually, and they avoid daylight so they need not see themselves!"

What better way to "hide" and yet be "involved" than by talking on the telephone! As soon as I began to talk to other parents about it, I found that we were all in agreement about the fact that teenagers often had far more intense and satisfying "relationships" on the phone than they were able to have "in person."

In an earlier age, the first tentative explorations of young people into the realm of adult relationships was probably made via the mail; now the telephone has almost replaced letter writing. Both kinds of communication offer an opportunity to try one's wings—to practice feelings of love and friendship; they are ways of experimenting with new and often frightening feelings. Teenagers are able to say things to each other that they are not yet able to say easily or comfortably face to face. The telephone permits disembodied voices to communicate with each other without the self-consciousness or shyness of being physically real and present for each other.

Adolescence is a period during which one must move toward adult relationships involving the strongest and deepest feelings. It is a time when young people are exploring their own feelings, finding their own special and individual identifies. When one still feels very young and very vulnerable, it is sometimes unbearable and impossible to be close to someone else—to look at them and to be seen oneself. The thoughts and feelings that one needs and wants to share are too personal, too overwhelming—unless one can share them in a such a way as to remain physically anonymous.

One mother observed, "From what my daughter tells me, she and her friends discuss some of the most intimate and painful problems with each other on the phone—a father who is out of work, an impending divorce. And yet when some of these friends come to our house, there seems to be much less serious and private talking. They giggle a lot and study a little, but I have the feeling that their deepest sharing is done on the phone."

In growing up we must all learn techniques and skills for relating to others. When you are still terribly unsure of yourself and don't yet know who you really are, when you are still too self-conscious to ever forget yourself in a genuine show of concern for someone else, the telephone can serve as a bridge across an abyss of fear and unreadiness, and through its use young people practice and prepare themselves for human relationships as adults.

Youngsters who wouldn't be caught dead reading a book of poetry can read poems to each other on the phone; teenagers who would die of shame to admit that they still enjoy fantasy and make-believe can play games with each other on the telephone, imagining the future, making up "silly stories." They can share thoughts and feelings that would embarrass them beyond endurance if they had to look at each other.

Our awareness of these factors may help us to be somewhat more tolerant of the disease telephonitis! It does not necessarily mean the elimination of all restrictions; that would be unrealistic and not at all helpful in the long run. There is still much to be gained in having to learn ways of living with other people, compromising, respecting their rights. Being given one's own phone in early adolescence, without any restrictions, can be an escape from necessary growth. Even if it is necessary to have more than one telephone line, it is questionable whether one line should be the exclusive property of a child. Such indulgence may rob a child of the opportunity to learn about life and living with others, encouraging the avoidance of those real-life relationships that sooner or later must take over.

The expense is an important factor for consideration; certainly there can be greater leniency when local calls are free. In large cities, parents must help their children to accept realistic limits in budgeting phone calls. If teenagers are old enough to earn money toward their calls, this may be one way to permit them to use the phone more extensively. Parents can acknowledge the emotional needs and the real gratifications that come from these telephone relationships by being willing to compromise. For example, they can make most of their own phone calls during the day and ask friends and relatives to call, whenever possible, in the morning or early afternoon. Then if a youngster wants to have a telephone visit of some length, the family can work out a time schedule so that after a long call, the phone is left clear for at least a half hour afterward so that any important calls can get through. One example of a compromise was the family who included as part of the allowance allotted to their teenage son money toward the use of public telephones part of the time in order to keep the family phone free.

It is also possible that in accepting the usefulness of the telephone to teenagers, parents will be able to get greater cooperation from their children about the matter of polite thank yous and occasional affectionate greetings to grandparents and other relatives and friends. Many parents have discovered that they can avoid a great deal of nagging about the necessity of writing thank-you letters by letting their children phone their thanks—and the results seem to be less stilted, more natural and spontaneous, which makes everybody happier!

Life has changed drastically in the past generation. People talk to each other about subjects that were once never mentioned in polite company—or for that matter even behind closed doors. Relationships are far more frank and open, and it seems logical that our young people would have to have time to practice and opportunities to begin relating in this intimate way by "long distance." If, however, they were to go on finding this the most satisfying of all "relationships," we might well become concerned. There are people who have "telephone personalities" even as adults and relate more easily on the phone than they do in person. Our present way of life even encourages this. It is not only possible but frequently happens that in our work or daily living we talk to people on the phone, often for years, without ever meeting. Those adults who continually choose this kind of relationship are stunted in their growth; the telephone is not a healthy or mature substitute for person-to-person contacts even in this automated and mechanized world. Experience in living, the normal processes of maturation, our own continuing interest and concern, will help our children toward the time when real relationships can be as rewarding and safe as telephone contacts.

When a youngster says, "I've got to run over to Peggy's house. Something wonderful has happened, and I want to see her face when I tell her," or a teenager on the phone says, "Bob, I don't

think we should discuss anything this important on the phone—
let's wait until study hall tomorrow," we can be sure that our
children, partly through the opportunity they have had for "disembodied communication," have gained the self-confidence, the
sense of personal identity, that permits them to move on to the
more genuine and deeply satisfying contacts of living and loving.

Stepmothers Aren't Wicked Anymore!

❋ A bright 7-year-old with a mathematical bent was very thoughtful one day. His parents had divorced several years earlier and both had recently remarried. "When so many people are getting divorced, then marrying someone else, won't there be more stepparents than parents?" he asked his mother.

"It sounds very reasonable to me," his mother replied. "At least I can see why you would *feel* that way."

Since about one out of every five children will be a child of divorce and about 75 percent of divorcees remarry within five years, the number of stepparents is certainly increasing at a rapid rate. Perhaps divorce doesn't create a lack of family life but rather a far more complicated family life as a result of this phenomenon, which is fast becoming the rule in our times.

To begin with, adults and children both bring a bagful of memories, fears, and fantasies to the new relationship, which means it takes twice the awareness to deal with the problems that arise—awareness of your own, often private, responses as well as your children's. Parent and stepparent are often so anxious to succeed in their new life that rather than face the traumatic move squarely, they pretend a family unit already exists. In fact, a family is just getting started, and denying the importance of what has taken place prior to the new marriage only makes dealing with it that much harder.

A new stepfather told me, "It hardly seems to matter how I try to deal with Danny. He's been so scarred by hearing his own father yell at his mother that he won't let me near him." A stepmother commented sadly, "Even after four years, there is still so much bitterness between Ed and his first wife, so much that is still 'unfinished business,' that my stepson, Alex, can't settle down and accept the fact that I'm part of his life. His attention is still focused on the feeling that I stole his father away, because he can't face the problems his parents had with each other."

It cannot be stated too strongly: When a child moves into a new family, he is taking his past with him, for better or for worse. He is also taking his wounds—which, regardless of kindness and support, just cannot heal overnight. Realizing this, one perceptive stepmother told me, "Those two boys I inherited were the biggest slobs I'd ever met. I almost lost my mind for the first few months. But I didn't make a fuss—then. I waited till things had sort of settled in, when the kids knew me and felt more at ease and were beginning to do well at school again. Then I lowered the boom: 'No slobs in my house—or else!' After six months we were all strong enough to take the gaff of setting rules and limits, rewarding and punishing, the normal things that go with raising children. *Timing* is what it's all about!"

One significant reflection of a child's past history is the degree to which he or she will test a stepparent. A stepmother recently complained to me, "Maria is wearing me out! She's doing everything she possibly can to make me lose my patience—maybe even say that I won't live with her. I'm trying so hard to remind myself that she feels her own mother deserted her by running off with another man and never even coming to see her. That feeling of being rejected will take a lot of undoing. Meanwhile she's behaving like a little monster. How long will this go on?"

The answer is that it can "go on" for some time, but the problem can be alleviated by the stepparent's acknowledging it. Remember, much of the behavior is unconscious on the part of the child, even if it doesn't seem to be. To clear the air it helps if either or both parents say, "It must be hard to trust a new mother and to believe she will love you and stay with you. But we are all going to work very hard to make that come true, no matter how you behave. You are a lovely child and it is not your fault that your mommy and daddy got a divorce."

In fact, the best way of handling all of the complicated feelings that each person brings to a new family is to *talk* about them, and since it is hard for children to articulate their feelings, the brunt of this responsibility falls on the parents and stepparents. "The way we survived," one father told me, "was by encouraging the children to feel free to talk about everything and by being aware that they might have hidden feelings about the past that we had to help bring out. And that's not easy. After all, we adults are scarred by what we have lived through, and I think at first I had a tendency to want to bury it. My kids were afraid ever to mention their earlier life, because they felt it would hurt Janet and me. But we found it was easier in the long run to 'let it all hang out' than to hope it would all just go away."

Part of the background history that children bring to their new families is not only the kind of life they experienced before the divorce but the preparation—or lack of it—for the new marriage. A friend of mine told me, "When I was ten years old my brother and I were sent away to summer camp. When we came home at the end of the summer my mother met us at the bus and calmly announced she'd remarried and that we were going to a new house. We knew the man she'd married and had met his two children once, but I remember feeling so betrayed. No matter how pleasant my stepfather tried to be to me and my brother, there was no way we could ever be close after that."

Clearly, it makes the adjustment easier if the introductions can take place long before the marriage and children are carefully briefed about what is going to happen. Even more important, the children need to have a chance to ventilate their feelings. The best way to help a youngster prepare for living with a new parent is to say, "We are bound to have some problems and we will work them out as we go along." Nothing is more likely to lead to strife than saying, "You are going to love Margot! She's so much fun to be with, and she can hardly wait to be your stepmother!"

One of the major reasons that history plays such an important part in the adjustment between stepchild and stepparent is that the child is bound to feel some conflict between old and new loyalties, even if the biological parent is no longer a regular part of his life. One stepmother reported, "I used to think it would be easier if Richie's mother just disappeared from the scene. While she still lived in the same town, we were rivals; Richie was confused about our authority and played us against each other. But when she moved away, he was so desperate to cover up his feelings of desertion that his loyalty to her interfered even more with my becoming his stepmother."

The issue of loyalty finds further complications when the relationship between divorced parents is still thorny. And these complications become even more convoluted when stepparents take on the role of adversary to the biological parent—a role that is all too easy for them to fall into, especially when they want their new children to like them. "I try very hard not to take sides," one stepmother told me. "But when I hear how Julie's mother screams at her on the phone, and then Julie tells me she loves me more than she does her mother, I find myself getting seduced into playing a role that I know won't help Julie—or me—in the long run. Her mother is still her mother, and if I run her down, sooner or later Julie will resent it."

Problems of divided loyalty also occur when a child does not live with a stepparent full-time. Cathy spends her winters in New York with her mother and her summers in California with her father and his new wife, Liz. At first Cathy seemed resistant to everything Liz tried to do: having her hair cut, getting new clothes, taking her to Disneyland—nothing tempted Cathy. Finally, Liz had an insight about what it might be all about. "Cathy," she said, "I'm not trying to take your mother's place. I would just like to be your friend." After that, Cathy relaxed.

There is an interesting and ironic twist that often emerges in relation to loyalty. If the relationship with the biological parent has been good and healthy on the whole, and if this parent is functioning reasonably well as a divorced or remarried person, the child need not feel guilty about establishing a warm and loving relationship with a stepparent. If the biological parent is in a lot of trouble, however, then the child feels a need to be protective, which makes it harder for the stepparent. It is terribly difficult for the child to accept the biological parent's shortcomings, and even more so when they are accentuated by the appearance of this new person who really can do a better job. As a result, stepparents are often likely to bear the brunt of fears and anger that are more related to the missing parent. In a sense the child is saying, "Don't you *dare* be a nicer person than my father (or mother), because then I will have to acknowledge his (or her) deficiencies."

Keeping this in mind, the stepparent must be careful not to get sucked into comparisons. When a child says, "My mother makes better pot roast," or "My father can play baseball," or "My mother never made me wash the dishes," it is no help at all to feel challenged or threatened and try to compete with this other relationship. It is more helpful to the child if the stepparent can simply say, "Everybody you meet has different good and bad qualities. Instead of comparing me with your mother (or father), I hope you will someday enjoy what each of us is like."

Some of the most likely—and often traumatic—problems facing both resident and nonresident stepparents have to do with discipline. One stepfather bemoaned the fact that he found it impossible to get his stepson to follow any of his rules. "Only my real father can tell me what to do," Chris announced grandly. At the end of his rope, Chris's stepfather finally replied with what he should have said to begin with: "In your dad's house, he makes the rules; in my house, your mother and I make them."

Disciplinary problems often arise in the home where children are just weekend or vacation visitors. This is because the "visiting home" is so frequently made unreal, a place reserved exclusively for fun and entertainment. To be truly healthy environments for children both households need to be real: *both* for fun; *both* for genuine relationships, serious work, and discussions.

It's not an easy task, but parents and stepparents alike need to understand and feel sure that they can play the role of parents without disturbing natural loyalties. It is not a competition but a responsibility to behave like an adult, whether one is the biological parent or not.

Where adults are competing with each other, names are often viewed as an indication of loyalty: Should a child call a stepparent by his or her first name? Should a child be adopted by a stepfather and change his or her last name? It is always a matter that ought to be discussed by everyone concerned, but this is only possible if parents can make it clear that they are not going to be hurt by a child's candid responses. There are enough serious adjustments to make without letting the matter of names become a major issue.

Other practical questions that come up are: Which parents go to the school play? Which parents go to a teacher's conference? Which parents choose a school or camp? These problems don't come up if one of the biological parents has abdicated primary responsibility. But these days, when divorces have tended to be more amicable, especially where the needs of children are concerned, they can be a real problem. The best approach is probably for adults to decide among themselves in advance about such matters as choosing a school or seeing a teacher. Sometimes it is possible for parents and stepparents to go together; in other situations, where it is not, parents and stepparents can take turns. Often children settle the question themselves. "I want Hal and Mom to come to the school fair," one 7-year-old said, "and you and Nancy to take me to the circus. Mom has always been to my school, but she never took me to the circus, so that's the way I want to do it."

On the surface it might appear that it would be easier for young children to adjust to new parental relationships, but there is no evidence to support this theory. It is true that very young children need mothering and fathering so profoundly that they may be less likely to "make waves," while older children may be quite open about their hostility, jealousy, rivalry, and anxiety. But little children have their methods of letting us know, too. One stepmother told me, "Jonathan was only three when Frank and I married and he came to live with us. He clung to me, wanted to be hugged a lot, was never disobedient. I was delighted—until he began to have awful nightmares, wet his bed, and wouldn't let me leave him at nursery school. I realized that he was suffering from the divorce and remarriage as any child would. But he was just too young to talk about it, so it showed up in other ways. A friend of mine just married a man with two teenage sons, and she's going out of her mind because they're expressing so much anger. I tried to comfort her by telling her that at least her sons were old enough to talk about how they feel!"

Some children seem to be born with an ability to ride the waves; others seem to be knocked flat by even the most insignificant changes in the environment. Some children seem to make a quick adjustment but have second thoughts six months later, while others appear to be totally incapable of functioning for a while and then suddenly begin to bloom again. Obviously, stepparents have idiosyncrasies, too, and their process of accommodation can also take a long time. In trying to assess what is happening, stepparents must first look within themselves to be clear about their own actions and reactions. They must get all the information they can from the biological parent about the ways in which their new child has reacted to other previous situations in his or her life. Over and over again, stepparents tell me, "It's so hard to know whether my child's behavior is due to the divorce or to his not liking me or is just the way he reacts to things in general."

The most important thing for children to feel, as they adjust to their new situations, is that the new marriage is a good one. Consequently, the most fundamental responsibility of a stepparent is to work at his or her new marital relationship, which also means getting away from children from time to time, enlisting the support system of grandparents and others to help out. In trying out their new families, children are not only testing the stepparent, they are also testing the marriage. Behind the behavior that appears to be "divide and conquer" is the question: Is this marriage really working, or is it too weak to withstand my behaving badly? It must be made clear to children that the marriage comes first, or there cannot be a good home for them. One stepmother told her stepson when they had a fight, "Listen, Joe, I love your father. I married a wonderful man! I want to keep him." Nothing could have been more comforting to Joe.

One thing that is especially crucial to discuss is the great worry that every member of the new family is likely to have in common: whether or not it will all work out or whether there might be another cataclysm. It does not help to tell oneself or a child that it could never happen again; nobody can know that for sure. What seems far more helpful for everyone is honesty: "We love each other and hope this is going to work out well for all of us. It will take a long time, and we need to remember to talk to each other about how we are feeling."

If this kind of open sharing and communication seems inordinately difficult, especially in the beginning, family therapy may be very helpful. There are times when any family can benefit from having a skilled counselor help them feel safe enough to share their genuine feelings. Implicit in all this is the realization that no matter how rough things are, they can get better. Time is truly the great healer. Nothing that happens is fatal. There *are* solutions and they *can* be found.

Helping Children Cope With Disappointment

❊ By the time I met Janet, her four children were all grown up and on their own. I was amazed to discover how resourceful they had all been in managing to work their way through college and even graduate from school, for their father had deserted the family fifteen years earlier and it had been a tough struggle to survive. As Janet and I became friends, I asked her how she managed to meet adversity with so much strength and creativity. "It all started with our trip to the Grand Canyon, in our backyard," she told me.

Janet's husband had been gambling for a long time before she found out about it. When the moment of truth arrived—when he had mortgaged their home to the hilt and used every other financial resource, even lost his own thriving business—he apparently had a complete breakdown and one day he just left home and disappeared. She told me, "It was during July, and for several months we had all been planning a camping trip through the national parks in the West. I thought George was just tired and had been working too hard, so I insisted he take a month's vacation. The children and I had pored over travel guides, maps, camping books; we read about the first explorers and found out what geological factors had created the canyons and mountains themselves. The day before we were to leave, when the children were full of excitement and anticipation, all hell broke loose; we found out what had been happening and George was gone. I was in a state of shock, of course, but all I could think of at the moment was that the children and I had to go on living and surviving—and it seemed to me that the first test of how we could do that was whether or not we had that vacation."

There was very little money left, but the camping equipment had already been bought and paid for, and Janet announced to her four wide-eyed and frightened children, "We are going on our trip! But we are going to do it in our own backyard!"

The children ranged in age from 7 to 15. The family lived in a house that had a half acre of wooded land behind it. She called a family conference to discuss what could be done. "We'll set the tent up in the backyard and live outdoors," she told the children. They were too shocked and frightened to be the least bit enthusiastic at first. "They were just humoring me in the beginning," Janet told me. "I guess they figured even if I'd gone crazy, I was all they had to cling to!"

She suggested that they set up some ground rules. Jenny, aged 9, said she thought they ought to be allowed to use the bathroom and the refrigerator in the house. Dennis said he'd build a better fireplace for outdoor cooking; Charlie said he'd put up the tent and carry out the bedrools and blankets. Sharon wanted to be in charge of cooking and reading the history of the places they were to visit. Charlie, the recreational director, was in charge of songs and games. Jenny would help Sharon with cleaning up after meals. They would make one trip to the supermarket and keep the food stored in the refrigerator but live only on what they had bought for a week. Jenny, Janet, and Dennis went shopping; as the day went by the children became more and more excited about the backyard adventure. Janet told me, "Eventually their dejection changed into excitement. I told them I knew they were scared and miserable about what had happened to us and to Daddy, but we couldn't change what had happened; we could only change what we did about it."

The biggest problem on the "trip" was the complaint that Sharon was burning the oatmeal! Every day the family would go over maps, figure out how far they would have gotten by car, plan their day around that locality, reading about it, singing songs, telling stories around the nightly campfire. One night Jenny zipped the tent zipper shut so tight that Sharon couldn't get out to go to the bathroom. In her frenzy to get out, she pulled down the tent on the rest of her sleeping family. The dog and cat went along on the trip. A few times the family decided that they would have stayed at a motel with a swimming pool, so they took a side trip in the car to a nearby public beach. They played softball and badminton and did daily calisthenics. "It was a terrific trip," Janet told me. "We went to Bryce Canyon, Yellowstone Park, the Grand Tetons, Glacier National Park—all inside our heads and through picture books."

I was so intrigued with this marvelously creative handling of a painful life experience that I almost forgot my initial question about how the children had become so strong and resourceful. But I finally asked Janet why that particular experience seemed so important. "Instead of running away from disappointment, we used it to create something new, something exciting—an adventure. Nobody tried to deny the pain we were experiencing, but we never let it defeat us."

Since hearing this story, I have found myself thinking a good deal about the meaning of disappointment in the lives of children. There is of course a broad range of disappointments that are bound to occur in a child's life, from such things as not being invited to a party to breaking a leg and missing a whole baseball season. Having to move involves disappointments, having to give up new-found friends, or not being able to perform in a school play. From the perspective of adulthood, we may know that these kinds of experiences are an inevitable part of living, but to a child who has had more limited experience with adversity, such events may take on gigantic proportions. They are, however, an important training ground for the larger disappointments that sooner or later come to all of us, and the ways in which adults help (or hinder) a child's ability to cope with disappointment can have an important influence on a lifetime pattern of dealing with the inevitable frustrations of living.

I recently had an excellent opportunity to observe the different ways in which children react to disappointment, and not at all to my surprise, their reactions tended to reflect the attitudes of the adults who were with them. I was standing on line at a movie theater when the voice on the loudspeaker announced that all tickets for this performance were sold out. There was a collective moan of pain, then I watched as parents and children began to walk to the parking lot. There was no mistaking a pattern; the loudest screams were coming from children who were being yelled at! "Don't you start crying, or I won't bring you back for another show" and "If you don't stop whining, you're gonna get a smack" brought forth louder shrieks of pain. A woman standing in front of me who had three young children with her said, "Isn't that *lousy* —we've been standing here in the rain for twenty minutes. I know how disappointed you are, kids—I feel the same way. Let's try to figure out what we can do this afternoon. We'll come back tomorrow, but meanwhile let's try to think of something we'd all enjoy. I know how disappointed you are." She and her entourage walked quietly to the car, deep in discussion of alternatives.

Of course adult attitudes don't account for all reactions to disappointment. We all seem to have different threshholds for frustration and different ways of handling our feelings. Some of the children just looked quietly sad. One wiry, active little boy stamped his feet and jumped up and down; a little girl ran toward the car in the parking lot, great sobs convulsing her. I heard her father say to her mother, "There goes Greta Garbo, giving another one of her great performances!" Since we had been next to each other on line and had shared the tension, he smiled at me and said, "Someday that kid is going to play Camille. She'll be fine by the time we get halfway to the ice-cream parlor!"

The ingredients for successfully dealing with childhood disappointments were all there in the drama of that waiting line. In general, children who took on the sympathy and compassion of their parents—who were allowed to express their feelings and whose parents shared their disappointment—pulled themselves together most quickly. In addition, it was clear that each of us has our own unique style for dealing with adversity. When adults acknowledge these differences in style, children are able to use their inner resources for recovery.

It seems to me that in every aspect of life, allowing ourselves and our children to have and to express our feelings is the first and most crucial issue involved in learning to cope with painful realities, whether this means a few brief tears, some colorful swearing under one's breath, or a quick, intense temper tantrum. What is most needed is our acceptance of the normal, human experience of disappointment. It's all a rotten shame, and we are sorry, too.

We also need to keep in mind the age of a child; it makes us judge more sensitively whether or not a child is reacting appropriately. The capacity to endure disappointments increases with age and experience. It is appropriate for a 3-year-old to weep inconsolably when a favorite toy gets broken; it is appropriate for a 7-year-old to howl loudly and long at having the flu on the day of a special birthday party; it is appropriate for a teenager to go into a mournful depression (for at least 48 hours!) when the girl he loves chooses another for the spring prom. It takes a lot of growing up before any of us are able to deal with such frustrations in a reasonable fashion. The trick is for *adults* not to react as if they were 3 or 7 or 13 years old—and that means providing sympathy, understanding, and leadership.

Giving children a chance to figure out alternative activities seems to be very helpful. It is comforting to a child to be helped to realize that there are other options to be considered, that all is not lost. Some of the discussions that went on around the movie theater had to do with seriously considering such alternatives as going to see the dolphin show; going for ice cream; going back to the motel for a swim in the indoor pool; going back to the house to finish the game of Monopoly; picking up some seeds at the hardware store so that as soon as the rain stopped they could start the vegetable garden.

Another general rule for sound mental health is that we are able to cope with almost anything if we don't feel as if we are totally helpless. The serious and earnest consideration of alternatives was a way of giving a child a sense of power over adversity; there were things he or she could do. Making choices offers a sense of control and autonomy. When a child has an intense temper tantrum about a disappointment, chances are that he or she feels there are no alternatives; all is lost. Caught in the emotion of the moment, he or she can't see any other possibilities. At that moment parents can be very helpful in helping a child gain control over his feelings by pointing out that there are other options and that the child can play a part in making the decision.

Sometimes parents seem to bend over backward in assuaging disappointment. It is one thing to offer a small comfort, such as some ordinarily frowned upon candy or an ice-cream sundae, but quite another to overreact to a child's pain so much that we give things, do things, that rob him of the opportunity to meet the challenge of the situation. For example, my friend Janet probably could have borrowed the money to take her children on the actual trip to the Grand Canyon. She didn't do that because that would have been an unrealistic response to a serious problem. There are times when we have to give up something we want; there are times when we have to accept pain. If we try to remove every painful experience, we are not helping a child learn to deal with such situations.

It is not easy to strike the most helpful balance between toughness and compassion. Saying to a child, "We have to move because Daddy's company is sending him to Chicago, and I don't want to hear any whining or carrying on," is no more helpful than saying, "Oh, my poor darling! You're going to have to adjust to a new school and new friends, and I don't know how you'll stand it!" The first declaration leaves no room for perfectly normal pain and apprehension, and the second message tells the child he or she is too incompetent to deal with reality. What might be much more helpful is something to this effect: "Hey listen, kids, we're all in this together, and it hurts a lot, but we're going to be able to deal with it."

When I was 11 years old I got rheumatic fever. In those days the only treatment was bed rest, and I was told I could not go to school for the rest of the year—about six months. It was a devastating shock, but my memories of those months are not awful at all. What I remember best was the newspaper that I edited from my bed. It was called "The Bed Post," and each week my parents and brother gave me news items, original poems and stories, and illustrations, which I then assembled. I wrote a weekly column myself, and every Friday the whole family would sit on my bed and read the paper out loud.

I began growing various kinds of plants from seeds with which I was familiar—grapefruit and orange mostly. I did a lot of clay figures and ashtrays; I learned to knit; I made puppets. I had lots of company. Toward the end of my imprisonment we had a "Family Fair," to which we invited everyone we knew and I sold all the things I had made that winter. I gave the money to an organization that provided recreation for poor children. I think it was about 68 dollars, which was a lot of money in those days.

I also remember the loneliness, the fear (would I ever get well?), the terrible disappointments especially at holiday times, when everyone else was going places and doing things. But it was not the disaster it might have been because my parents assumed I had the creativity to deal with it constructively. Even now, I can feel a sense of pride over my victory; it was not a wasted time at all. In fact I am sure that experience contributed greatly to an inner sense of competence.

Adversity, after all, is an intrinsic reality of living, and the disappointments of childhood are a training ground for discovering that the tragic in life can hone us to a fine edge, help us become more than we have ever been before, not less.

Children react so much to our expectations. If we expect them to be stalwart in their suffering, this is more than likely to be the case. Anytime a parent says to me, "Oh, God, I don't *dare* tell Dorothy we can't go to the beach. She'll just scream all day!" I know that a self-fulfilling prophecy is in the making. When we assume that a child is strong, reasonable, and resourceful, the child feels a sense of pride in our expectations: "If they think I'm really so strong, maybe I am!"

But there is a catch in this approach. Having confidence that a child can meet the test of painful reality is different from *ordering* such behavior. Anytime an adult tells a child, "You are too big to behave like such a baby," I know there is going to be a great deal of regressive behavior. It sets in motion feelings of exhaustion and self-doubt, because the truth is we never get over needing to behave in babyish ways some of the time. The message is totally different when we say, "It's so painful to be disappointed this way at your age; I know how awful you feel. But I also know that you are a pretty strong person, and you will get over this feeling of sadness."

How children react to disappointment also depends on the quality and kind of disappointment. One little girl had been looking forward for many weeks to being a flower girl at a wedding. When the wedding was canceled, we all wondered how Sarah would survive this great disappointment, what with the new dress and fancy shoes and flower basket all ready and waiting! Sarah was very philosophical about it for a 6-year-old. "I guess they shouldn't get married," she said, "if they don't want to." The disappointment was less than the adults expected partly, I'm sure, because Sarah knew she would still be going on a vacation trip with her parents!

There is another way in which adults set the stage for the quality of a child's disappointment, and that has to do with our attitudes toward competition. If the baseball team loses three times in a row, Marty takes it in stride. He kicks a wall or two, curses under his breath, and suffers with his teammates, but he is not destroyed by this series of events. Julie, on the other hand, comes out of the locker room after a statewide gymnastic tournament totally devastated. Her father has made so much of her winning that she no longer senses any pleasure in the activity itself; winning is everything. If we ourselves see any kind of winning over others as a necessary victory, our children's disappointments are going to be entirely out of proportion, whether the competition is for grades or points in a tennis match or becoming class president. When we stress the fact that the only genuine and meaningful competition is with oneself—did we do the best we could?—the inevitable times of losing don't become major disasters.

One of the best ways to prepare a child for disappointment is to help him enjoy his own company from the earliest years of life. Disappointment in childhood usually has to do with not being able to do something or see someone. Ultimately it may involve spending time alone, and if a child sees this as an empty wasteland, the disappointment is bound to be more intense. The inner satisfaction of knowing that one can enjoy one's own company is an important antidote to having to miss a school picnic or a camping trip. These days parents have a special obligation to see to it that children can tolerate an absence of spectator entertainment, for it abounds everywhere. Of course the television set is a prime example of a way to remain passively dependent on being entertained by others; television-watching needs to be a controlled activity. On the other hand, I am not one of the zealots who want television removed entirely from the lives of children. When a child has a fever and is naturally listless, it seems legitimate to use the resources of the environment to let him or her watch more "junk" than one might ordinarily sanction, because another clue to making disappointments more bearable is to allow for compensations. Moments of dismay are a great time to break the rules! When the doctor says the cast can't come off for another two weeks, it is time to have a hot dog and a soda, even if these are "verboten" in the house. If Daddy has emergency business problems and can't take his child to the baseball game of the season, it may be time to throw caution to the winds and allow a youngster to buy five comic books.

There is nothing whatever wrong with sweetening the pain; this is not spoiling a child. What it is is a lesson in compassion; you are letting your child know that you are sensitive to his or her suffering and want to offer some perfectly appropriate cheering up. The kinder we are and the less we use such opportunities to demand square-jawed toughness, the more likely it is that a child will be a good sport. We all thrive on sympathy and tend to become our best selves when caught in adversity with someone who really loves us. Ultimately, we can stand just about anything if we know we are not alone, that others care what happens to us.

When children seem to overreact to disappointments routinely, then we are probably dealing with a "hidden agenda"— issues that really have nothing to do with what is going on at the moment. It may be that a child has felt too pressured to succeed at tasks that are too difficult. His behavior in any situation then becomes more babyish, for the struggle to measure up is just too overwhelming. Sometimes emotions get directed into safer channels; a child who carries on wildly over a canceled birthday party because of a sore throat may have found a necessary (and safer) outlet for the pain of observing that Mom and Dad seem to be fighting all the time, and suppose they decide to get a divorce? This question contains so much agony that the child cannot express his feelings directly. When some minor issue comes up, it's greeted with a flood of tears that was just waiting for an excuse. When a child seems unable to bear the normal disappointments of life, it may be time to explore the possibility that some much bigger terror is waiting in the wings.

Agonizing disappointments are a special category. They are the major crises—tragedies even—in which a sense of disappointment is only part of many other feelings, such as the anxiety or crushing pain a child experiences when parents separate, a favorite aunt dies, or the family pet is run over by a car. In such cases we need to help children to accept their genuine grief and to experience a period of mourning; we need to help them understand that feeling deeply sad is a normal and necessary reaction that is not to be feared. *Not* to feel sad when such feelings are appropriate is far more hazardous to one's mental health.

When Janet and her children took their backyard "trip" out West, there was room for sadness, for the expression of anxieties, for discussion of the future. She told me, "While we had some hilarious times together, we never tried to pretend that something awful wasn't happening. We'd sing around the campfire at night and then all cuddle close together and talk about how we felt and what we were going to do when our 'vacation' was over. I encouraged the children to tell me what they were feeling and to ask me any questions they wanted to. Sometimes, late at night, we'd all lie in the tent in our sleeping bags and cry. On the last day of our trip, when we were pretending to be driving back home, we talked about what would happen when we got there. I assured the children that we would manage, that life would go on. They would see their friends, go to school, be safe with me until they all grew up and could take care of themselves. We never had to *pretend* we were having a good time because some of the time we really were having fun and some of the time we were frightened and upset together. I guess it was just real life going on." And that of course is what disappointments are—real life going on. Developing the strength and the fortitude to deal with them adds to our zest and delight in the equally real experiences of joy and fulfillment.

The Trouble With Santa Claus

❋ I realize that anyone who questions the sanctity of Santa Claus may well be stoned in the streets. However, I've been having some increasingly pervasive misgivings about the man in the red flannel suit, and on the basis of these doubts I've been doing a little research.

Two things bother me about the Santa Claus we have invented. The first is that when our children "find out" they may quite logically feel betrayed and confused. Lying is, generally speaking, a manipulative way of relating to children, and we *do* lie about Santa Claus when we say he is a real person. My second complaint is that Santa Claus has become judge and jury rolled into one, weighing a child's value and deciding if he's worthy of punishment or reward.

My research into these two issues has been informal but, I think, enlightening. I asked as many adults as I could how they felt when they learned "the truth" about Santa Claus, and I also went snooping around shopping centers and department stores, listening in on what the Santas were saying to children. The results of this investigation have confirmed my growing uneasiness and given me the courage to speak out. It's not that I'm not crazy about Santa Claus, but I think it's time we put him in his place.

I was genuinely surprised to discover how bitter some adults still were about their childhood experience with "the moment of truth" about Santa. Those who needed and most wanted to believe that he was a real person were the angriest. A man who had grown up poor, in a ghetto tenement, told me, "Man, I *had* to believe in Santa Claus 'cause what else was there? I *believed!* I didn't mind Santa Claus not listening to me about what I wanted half as much as when some kid told me he was my grandmama. I was so sad I almost killed him. I've never gotten over how bad I felt."

A woman musician told me, "I felt tricked, misused—made a fool of. It was a double shock—I lost Santa Claus and I also lost faith in my parents for a long time." A grandfather said, "For me the worst part was it seemed I'd been lied to. If only my parents had left me alone with the story of Santa Claus—you know, the reindeer and the chimney and all that—I'm positive I would have realized that it was a nice fairy tale, but they kept insisting he was real, making such a point of it that it seemed different from any of the other fantasy-reality problems I had to come to terms with."

The adults who showed the least emotion were those who said they had always known it was a story or those who said, "Well, I think some part of me always knew it was a game, even when I still believed." What interested me especially was that the people who had had pleasant, ambiguous, uncertain attitudes about Santa Claus are the ones who still like the idea of him the most. Those at the two extremes—the ones who had never for one moment been allowed to believe he was real and those who had believed until a rude awakening at 5 or 6—seemed least likely to be Santa devotees. This provocative development has led me to the conclusion that the first trouble with Santa Claus is that in this case— and with no other fairy tale—we have allowed ourselves to completely forget how children think and feel. I wonder why we have made a special case of Santa Claus, why we seem trapped in extreme positions for and against "reality"? We don't do that about any other children's stories.

When I read *Mary Poppins* to my daughter, I never felt compelled to explain that real people can't fly. *Winnie the Pooh* was just there to love; nobody discussed the scientific validity of his existence. When we tell our children traditional fairy tales we seem to make the accurate assumption that they know perfectly well these stories are not real, but "truer than true."

We have lost our cool when it comes to Santa Claus, however. I can still recall clapping like crazy when Eva Le Gallienne as Peter Pan pleaded with me, personally, from the stage, to try to save Tinker Bell's life; my mother was clapping wildly too, but I didn't think she was lying to me. Nor did it ever occur to me that Peter Pan was someone you could invite home to dinner. There was the normal, tacit understanding between parent and child that some things just don't have to be analyzed and talked about—they just are.

I think it's time to put Santa Claus back where he belongs—in the natural, childlike department of fantasy where he can be thoroughly enjoyed and understood along with all the other beloved characters who peopled our lives so wonderfully, but whom we understood did not have social security numbers. Yes, Virginia, there is a Santa Claus and he is one of the best and nicest fairy tales of them all. He is full of love and tenderness, and most of all he reminds all the grown-ups that children are the very greatest treasure in all the world. In the dark of winter he tries to fill all the children everywhere with wonder and delight and joy, because that's the kind of thing grown-ups wish they could do for children all of the time. He is magic—and children understand about that better than we do.

The second trouble with Santa Claus has to do with allowing him to make judgments about our children. As I listened in on Santa Clauses talking to children in toy departments and on the street, I found that with very rare exceptions they all asked the same question, "Have you been *good* this year?" Fifty years of mental health education down the drain every December! I spend most of my working life trying to convince parents and children that there is no such thing as a good person or a bad person, that we are all human and imperfect but worthy of love and understanding. Along comes Santa Claus and there we are all over again, with these simplistic, dehumanizing notions about human behavior. Children are sometimes lovable, sometimes nasty, sometimes kind, sometimes mean, sometimes responsible, sometimes impulsive;

that's what it is to be a child. Grown-ups are for helping children to become civilized—and this is *never* accomplished by withholding love. To deny love and approval is to deny the whole meaning of Christmas, which has so much to do with forgiveness for human weakness.

We need to rethink the Santa Claus game because of these two essential problems. First, many children eventually feel they have been lied to and manipulated, and secondly, the Santa Clauses they actually meet often have little or no understanding of the meaning of love and mercy. It seems to me that both problems can best be handled by allowing children to become full partners with us in the creation of their own personal, special, family interpretations.

When my daughter was asked by a department store Santa Claus, "Have you been a good girl this year?" she replied with conviction, "Nobody's good all the time." It was one of the few times I felt I was doing a good job! Statements and attitudes by "men dressed up in Santa Claus suits, to make this a time of special fun," can be an important and often revealing topic of conversation for parents and children—and the fact that these are men in costume will *not* destroy a child's pleasure, any more than seeing a ghost at the door at Halloween is spoiled by the knowledge that it is really the boy next door.

It seems to me that the reason the issue of fantasy vs. reality has become so muddied in the case of Santa Claus is not so much that this is a special case but that we have made it adult oriented. Once we begin to share it with children, it gains proper perspective. It may seem at first glance that Santa Claus is a special case because children write him letters and even leave food for him near where the stockings are hung. But think for a moment of the "absolute reality" of your last tea party with a youngster. You're sitting on the edge of a sandbox and daintily eating a fantastically delicious upside-down chocolate-pineapple-nut pie just recently "baked" in the sand pail. Or you are sitting at a tiny table in a doll corner, eating with a toothpick-size fork, while your host or hostess announces each succulent course from soup to nuts, being lifted invisibly from a toy stove. Maybe you don't believe in the reality of this experience, but the child certainly does. We underestimate the degree of total commitment a child has for his fantasy. It is one of the reasons we sometimes erroneously think a young child is lying, when actually he is caught up in a kind of never-never land —half reality, half his own wishful fantasy—with a very, very dim line of distinction that he will (he really will!) outgrow by the time he is 7 or 8.

When we play these games, I don't think any of us ever feel we are "cheating." The rules are tacit and well understood. It is make-believe, but from the child's point of view, the less said about that, the better; he's *in* the world of make-believe and he wants your companionship. I feel that we can enter into the fantasy of Santa Claus in precisely the same way, letting the child take the lead.

If we give all the particulars rather than letting the child develop his own fantasy, we are running the show too much; if we let the child make some of the decisions, this will help him decide for himself when he is ready to give it up. For example, instead of telling a child where and how Santa Claus lives and works, we can ask the child to tell us what he thinks—how he'd like it to be. From the adult viewpoint it may seem that we are robbing the child of something, but it just isn't so. In the realm of fantasy, the closer a story approximates a child's own wish-fulfillment, the more he will enjoy it.

Asking a 4-year-old to tell his own personal story about Santa Claus can elicit this kind of tale:

"Well, you see, he has a big house, it's really like a castle, and he lives there all alone. Nobody is allowed to ever bother him or tell him what to do. He just sits and watches TV and eats TV dinners, and every once in a while, he waves his magic wand and the whole house gets full of toys."

It doesn't take a psychoanalyst with five degrees to see what that's all about! Each child is so different in his needs and expectations that it would be foolish to set up a system of techniques for dealing with Santa Claus. The only general advice I can give is to treat it as one would any other fantasy experience one shares with a child, and in doing that, one can leave it to the child to make most of the decisions. If one starts with something like, "Santa Claus is the story about a wonderful, jolly man who loves all children and wants them to be happy at Christmastime," then the decisions about what forms may develop can be left to the child to decide. Let him decide about letter-writing, about where the letter should be mailed. Left to their own devices, I am certain children would be delighted to mail their letters in the hole in the tree, floating on the stream in the woods—or handed to the postman. All have equal validity when you are 3 or 4 years old. Leaving something for Santa to eat comes under the perfectly appropriate heading of eating mud pies and calling them devil's food cake; it's fun, and parents can eat them themselves, just as they pretended to nibble at the mud pies.

As for the crucial question of who brings the presents, that is again a problem from an adult's point of view, not a child's. If one says something to the effect that "part of the Santa Claus story is that mommies, daddies, grandparents, aunts, uncles, cousins, and friends want to have a special time to bring surprises to children, just as Santa Claus would want them to do," that's enough for children. You have stated your reality and they can now dream it any way they please!

A very important consideration in taking the manipulative quality out of the Santa Claus myth is not only that it allows the child to make his own individual fantasy but that it means he can be a participant sooner. The passivity of simply allowing adults to run the Christmas show means that children actually play a very minimal role in this family experience—and the less one participates, the less the event really can mean. For example, I recall a young mother I once met who said to her 4-year-old son, "You will know you are growing up when you can feel Santa Claus inside yourself, and you want to make other people happy and give them presents and love."

In one affluent Westchester nursery school the children make gifts to give to children at a day-care center in Harlem. The less privileged children also make gifts for the Westchester children, and while the adult might make a distinction between toys and ginger cookies, the children do not; the exchange is the important part of the experience and it is, indeed, the beginning of "getting Santa Claus in your heart." That's where he belongs—and you will be amazed at how willing and ready your children are to accept and enjoy that lovely idea.

Baby-Sitters Are Not Substitute Parents

❈ When my daughter was young we moved a number of times. As soon as the barrels and boxes were unpacked, I put an ad in the local paper for baby-sitters. I interviewed until I had a list of from five to ten sitters whom I felt I could trust implicitly. I tried for some variety, for different occasions.

First of all, I wanted two or three who were mature, motherly women who were raising or had raised children of their own and were relaxed about the whole thing. When they came to be interviewed, I watched very carefully to see how they approached Wendy. If they tried to force themselves on her, the interview was very short. There was always one chief baby-sitter, with whom we had a steady, enduring relationship and with whom Wendy was able to develop a greater intimacy. During the years when Wendy was 2 to about 12, this was a lady whose name was (really) Mrs. Smith. She had six children of her own, and was unruffleable. When she came to be interviewed she left Wendy completely alone. "When she's ready, she'll talk to me," she said calmly. When I said Wendy was not yet toilet trained, she said, "That's okay. That's a parent's business, not mine." I asked how she felt about children and food. She replied, "I don't think it's up to me to worry about that." I couldn't have agreed more! Mrs. Smith let Wendy get away with murder—and I thought that was just fine. She stayed up later, ate what she felt like eating, went to visit Mrs.

Smith's house, where everyone catered to her. I feel that this is quite legitimate for when parents are away. Discipline and doing what's good for a child is the parents' job and nobody else's. When parents are away, and assuming this often feels like a deprivation to a child, there ought to be other compensations. It was my and my husband's responsibility to worry about things like nutrition and bedtime. We were around enough to keep things on an even keel. And Wendy understood perfectly well that baby-sitters are not parents. Of course I am talking about the unimportant details. A sitter certainly must take responsibility for disciplining where danger or the rights of others are involved.

There were always three or four mature, experienced women on my list. They were the ones I called if Wendy woke up with a fever on a day that I had to go to work, or when we wanted to go away for three or four days. I knew that they could deal with emergencies. Then there were younger people on my list, both male and female, teenagers who were great when we were going out for an evening, who were willing to play with Wendy and be companions rather than adults in charge of her. Once in a while we took a teenage baby-sitter with us on a vacation so that Wendy could have someone to stay with her if we went out for the evening. Once in a while this backfired, but the story became part of the folklore of the LeShan family. None of us can hear the word *Nantucket* without remembering the summer that we went to Cape Cod with Wendy and a baby-sitter. We took a boat trip to Nantucket Island, and though Wendy turned out to be a great sailor, her baby-sitter was so seasick that the whole miserable day was spent taking care of her!

If both husband and wife are working people, good sitters are an absolute necessity. We need to have great confidence in them. It is well worth the time it takes to do a thorough job of interviewing and investigating. There are bound to be crisis times when you must have a sitter and two or three are busy; have a fourth and a fifth on your list.

Some major criteria for selecting a baby-sitter are: Does your child like to spend time with this person? Does this person make your child feel uneasy or very comfortable? Does your child look forward to her coming? And if anything frightening or dangerous happened, would she make your child feel safe and would she know what to do in such an emergency?

The only serious trap I know of that many parents seem to fall into is that of trying to find a baby-sitter who would do exactly what they would do, insist on the same routines, follow exact instructions about discipline, and in general be a carbon copy of them. Assuming that one is a reasonably good judge of character and that the sitter one chooses is a good, kind, decent person, I think one must allow the sitter to be him or herself, to react with spontaneity, not self-consciously watch every word or action. And if we openly face the fact that most children, under most circumstances, would prefer the company of a parent, we need to make allowances. Sometimes, of course, a sitter will have to be instructed to administer a foul-tasting medicine, or not allow a child to eat sweets, or refuse to let a child watch a television program that deeply offends our sensibilities. There are, of course, such legitimate realities. But in general, I think we do better if we allow the baby-sitter to be a treat instead of a treatment.

Six Signs of a Good Teacher

✽ Jason Martin, aged 10, arrived home from school one day, and in between having some milk and cookies told his mother, "School was terrible today because Mrs. Wells was in one of her moods." Mrs. Martin made a mental note to discuss Mrs. Wells with her husband that evening and to make an appointment with the principal of her son's school. Moody teachers were not her idea of good elementary-school education.

Mrs. Martin's fears were unfounded in this particular case. She could have gotten a clue from Jason's tone of voice. He was not upset, anxious, or frightened—he was just stating a fact. Mrs. Wells was apparently unusually irritable and impatient that day and as a result had treated one of the children unfairly. Just before dismissal, she had apologized to the class and told them that there were times when she got into a bad mood but she was sure she'd be feeling better the next day.

Mrs. Wells actually had one of the most important characteristics of a good teacher: She was honest with the children; she admitted her vulnerability—even failure—and she expected perfection of neither herself nor the children. Parents are sometimes inclined to think in stereotypes when they evaluate their child's teacher and to let words get in the way of seeing the person rather than just an image. One parent believes a teacher ought to be strict. Another thinks a teacher must have patience. Yet another parent describes a good teacher as "someone who is always in control of the class and can make the kids work." The trouble with such descriptions is that they leave too much out of the picture. No parent wants to be measured by a set of rules; we know perfectly well from our own experience as parents that we behave differently on different days; that a child's behavior evokes different reactions; that a great many outside factors not directly related to the child influence our behavior.

Parents are quite right to be concerned about whether a child's experiences with a teacher are happy and comfortable or frightening and demeaning, but snap judgments of teachers can often be misleading. It seems to me that in order to make a reasonable and sensible evaluation of a teacher's ability and performance, parents need a list of solid criteria that will take them past the simplest, most superficial responses and judgments. Here are some examples of instances in which deeper probing was called for and the criterion I derive from each situation.

Kim, aged 9, commented at bedtime, while reading a story to her father, "Mr. Leonard says he's as dumb as we are!" Kim and her family happen to be black, and her father was infuriated by the word "dumb"; he saw it as a racial slur. He had never met Kim's teacher, but he stormed into the school the next morning. To his surprise, Mr. Leonard was also black. Mr. Leonard explained to Kim's father that in a discussion about learning the day before he had written a word on the board that he almost always spelled wrong; then he wrote down a math problem and admitted he didn't know how to solve it. He then read the class his favorite poem and admitted he'd never been able to memorize it. "I got to be a teacher," he said, "without having to know everything; I still go on learning and I'm a grown-up. That's all I expect of you —to keep on trying, knowing you have to fail sometimes at some things."

A good teacher is a person who can admit failure, who knows how anxious children get about doing well, and who sees learning as a lifetime process.

When Grandma came to visit and asked David, aged 5, what he was learning in kindergarten, David replied airily, "Oh, we don't learn anything—we just play." Grandma wasted no time in urging her daughter to look into this situation; her neighbor's grandson was learning how to read in nursery school! David's mother visited the class the following week. She joined the youngsters on a field trip to collect different kinds of fall leaves. She saw the children help their teacher look through a book of pictures in order to identify the leaves. She saw them make posters with name labels to put up on the walls. Later the teacher read a story to the group, and at the mention of a blue sky, one of the children asked, "What is the sky made of?" The teacher said that was a wonderful question and promised the whole class a trip to the school library the next day to see if the librarian could give them some books about the sky. In the course of the day they painted, sang a counting song, built with blocks, climbed the jungle gym, baked cookies, and took off and put on their outdoor clothes, among many other activities.

A teacher of young children is someone who makes use of a child's natural curiosity, carefully observes a child's readiness, and sets the stage for learning skills by making learning the most exciting game in town.

Jeff's parents came home from their first teacher conference in a state of shock; they couldn't believe what they had heard. Jeff, aged 12, an affable, bright, capable child at home, was failing in school. His teacher had showed them a file of test scores and the results of a group I.Q. test that put Jeff at the lowest edge of normal intelligence. The teacher had made it quite clear that he blamed them for Jeff's poor work; she had simply assumed that they did not encourage his learning and did not realize how serious his limitations were. It was as if Jeff were a Dr. Jekyll and Mr. Hyde character. They were devastated; they were also extremely self-conscious with Jeff when he came home from school; then they got very angry and said he'd have to stay in and work on his homework assignments every day after school. What they overlooked completely was that the teacher had not shown the slightest interest in hearing anything about the Jeff *they* knew. He had assumed, without questioning, that something was very much amiss at home.

A good teacher looks at the child first and the tests second, and wants to know everything possible about other aspects of a child's life and behavior. Such a teacher never blames children or parents for school problems without knowing all the facts.

Peggy's mother was appalled when she visited her daughter's sixth-grade class: Tables and chairs were scattered about in disorder, covered with all kinds of papers, books, and materials for costumes; the window sills were crowded with plants, a fish tank, more books in haphazard piles, a sewing machine, someone's guitar, and a large pile of shoe boxes; the children were all moving about the room, talking to each other, and the teacher seemed unperturbed by the chaos. Peggy's mother could not see how the children could be learning anything in such an atmosphere. In fact, the children were deeply engrossed in fascinating projects. They were reading up on the Middle Ages because they were doing an abridged version of *A Connecticut Yankee in King Arthur's Court* at their next assembly, and they had been collecting shoe boxes for a trip to gather rocks for a study in geology. The teacher was helping the students learn to work on their own, apart from formal study.

There is no greater teacher of children than the one who has the capacity to tolerate un-order and not to confuse it with dis-order. A teacher who can establish freedom with responsibility in a classroom and live with the necessary fluidity this creates is a terrific teacher.

Kurt's mother almost had a fit when he casually mentioned one day that he had heard that his high-school biology teacher was a homosexual. She began calling other parents and arranged to have a meeting with the school principal. Her position was that if the rumor was true, the teacher would have to be fired. She was making a big mistake.

Nowhere in my list of criteria for judging a teacher is there any place for making such a judgment on the basis of sexual preference alone. There are excellent teachers of unorthodox sexual preference and terrible teachers of conventional sexual preference. The only important factors in this connection are whether or not a teacher keeps private relationships private, and whether or not appropriate student-teacher relations are maintained. We don't protect young people from all the complexities of human choices by denying their existence but by communicating our own values and attitudes in a positive way.

Pete seemed reluctant to go to school one day and told his father that Miss Murphy was so strict it made him nervous. "She whispers," Pete said, "so you have to keep absolutely still or you don't hear the stuff she's teaching or the homework assignments, and she just looks at you with those piercing eyes that go right through you!"

Pete's father was upset by this report. All he needed, he thought to himself, was a cruel and inhuman math teacher for his 13-year-old son. He and his wife were divorced and Pete was living with him. It was difficult to supervise his son, do the shopping, and hold down a taxing, time-consuming job. Pete, an only child, was left on his own much of the time, and the apartment was often a wreck. At his office the next morning, Pete's father called the school principal, who laughed when he heard Pete's comments. "Old Battle-Axe Murphy puts on a good act," he said, "but believe me, she's a pussycat! As a matter of fact, she's talked to me about Pete. She feels there is too little discipline in his life right now and that what he needs is a feeling of success. She's putting pressure on him because she wants him to have a sense of accomplishment, which he also badly needs right now."

There is no way of judging how good or bad a teacher is by the way in which he or she conducts a class. Each teacher has a unique style, and even the strictest disciplinarian may be making it quite clear to the children that they are deeply cared for and valued as persons.

Teachers, like parents, are complicated human beings with strengths and weaknesses, talents and limitations, good days and bad days, special sensitivities and unique assets. One of the most important lessons of childhood is that adults are vulnerable and imperfect, just as children are, and that making allowances for each other is a necessary part of growing up and becoming a mature person.

The best teachers are the ones who are struggling to become more than they are, on any given day, and who demonstrate to their students that this quest to learn and to grow, to accept failure and go on to new challenges, is what life is all about.

How to Prevent a Child
From Being
Sexually Molested

✳ When I was about 12 years old and riding home from school on a subway, a man exposed himself in the empty vestibule area, then tried to sit down next to me and touch me. (In the 1930s, subways had an entrance and vestibule at each end of the cars.) It was midday, and there were only two young men in the subway car. They both seemed to think the situation was hilarious. At first I was too stunned to move, but when the man sat down next to me and his hand moved toward my lap, I leaped up, gasped, and ran for the door as we luckily came into a station. I completely forgot that I was supposed to be on the way to the dentist, was too frightened to get back on the subway, and literally ran several miles to get home. I felt sick to my stomach and terrified, and all I wanted was to get to my mother and tell her what had happened to me.

Fifty years later the whole event is still vivid in my mind, but now that the subject of child molesting is out of the closet and people are talking about it, what I find important about my own experience is that it never for one moment occurred to me *not* to tell my parents, and that was at a time when *nobody* talked openly about such matters.

Preventing a child from having encounters with sexual deviates —or seeing to it that if such an event should occur parents are the very first to know about it—depends entirely on parental attitudes and guidance. Now, looking back, I've been trying to assess just what the qualities were in my relationship with my parents that made me feel able to tell them. It seems to me that there are some general principles that parents need to think about if they want to be sure their children will run to them—or, just as important, know when to get home before anything happens.

The most common reason a child may not report a disturbing or confusing incident to a parent is that he figures that whatever is happening is his own fault. The most characteristic reasoning of childhood goes something like this:

- "I must be real bad or this person wouldn't be hurting me."

- "It's all those secret bad thoughts I have—this person knows about them."

- "Grown-ups know everything and I don't know anything, so it must be all right, even if I don't like it or it makes me feel funny."

The first thing we need to make clear to all children is that they are *not* guilty of some crime because they are childish; that being childish is the name of the game when you are a child. Every child is special and beautiful and full of wonderful surprises that are unfolding every day, and when unpleasant, confusing, or painful events happen—from not being able to control the impulse to bite the baby to running into the traffic or having nightmares—a child should understand that these are all part of being a perfectly normal youngster. And when a parent yells or spanks, it is as much a measure of adult fallibility as it is one's own normal immaturity. When I ran home that day, it never occurred to me that this event was in any way my fault, and that was the important ingredient in my running to the right place.

The second most important attitude necessary for self-protection is a comfortable awareness of one's own sexuality, without guilt. Another memory I have of childhood is the night I called my mother into my bedroom when I was about 4 years old and told her that "my hand smelled funny." I had been masturbating, and

I guess I became overwhelmed with guilt and wanted to be punished. My mother said, "I guess you've been touching yourself, and that's a nice feeling. It's all right when you're in bed alone." She put some talcum powder on my hand, and that was the last discussion we had about masturbation. By the time I was 12 I knew everything I needed to know about menstruation. I had been given books on how babies are conceived and born, and most important of all, my parents had talked to me about love. I had excellent role models for gaining an understanding of sexuality through observing my parents' feelings for each other.

If there had ever been an episode in which someone wanted to "play doctor" with me in a somewhat intensified fashion, if someone had tried to take me for a ride in a car—even if there had been an attempt at rape—it would never have occurred to me that my own sexuality was responsible. It seems to me that sex education in its broadest terms must begin in infancy, in the pleasure we take in kissing and hugging a baby and the pleasure a child takes in the natural sensations of touching him- or herself. Curiosity about what boys and girls are all about is in high gear by the age of 3 or 4, and it is sheer cowardice and rationalization to take the attitude that "the time to tell is when children ask." We are busy teaching young children about themselves and the world they live in all the time. Where's the logic of leaving out this crucial and vital issue?

The important consideration in beginning to teach children about sex at an early age is that we have the opportunity—the responsibility—to teach values and attitudes as well as facts. My mother's message about masturbation was very clear: It's normal, it's pleasant—*and it's private.* We have the opportunity in a direct give-and-take discussion with little kids to tell them about social customs and good human relationships. I remember the day I was visiting a friend and we discovered that her 5-year-old was in the garage with a neighbor's little boy, who was exploring her genitals. My friend said, "I know you both want to learn about your bodies, but you know, when grown-ups go to visit each other, they don't take off their clothes. That's something special and private, and is only done when a man and a woman love each other and are all grown up. For now, what we can do is go to the library and get some books and talk about boys and girls and babies."

The parental attitudes toward a child's sexuality can make an enormous difference to an adolescent girl who feels very unsure of herself and probably wants to postpone sexual encounters for a while but is needled and pressured by her boyfriend. If she is ignorant of the facts, she might not understand that she could get pregnant from one sexual experience. If her parents have viewed her growing up as frightening and dangerous and take the attitude that she might potentially be "a bad girl," she is likely to assume that it is her own "filthy sexual urges" that have created this situation and she has no right to say no. If, on the other hand, she is fully aware of the fact that when she is more mature her mother will see to it that she gets the necessary information on birth control and that her emerging sexual feelings are normal, she will be far better prepared not only for the entreaties of her peers but for any blandishments from older men, strangers, or relatives.

This brings me to the next way of protecting young people, and that is teaching them about emotional illness and mental aberrations at a very early age. When my daughter was only 3 or 4 years old and either an adult or a child we knew behaved in some strange or antisocial or self-destructive way, we simply said, "He has hurting feelings inside," or "She can't stop herself from doing what she's doing because of a special kind of sickness that is in her feelings." Very young children can understand this. They know darn well there are times when *they* lose control and behave strangely because of hurting feelings. There are hundreds of everyday examples we can use, such as, "Remember the night you had that terrible nightmare and you were so scared and you thought something bad was in your room? Well, that's one kind of hurting feeling." Or, "I'm very sorry I screamed at you and hit you—I'm having a very bad day. I'm tired and upset, and I have a lot of hurting feelings. It wasn't your fault, and I'm feeling better now." These are concrete lessons in mental health, and the reason they are so vital in connection with child-molesting is that more often than not such episodes involve relatives, friends, and neighbors. If a child has learned that we never make moral judgments of people who are emotionally disturbed—we just see to it that they get the help they need—it is far easier for him to report sexual advances without feeling like a monster.

A friend once told me of how devastated she was when she began to realize that the grandfather she adored not only seemed to be touching her in unusual and disconcerting ways but was having an erection. She was shocked, disgusted, deeply hurt—but most of all, she felt she could never tell anyone. "I was sure my grandpa was committing some sort of crime and that if I told anyone he'd be sent to prison. I had always loved him so much, I would rather have died than do such a thing to him."

If that grandchild had been taught to understand that nobody is good or bad but rather sick or well and that there is nothing a human being can feel or do that hasn't been felt and done by others, she might have been able to tell someone, knowing that nobody would want to hurt Grandpa.

If sexual deviation is presented as an illness, it takes a good deal of the potential poison out of the situation. A sick person is less frightening than an evil person. A sick person is someone who needs help, not punishment, so it's okay to tell. And someone you love and respect need not be lost to you.

There are, of course, situations of such pathology that neither child or parent can handle them. In some cases, both parents may actually be involved in the molesting of a child, one actively, the other by silent consent. In some really sick marriages a child can become the source of titillation and stimulation to the adults. In such situations one can only hope there will be some relative or teacher to whom a youngster can turn. We need to give children all the facts so that, if need be, they can feel free to come to us about "Uncle Joe doing funny things," or the baby-sitter who "makes me take a bath every time she comes and wants to play with my penis."

The degree of sexual molesting of children is something that we are just beginning to reveal to ourselves, especially the fact that it can strike very close to home (or in it) among people who seem normal in every other way. When he first began analyzing patients at the turn of the century, Sigmund Freud was so appalled by the stories his patients told him that he invented the theory of the "screen memory." When a patient began to describe sexual overtures or actual practices involving a parent, Freud assumed that because this seemed unthinkable to him, it must have been a sexual fantasy on the part of the child. Today's psychotherapists have no such illusions. The stories they hear have the ring of truth, and we now know that such activities are far more common than was previously thought.

Whenever a child reports such events, we need to listen quietly and with great sympathy and respect; we need to be reassuring and make it clear that it is not the child's fault or problem, that this is something adults have to deal with. It's also important to do some quiet checking; occasionally a child's fantasy life gets out of control. Many years ago when I was a child-welfare worker in a rural area, I was called into a case where a 9-year-old girl was accusing her adoptive father, a farmer, of coming into her room at night and "doing things to her." The farmer's wife listened quietly, but she felt certain the story wasn't true. The next night when her husband was snoring peacefully, she went into the little girl's room and put a pail of water at the door, then slept with the child. After three nights she and I met and talked. I discovered that the child had many symptoms of emotional disturbance and that before being adopted, and until the age of 5, she had probably seen a good deal of violence and may well have been molested by an alcoholic father. In a series of tests and interviews it became clear to me that this child was reliving old nightmares and that the farmer was not really going near her at all.

We should never assume that the story a child tells us is impossible, but if we have real doubts, we need to do some checking. If the story is a fantasy, then we need to get the necessary help to find out why this is happening and to make it clear to the child that he or she is not a liar and not bad but hurting in his or her feelings. When we use this mental health approach, it becomes far easier to teach precautions without terrorizing a child. If children were taught that sometimes a person who is really sick in his or her feelings can look normal and so they must never, ever, get into a car with *anyone* without telling a parent about it, chances are many attempts at sexual abuse could be thwarted. When a child says, "I have to go and tell my mother first," that is the end of the encounter.

When we warn children never to go anywhere with strangers and to report any strange behavior wherever it occurs, and whoever it involves, there is no reason for them to become unduly fearful or suspicious when we explain (quite truthfully) that most grown-ups are healthy, responsible people, but a very few adults can be very sick indeed, and it is because of those few that we have to be careful.

Once an episode is reported to a reliable and trusted adult, it ought to be made clear to a child that he or she is not responsible for whatever actions must be taken, that it is the grown-ups' business. In some cases a child may have to appear in court, but the process that leads to that eventuality is up to the adults. Children cannot be asked to carry the heavy and complicated burden of dealing with the problem.

Sooner or later most children will have some kind of experience with sexual deviation, the most common being the flasher—the "nice-looking old man in the raincoat." It is important that a child report such experiences for many reasons, but one of the most important is the need to be reassured and comforted, to be allowed to have the appropriate emotional reactions to a traumatic experience. When I finally reached home that day when I was 12, I dissolved into tears, swore that all men were filthy, dirty beasts, and that I would never, ever, have sex relations with anyone. After I'd calmed down a bit and there had been some discussion about having a little compassion for a sick person, my mother quietly commented, "You know, your *father* is a man!" I know that clarified the picture immediately, for exactly 10 years later I married a man very much like my father.

Part X

✳

SUMMERTIME

✳

A Time to Loaf

❋ "What I like doing best is nothing," Christopher Robin told Pooh. "It means just going along, listening to all the things you can't hear and not bothering."

Children haven't really changed since the 1920s, when A. A. Milne wrote *The House at Pooh Corner*. Christopher Robin could be the spokesman for thousands of today's children. When asked the other day how he'd like to spend the summer, a 5-year-old unconsciously echoed Christopher Robin. He said wistfully: "I'd just like to sit in the noonday sun and do nothing."

Every one of us, adult and child alike, needs some such moments. It seems safe to predict, however, on the basis of current statistics on vacation plans, that few of our more "privileged" children will have much time on their hands this summer. A great many children will be as pressured, hurried, and overorganized in summer as they were in winter. More and more camps are beginning to resemble schools. For the gifted, there are camps that specialize in every variety of intellectual pursuit from advanced science projects to composing symphonies. For the "underachievers," there are camps designed to set them straight with individual and group tutoring—and an hour here and there for a quick swim.

Camps are not the only summer programs bent on education and enriching. Stay-at-homes are also being given lessons in everything under the sun. And the affluent are taking their subteen children to Europe for the contemporary equivalent of last century's Grand Tour.

We do not dispute the fact that some fortunate children will have wonderful summers planned by their parents to permit them to indulge in that most precious commodity of childhood—child's play. We only wish that more children could enjoy this kind of summer.

If you ask children themselves—and we did—what they would like to do during the summer, it appears that many of the youngsters who will be provided with the most stimulation and excitement would prefer to be in their own backyards in a wading pool doing absolutely nothing about improving themselves. Not that they aren't inclined to argue with their parents' plans for them. One typical response began: "The first thing I'd like to do is listen to my parents' suggestions since they usually know what I want." And there were a large number of adult-oriented responses, such as: "I'd like to travel through Europe . . . go to a camp in Switzerland . . . study a foreign language . . . become a champion tennis player."

Many of the children we queried seemed adjusted to the summer culture of doing something "useful" every minute, but there were some poignant exceptions. Nursery schoolers said it this way: "I want to grow my own flower . . . fly a kite all by myself . . . play in the sand." Grade schoolers said: "I think I'll ride my bike down lonely roads . . . I want to go fishing, but I don't want to catch any fish . . . I'd like to stay in bed all summer long."

In a group of fifth and sixth graders asked to write compositions on "The Perfect Summer Vacation," a goodly number revealed that their dearest wish was to get away from it all, especially from compulsory activities. This is how some of them put it:

I'd like to take a real long hike alone lasting through the entire summer. At times I might take a boat out on the lake for a couple of days and catch a lot of fish. Then I would take my catch and sell them.

This way I would be able to feed myself and have fun at the same time. You would never believe that what I'm really doing this sum-

mer is going to camp with an hour-by-hour schedule. *That was the summer that was.*

My perfect summer vacation would be to live on a desert island for two months. I would like to have a little house with a door and a fireplace and a television set. The island would have palm trees and monkeys. All day I'd play with the monkeys.

The perfect vacation for me is to have a little boat in which I could go out on the sea whenever I got the urge. No one would be around to bother me.

I would go roaming through the woods with my dog without a care in the world. Nothing would disturb us till I returned to school in September.

To rest in quiet in a comfortable country house is a good summer vacation. I could forget my problems and just loaf around or read. . . . Then I would work in my garden growing vegetables and flowers so I could have a relaxing place to look at. I would lead a simple life.

This summer I intend to fix my bike up so it will be the fastest on Ridge Road. Then I am going to make a go-cart with a motor on the back of it. Summer is when you can do whatever you want.

I would like to be a beatnik and walk around with my bongo drums. I would learn the cool English of the beatniks and hang around with my friends.

A perfect summer is doing what you want to do without fighting for it. Think about it. All day not being bossed around by parents or relatives—lying on the couch, sipping lemonade. Freedom, that's the word.

It would be foolish and destructive to suggest that we encourage a summer vacuum—limitless time in which children would have no stimulation from their environment, no satisfaction in accomplishment. Nostalgia for a simpler world in which children could run freely through the woods and fields and find their own adventures doesn't help. The world we live in is crowded, complex; it presents us with hazards that demand greater supervision than ever over the activities of our children.

There can be no turning back, but within the challenges of the present, it must still be possible to find ways to let children have some of the necessary pleasures of childhood—the private explorations, the lazy dreaming, the simple joys of being at home in a natural world. Whether a child goes to camp or to a resort, is taken on a trip or stays at home, he can be given some free time—with no strings attached. Many parents are uneasy when a child seems to have nothing to do. They nag when a 12-year-old sits indoors reading on a fine day; they get fidgety when a 5-year-old spends the morning tossing pebbles at a target; they're inclined to think it sinful when a 10-year-old sprawls in front of the TV set all afternoon (chances are his mind is a million miles away and the programs are just a background for his daydreaming).

We need to be more concerned about the child who can't bear it when he has nothing to do. We need to retrain ourselves to recognize that often the world is pushing us and our children into activity for the sake of activity. It is not necessary to break the habits of years in one day. Our overorganized youngsters may react with "withdrawal symptoms" of anxiety, irritability, and discomfort if we suddenly insist that they spend time alone or leave them without their accustomed planned activities. They may need help and suggestions for activities for a while, but if they are provided with a relaxed environment and allowed to respond freely to play materials that encourage them to use their own ideas and imagination, they will eventually get the hang of it.

Some children are gregarious and outgoing. They need more play with others. Some are bursting with energy and enjoy physical exertion and competition. But all of them need some chance to "goof off." Fields must lie fallow for certain periods, and so must children. A plateau period in development will usually result in a richer development later on. The children who may seem to have accomplished the least during the summer are often the ones who are "rarin' to go" and ready for achievement when they return to school.

Sending a Child to Camp

❄ What I remember best about going away to camp as a child was that I was always terribly homesick—and I had a perfectly marvelous time! If this common ambivalence were made clear to children, I suspect there would be much less tension and anxiety —especially for parents.

When a child first begins to talk about going away to camp, parents may put up some resistance. It's a new idea and they need time to get used to it. But after a while they discover that the child's best friend is going, the camp is highly recommended, and the cost is well within their budget. Gradually parents begin to enjoy the idea. Mother thinks, "With Suzy at day camp and Bobby away for two whole months, *I* could have the best vacation I've had in twelve years!" Father thinks, "Imagine coming home to a quiet house, with plenty of time for a peaceful drink before dinner and —even better—a whole evening alone together!" Camp begins to sound better and better every day!

At first the child is wild with excitement—it's all he or she can talk about. But about two weeks before camp starts, it begins to dawn on him that camp means going to live with a bunch of strangers for a long time and that parents, pets, and perhaps siblings will be staying behind. Suddenly the youngster decides that maybe camp isn't such a good idea after all.

Mom and Dad feel guilty because they've begun to look forward to it. They either get angry ("This is a fine time to change your mind when we've already paid the first installment!") or their guilt causes them to panic. Are they pushing this child out of the nest too soon? Have they made him or her feel rejected and unloved? What in the world do they do now?

"I can't understand it," a parent usually says. "It was all her idea and she seemed so happy. Now she cries and says she doesn't want to go." Both parents and children need to understand that mixed feelings are perfectly normal. A child can be overjoyed by the prospect of fun and games at camp and still be terrified at the thought of leaving home. Parents have mixed feelings too. While the promise of extra peace and quiet is very appealing, camp is often the first long period of separation. It forces parents to notice that children are growing up and away—and that the parenting role is beginning to change.

Recognition of these feelings and the reasons for them can be helpful to both sides. One mother told me that she explained the meaning of "ambivalence" to her 9-year-old son. "I confessed I was feeling that way too," she said. "He seemed much relieved and decided that in spite of being a little scared, he really did want to go to camp."

It's also helpful to a child going to camp for the first time to know that he can always come home. A child's first weeks at camp are not a good time for parents to plan a trip to Europe, renovate the house, or sign up for the summer session at a local college. It is reassuring to the child to know that plans can be changed if necessary, that the decision to go to camp is *not* irrevocable. Parents might say, "Look, we want you to really give it a try. You might feel very homesick at first—lots of kids do—but you'll probably love it by the time the first week is over. If not, you can come home. It won't mean that you've failed, just that you're not quite ready for camp."

Many parents make the mistake of overreacting to the first signs of distress. When they hear a child crying over a long-distance phone, they feel guilty for having deserted their young. It's important to remember that a child is not necessarily miserable just because he or she sobs at the sound of a parent's voice. The loneliness felt at such moments often passes quickly. Ten minutes later the child is likely to be part of a singing, giggling group toasting marshmallows over the campfire.

The most important factor in helping a child have a good camp experience is to choose the right camp. That requires knowledge of your own child as well as of the facilities, activities, and philosophy of various camps. You certainly don't want to send a shy child to a highly competitive camp or a bouncy, active child to one that specializes in weaving and nature study. Parents should also learn the size of the camp, the age range of the campers, and how structured the program is. Some children like to have every minute planned for them, while others need time to daydream, watch the birds, and just be alone. All anxieties—your own as well as your child's—should be candidly discussed in advance. You have a right to expect the camp staff to be sympathetic and willing to deal openly with any problems that may arise.

Most parents have a good idea of what's right for their child and manage to choose a suitable camp. The problems arise when the child makes up his or her mind before parents are even consulted. The chosen camp is often one that a best friend has gone to and adores. It's important to point out to children—especially those in grade school—that friendships blow hot and cold very quickly. Their best friend in March or April may turn out to be their worst enemy in July. Choosing a camp *only* because a friend goes to it is very unwise; there must be other positive considerations as well.

Recent research in child development reveals that children seem to be born with their own specific ways of coping with new situations. Some react the same way at 8 or 12 as they did as infants, no matter how different their environments may be. For example, a baby who screams bloody murder when someone shakes the examining table grows up to be a child who cries for an hour when left with the first baby-sitter, wails and hangs on to mother the first week of school, and suffers terrible homesickness the first week of camp. Such a child is not necessarily disturbed. After crying as if his heart would break, he ends up having a lovely time with the baby-sitter; after the first two weeks in school, she's as well adjusted as anyone else in the class.

If your child copes with every new situation in this dramatic, nerve-wracking way, it is appropriate to remind him of this fact as camp approaches. One father put it very directly to his 10-year-old. "Listen, George," he said, "you know perfectly well that you approach every new experience as if it were going to kill you! You've been doing that since you were a baby. In all likelihood, you'll hate camp the first week and plead to come home—and then you'll have the best time of your life. We should all be used to this by now!" It is usually reassuring to a child to know that his parents understand him that well.

Other children react to new situations in other ways. At one extreme are the shrinking violets who takes two weeks to talk to anyone; at the other are the bossy children who meet every new situation (and conquer their anxiety) by taking over and telling everyone what to do. If such characteristics have shown up at each new crossroad in the past, they will surely be there when camp starts.

Another type is the delayed reactor, the child who appears to be getting along perfectly for several weeks and then comes apart at the seams. This is the child who cried after his parents came home, not when the baby-sitter arrived. Such a youngster seems to be taking to camp better than all the others but falls apart later when everything is just dandy. This method of coping with new experiences is not as illogical as it may sound; the child merely controls all his anxiety until things are going so well that he feels safe to let it out! When parents are aware of their children's coping styles and talk to them about what is likely to happen at camp, adjustment usually proceeds a lot more smoothly.

Sometimes a child's adjustment to being separated from the family is hindered by parents who aren't ready for the experience. One camp director told me about a mother who'd suffered so much separation anxiety herself—she'd been sent away to camp from the age of 4 and to boarding schools from age 7—she could not believe that a healthy, happy child reaches a point of truly *wanting* to leave the family nest. "Her daughter was a little homesick," he said, "but she would surely have overcome it if her mother hadn't called every day and written letters about how lonely it was at home. Poor Jill had to feel miserable and want to go home for her mother's sake!" This is an unusual example, but many parents do give a child the unconscious message, "You'll hurt my feelings if you can get along without me."

It's always a good idea for parents to examine their own feelings ahead of time and perhaps even discuss them with the child. "When I was ten years old," one mother told her daughter, "my parents sent me to a camp I hated, and they made me stick it out. I've always felt nervous and uncomfortable about sleep-away camps because of that. I'm confident that the camp you're going to is a good one—not at all like mine. I know you're ready and eager to go, but I still get butterflies in my stomach, as if *I* were going instead of you." Such a statement can often clear the air.

"Hidden agendas" can also influence a child's readiness for camp. For example, a father, disappointed that his son is not interested in competitive sports, hopes camp will solve that problem and "make a man" of him. Some parents expect camp to change a basically shy child into a social butterfly. Others hope the camp will be able to remake an unhappy and rebellious child. Camp is not the place to which a family should turn to solve serious emotional problems; such goals are unrealistic and unfair to the camp. The only suitable goals are for a child to have a good time, to become more independent and sure of himself, and to enjoy developing new skills. Camp certainly can be a place for exploring new interests and gaining in self-confidence, as in any new experience. But traditional camp programs are not designed to handle serious emotional problems.

Some camps are specifically designed to deal with problems, of course. Some cater to campers with physical disabilities, others help children deal with learning problems, and still others are for children who need to lose weight. These camps can be very helpful, but only if the child *wants* this help. One 12-year-old who was thirty-five pounds overweight pleaded to go to a special weight-loss camp. As he put it, "It will be much easier for me to diet in a place where nobody knows me. I'll also be much less self-conscious if all the other kids have the same problem." In this case, the parents were wise to allow their son to go to the special camp.

Karen's parents, on the other hand, decided to send her to a camp that offered tutoring in arithmetic—much against Karen's wishes. She was having a miserable enough time in school; more pressures at camp could only add to her anxieties and feelings of failure. It is important for parents to realize that sometimes the best way to handle a problem is to do nothing at all. As a rule, I believe in allowing children to escape completely from school problems during the summer months. This is *not* a waste of time. Children need to let go, to relax, to have different life-enhancing experiences without all the pressures they have to deal with the rest of the year.

Age and maturity are important factors to consider in deciding when to send a child to camp. I don't think many children under the age of 7 or 8 are ready to be away from home for long periods. The younger the child, the smaller the camp ought to be. For a young child or a first camp experience, two weeks to one month is usually better than eight weeks. The number of children per counselor is also important for young children who need surrogate parents more than buddies. When my own daughter was young, we sent her to a camp where every child was given a farm animal to take care of—a baby lamb, a duck, a young rabbit, or the like. Feeling needed by something even more vulnerable than she was a help during the first weeks. Older children need less tender loving care, but they still need some. It takes a good deal of thought and careful exploration to find the camp that will best suit an individual child, but it is well worth the research.

Perhaps the most important factor in a child's readiness for camp is how he feels about himself and how he thinks his family feels about him. Children who feel unlovable and unworthy don't enjoy being sent away. Children who are worried because their parents have been fighting and talking of divorce are not enthusiastic about leaving home either. At first they may think it will be a great relief to get away from family problems, but after a while the anxiety comes back full force. It is far better to talk about family problems before camp is even considered. "Grandma is very sick and Mother needs time to take care of her," or "Mom and Dad are upset and need time alone to work out some problems" or

"Mom is very weak from the operation and needs to rest all summer." Children can deal with such worries if they know what they are. To be left with free-floating anxiety, far away from home, puts an impossible burden on both the child and the camp.

During my own first two weeks at camp, I wrote my parents every day that I would die of homesickness. Looking back, I don't know why they put up with me. By the third week I had the lead in the play, had passed four swimming tests, and had learned to paddle a canoe. I remain eternally grateful for the skills I learned and for the reverence for nature that began during those years. I cried when my parents arrived on visitors' day, and I cried when they left. By the end of the summer, I cried for two days saying good-bye to my bunkmates and counselors. I guess my parents knew that was just my style. I was ready to go to camp all right; I just had to do it in my own histrionic way. All children and parents get ready for such experiences in their own ways. Maybe readiness is really the capacity to let it all happen the way it comes naturally.

Visitors' Weekend at Summer Camp

❋ The trouble with visiting our children at sleep-away camps is that we feel so guilty about being glad they are there that we tend to overdo the parent bit.

There's our Tom or Suzy, winning the relay race or the bubble gum contest, finding a new best friend every third day, adoring not washing their ears all summer, and having a wild crush on the dramatics counselor—and suddenly we blow it all with our verboten care packages, our worried comments about it really being much too cold for swimming—these counselors are just too young to be responsible—and our sighing about how empty the house is. By the time the weekend visit comes to an end, the camp director wonders how much of a loss he'll take, selling this damned camp in mid-summer, and the child you leave behind is homesick and weeping and has a terrible upset stomach as well.

American parents offer their children more privileges and pleasures than any other parents in the world. At first it may seem illogical that they are also the guiltiest parents. But we have been well trained at self-flagellation. We think to ourselves, "Perhaps I'm giving my child too many *things* and not enough love; perhaps sending him to camp is not to widen his horizons but rather expresses my deep, unconscious feelings of rejection." We *talk* a good line about the joys of comradeship around the campfire and the lifetime assets of knowing how to play tennis and swim well.

But deep-down in our hearts, we know we are also thinking about a return to those preparental candlelit dinners. And to be absolutely candid about it, we are also experiencing that fantasy about how the candlelight might lead to other things that are so much better done without three kids sleeping (?) down the hall.

You have waited fifteen years, until your youngest was 9, to spend two months alone in this house; a chance to listen to music and have a drink on the terrace, and talk of the day's events without a single interruption—no fights, no spilled milk, no wounded feelings, no nagging for a second bedtime story, not a yell, not even a kick in the shins under the table. Ah, the luxury of being able to walk around the house with no clothes on—and the sheer heaven of being able to have a fight and scream and yell at each other without worrying about traumatizing the children. You feel in your Puritan heart that no one could have such pleasures without having to pay a price for them, so in order to bear our happiness, we make ourselves (and our children) miserable on visiting weekends.

There is that poignant first hug, that whispered, "My arms have felt so empty." There is the fervent report on how we feel, that terrible lump in our throat when we pass the empty bedroom. We bring along a bacchanalian feast—no items allowed unless guaranteed to increase tooth decay and cause vomiting within the next twenty-four hours (the camp director's letter begged and beseeched, but how could our child possibly live for eight whole weeks without his favorite double chocolate cake or a chopped chicken liver sandwich?).

We arrive at camp two hours before the instructions say we may set foot on the grounds. We curse and broil in the noonday sun, miserable in our city clothes. The instructions also said wear blue jeans or slacks, but there are several Very Important People who have children at this camp and we must try to make a good impression—you just never know. We manage to work ourselves up into a wild, raging anxiety about whether our child feels rejected or unloved. Tears leak from our eyes as she loses at archery, does an Indian war dance, shows us how she's learned to canter, or presents us proudly with a silver ring she's made for us. We keep hugging and kissing and holding on for dear life, through animal feeding time, boating, and weaving—and finally we get through to her. By seeming to be lonely and miserable, by worrying so much, our child begins to feel bad about not feeling bad enough. How could she be so mean as not to be homesick? She begins to feel the faint stirrings of memory; she remembers her room and her Teddy bear —and how Mommy fed her chicken soup when she had the mumps and felt so awful. Her heart begins to flutter and her legs get all trembly. Her nose begins to run, and by the time she's sobbing and clinging to us, it's two hours past visiting time, and we cannot bear to leave. *What kind of a rotten camp is this, anyway?*

Some children are sent to camp too soon, and some for the wrong reasons. If there is real trouble, of course, we've got to take a look at it. But most children like camp if we have chosen wisely, and the idea of parents having a chance to renew an old and maybe frayed romance is wonderful! In the long run, it is surely good for children to come home to parents with secret, bedroomy eyes, cherishing enough fun-with-our-summer-affair to last them through the rigors of another winter of family togetherness. For most children, living in a child-centered world with children-loving people is a good adventure. And camp is just another place where you learn the truth about life—that there is much that is fun and joyful and much that is tedious or frustrating, and even sometimes quite painful. Separation is a reality of growing up, and camp can be one of the most painless ways of learning about it.

Leave the ten-pound box of Barton's Pecan Patties at home; leave the seven-layer cake, the carton of sardines, the six-pack of Cokes. Leave the weepy, lonely feelings there, too. And most of all, leave the guilt behind. You've a right to like being without children for a while. What you can bring to your child in camp is interest, enthusiasm for what he's learning and doing, pleasure in his triumphs, compassion for his hardships, and a nice, healthy enjoyment of his company for a few hours before you sneak back to your sinful love nest in the city or suburb. Camping is almost as good for kids as having parents who want and need to be alone together.

Part XI

*

CONCLUSIONS

*

Not Guilty!
The Important Difference Between Guilt and Regret

❉ The divorced and working mother of two teenage daughters told me how anxious and guilty she felt when it was necessary to send one of her children to the doctor alone, or when she had to leave a child home alone with a bad cold. "Since my job involves running large corporate conferences, there are times when I simply cannot leave work—unless, of course, some major disaster occurred —and I seemed to be drowning in guilt most of the time. I'd come home, and instead of sitting down and playing a game, or making something special for dinner, I'd tell my kids what a terrible mother I was. One day Angie [14 years old] looked at me very solemnly and said, 'Mother, your guilt is a great bore; we don't need it. We know you are concerned about us, and that's enough.'"

Angie was a very smart child. Guilt is one of the most useless of all human emotions because it has a paralyzing effect on us. We feel so guilty, so unworthy—so *hopeless*—that we become unable to take the actions we need to take in order to change whatever it is we're feeling so guilty about. I belong to the original, exotically neurotic generation of guilty parents of the 1940s and '50s. There have been few excesses since to match ours. This came about because we were the first generation to be told that environment was much more important than heredity, and if our children had certain unique and mystifying peculiarities, it was because we were doing something wrong. When our children were happy and successful, we assumed it was just good luck. When they were impossible, difficult, unhappy, and failing, we knew absolutely it was because of our imperfections as parents.

We were struggling under the oversimplifications of the first discoveries of psychology, long since modified by wiser heads and further research. For example, I felt guilty because my child had colic—obviously a psychosomatic reaction to poor mothering. I recently read a research report that proves that while colic may make mothers crazy, mothers don't give babies colic. In a study on prenatal and postnatal adaptation, the Group Health Association in Washington, D.C., and the National Institutes of Health found no demonstrable psychological differences between the mothers of colicky and noncolicky babies.

At the University of Rochester, additional research suggests that children who are "born difficult" can transform a normal parent into an emotional mess! Another study, in which an attempt was made to try to figure out why some children are invulnerable to stress and others crack, indicated that parental handling is only one part of the complexity and mystery of the nature/nurture forces involved. And finally, I have just finished reading another report of the National Institutes of Health that explores the range of "normal behavior" in growing children. I felt guilty when my child lied or stole or played with matches, smoked, failed in school, played hooky, had nightmares, or was selfish. Now it is being proclaimed that there is almost nothing that happens to a growing child that cannot be judged as within the normal parameters of "just growing up." I have the feeling that I spent a great deal of time feeling guilty unnecessarily, and my 32-year-old daughter is only too eager to assure me that this never did her any good!

The conclusion I have come to over the years is that guilt is not useful in *any* situation but *regret* is one of the most essential of all human attributes.

I have discovered, in many conversations with my now-grown daughter, that she was often least traumatized by the things *I* felt most guilty about, such as being impatient or unreasonable, and most traumatized by the things about which I felt most pleased and proud. When she was 2 years old, we bought a suburban home near a well-known private school in order to provide the richest resources for our child's healthy growth. It took us about twenty years to pay back my father's loan; we both worked desperately hard for these luxuries; my husband despised commuting into the city every day for twelve years. My daughter now tells us that she hated the school and the neighborhood! I regret now that we didn't have enough sense to recognize that our child would be happy if we were happy too, and that our grim determination to satisfy her needs and ignore our own poisoned the whole experience.

As I look back now, over more than three decades as a family counselor, it seems ever clearer to me that guilt was and still is a dangerous luxury. If you hit a child in a moment of anger and are then overcome by inordinate guilt, you simply fall apart; you become depressed, remote, self-punishing. You may fall down the cellar stairs—or you may even yell harder and louder and more unfairly as a way of disguising those painful guilt feelings.

If you hit a child in a moment of anger and immediately regret it, you can do something about it. Regret leads to saying, "Hey, I'm sorry. That was a mean and unnecessary way of showing how angry I was. Let's sit down and talk about why you have to let me know when you're visiting a friend's house and I don't know where you are."

Most of the serious psychological damage that occurs to human beings occurs because our parents had a large residue of guilt from their childhood ("you're a bad boy," "you're a naughty girl") and passed that along to us; it is natural for us to pass this on to our children. Generation after generation, we continue to raise children who feel inordinate guilt about the most normal of childlike behavior, and what they discover as adults—perhaps most frequently when they may get to a therapist's office—is that their chronic headaches, their inability to adjust to marriage, their job problems, their depressions, all stem from guilt feelings they had as children.

When I felt guilty for my shortcomings as a child, what I was telling myself was that there were ways in which I was a great disappointment to the people I loved. That is an awful burden and leads to feelings of hopelessness and self-hatred. I felt guilty long before I became a parent. I felt guilty whenever I failed to measure up to my parents' expectations. I felt guilty when I failed a test in school (I wasn't living up to my teachers' expectations). When I worked twice as hard as the child sitting next to me in arithmetic class, but she got the higher mark, I felt guilty for being stupid. If I tripped more often than I kicked in a hockey game, I felt guilty for being so uncoordinated. This practice led to perfect when I became a wife and mother; if my husband was depressed about his work, I felt guilty; when my daughter had a nightmare, I felt guilty. The more guilty I felt, the less constructive I became in my behavior. If it was my fault that my husband's work wasn't going well, I felt far too upset to be sympathetic; if it was my fault that my daughter had a nightmare, I felt too awash in guilt to pay attention to her need for reassurance. Since I was such a rotten person, it was hopeless to try to do better.

Feeling guilty as a child is the natural consequence of being young and inexperienced. We simply did not have enough information to know that it is normal to be childish when one is a child —to make mistakes, to be imperfect because one is human. We assumed, through lack of mature brain synapses and limited life experiences, that everything bad that happened was our fault.

I would like to suggest a *total moratorium* on guilt! This is not to suggest irresponsibility or lack of concern or compassion in human relations. Quite the opposite. Guilt makes us feel unworthy, useless, no good. How can such a person improve or make amends? When we regret something we have done, we are admitting failure, *but we are not conceding that we are worthless.* Regret implies a capacity to learn from one's mistakes and to make restitution. As my dialogues with my daughter continue, and I find things I now regret having done or not having understood, my reaction is to be grateful that I have grown so much, that I am so much wiser now —and that, regretting past mistakes, I now have so many opportunities *to do things differently.*

There are excellent and exciting things happening these days in the area of rehabilitation of such crippled and damaged people as child abusers, alcoholics, delinquents, and victims of drug abuse. In all such situations rehabilitation begins with restoring feelings of self-worth. For example, punishing a parent who hurts a child never helps to solve the problem; it only reinforces underlying feelings of self-hatred and guilt. Giving loving attention—nurturance—to the parent is what starts him or her down the road to recovery and more constructive behavior. When such a parent feels loved, accepted, and respected as a struggling human being in great pain, he or she begins to have the strength and the courage to regret past actions and to move forward to a different kind of behavior.

Whether others help us to find this more constructive avenue to better human relations or we do it alone, the fundamental issue is, "I am not intrinsically a bad person; I can change because there is good in me."

A friend of mine was suffering terribly over the death of her mother. Her grief was of course completely understandable, but the mourning period was very prolonged and she seemed unable to move on with her own life. Every time we met, she told me again about the circumstances of her mother's death. Her mother was in a small hospital several hundred miles from where her three children lived. She had a sudden stroke and the doctors said she could not be moved. The daughter, however, felt that her mother was not getting the best possible care and wanted to move her to a well-known rehabilitation center in New York, but the doctors told her that the trip might kill her mother, so my friend postponed the decision about making the move. When her mother died, she felt terribly guilty. "If I had gotten a special ambulance and moved Mom to New York, she might not have died," she wept.

Most of us have a strong tendency to want to play God; it is part of our underlying feelings of guilt because we are not perfect or all-knowing. There is no way to know whether her mother would have survived the trip. In trying to help Barbara experience her grief but begin to move back into the world of the living again, I said, "It is appropriate to regret that you did not have the powers of foresight to predict what might have been the better way, but you are only human, and whether you could have saved your mother or not, feeling guilty now won't bring her back to life. Take your regret and learn to use it for good. Volunteer to work in a hospital with stroke victims, help to save others." Guilt was immobilizing a good and decent person who needed to use her regret as a springboard to useful new action.

An older woman was reminiscing with me about her marriage of forty-one years. "I think I learned the most," she told me, "when I finally understood what Matthew meant when, after a very brief affair, he told me that he didn't feel guilty, but he regretted hurting me. At first that made me so angry I wanted a divorce; later I learned that regret was a positive force for helping us to find out what had happened between us and to begin to deal with mutual problems. Guilt would probably have destroyed both of us. If I had forced him to feel guilty, he would have ended up hating me."

Regret allows for the process of restitution. It makes us capable of taking action. We are not bad people, we just don't know everything. But we can learn from our mistakes and go on. Restitution is a far more useful social resource than punishment. In dealing with juvenile delinquency, for example, some judges are now experimenting with a new approach. Instead of sending a young person to prison, which merely reinforces feelings of self-hatred and hopelessness, the court finds jobs for them and requires them to pay back the money they have stolen. The pride in restitution is a way back to feeling good about themselves, and therefore capable of functioning in more positive ways. One might say that regret is a kind of healthy and realistic form of guilt. Unlike neurotic guilt, regret does not allow you to escape into passivity but makes you feel capable of changing.

Many years ago in a child-study discussion group, a mother commented, "I feel so guilty, I just can't think or do anything!" At the time I was a young mother myself and I knew exactly how she felt, so I just sympathized with her guilt feelings. I was not yet wise enough to say what I would say now: "If guilt keeps you from thinking or acting, then it isn't going to help you learn from your mistakes and grow. How about regretting what you did, forgiving yourself for your human frailty, and deciding what you would like to do about the situation?" I don't feel guilty because I was not as helpful as I wish I'd been to that mother at the time we met. I regret that it took me so long to learn how useless guilt can be. I hope I'm making amends for it now!

The Family Is Not Dead

❈ If one is not exceedingly careful, one is likely to get the impression that the family, as a human institution, is suffering from a terminal illness. It is difficult to open a book or magazine or turn on the television set without being assured by any number of prestigious experts that we have become a race of hedonists—selfish, self-centered, undisciplined, unable to deal with the slightest frustration—and certainly too immature for marriage and parenthood.

My response to that is a deleted expletive! What I see happening is that the family is *changing*, which is entirely different from *dying*. In a time of enormous, rapid social change, the family as a social institution is doing exactly what it has to do—finding ways of adapting to new conditions, new ideas, new modes of thinking and being.

A lot of people are living together instead of getting married. Some people are living together for a long time before getting married. And while all this is going on, even more people are getting divorces. What I think is happening *less*—is really on the decline—is miserable people living together in unhappy, destructive marriages. I think all these things are happening for a very good reason. We don't need each other for mere physical survival anymore, so we are trying very hard to restructure our relationships to each other so that we can be together for love only—and that is the hardest task human beings have ever set for themselves. It's so beautiful and so courageous that I could cry. In fact, I frequently do.

I don't deny for one moment that there are still great pain and sorrow in many relationships. Just as many unmarried couples as married ones end up hurting each other. Living together first is no guarantee of marital bliss, and you may be sure that I know the initial anguish of children who must live through a divorce. As for their parents, I am infuriated by the notion that it is weakness and irresponsibility that leads to many separations and divorces. On the contrary, it seems to me that in the majority of cases, divorce has come to represent the maturity and courage to face an agonizing period of self-examination, upheaval, and ultimate growth. Not always, of course; when young people marry impulsively, they are likely to divorce impulsively as well. But when people with children divorce, I think we can assume that at least one of the partners is well aware of the trauma to be endured and conquered. The point is that people always did and still do bring their unique strengths and weaknesses into any living situation, but the presence of unmarried couples and single parents is no reason to throw in the towel and decide that the human race has come to a bad end. Our expectations are higher than they have ever been; we don't want to live with anyone unless there is love—not some silly idea of romantic love but the kind of love on which people can grow, the kind that nourishes the soul; the kind of loving in which people want more for each other than for themselves and want most of all to enhance their own lives by helping someone else to become all he or she can be.

If you want to be reassured about family life, just spend a day or two in any airport and watch the arrivals and departures. The grandmas who look as if they are going to burst a blood vessel in anticipation of the hugs and kisses on the other side of that gate; the unspeakably poignant, private look between a man and a woman finding each other in the crowd; the exchange of a shy, secret look between a husband and wife while the kids climb all over a returning daddy. It's all still there—sometimes even in traditional forms, but what is important to remember is that it is all still there in *untraditional* forms as well: the single parents in San Francisco who have banded together informally so that all the children in the neighborhood have at least half a dozen surrogate parents; the church in Oregon that organized a foster grandparents' plan so that young families living far away from blood relatives could adopt grandparents for Thanksgiving and Christmas, for baby-sitting, for mutual loving. There is a new informality in every neighborhood, on every job, which helps the mobile families of today who must move so often to feel at home quickly, to help each other. A father once told me, "We have had to move ten times in the past sixteen years. Dennis grew up thinking that he had aunts and uncles in every city we moved to, because wherever we went, people were there to help—quickly, easily, comfortably."

I think I began to learn that the family was merely changing, not dying, when a grandmother in her late seventies, suffering from a heart condition, walked up five flights of an apartment building (very, very slowly) to visit her 20-year-old granddaughter who was living with a young man. The grandmother loved them both, and while this new life-style scared her and made her uncomfortable, love transcended change. She came for dinner, panting for breath, admiring the apartment and the meal, bringing the gift of an electric coffeepot. Fifty years ago, she could not have *imagined* tolerating, much less understanding, such an arrangement. But she loved and was loved, and that was all that mattered. I know such things happen; that grandma was my mother visiting my daughter. Love goes on. Sitting in the park the other day I saw a very old man and a very old woman holding hands. People are going to go on holding hands. I'm glad, because it is the most civilized of all human gestures.

The Importance of Finishing Unfinished Business

❋ A 55-year-old man stood on a dock in New York harbor weeping quietly as he watched a Russian freighter, the *Odessa*, making its way out to sea. He later told me, "That day I had some business to take care of nearby, and I noticed the name on the side of the boat. When I saw the name, the first thing I thought of was that was where my father had come from when he was a little boy. All of a sudden I started to cry—I had a feeling of such profound sadness. As I watched the boat going down the river, I felt as if I was saying good-bye to my father maybe for the first and last time."

John's father died when he was 5 years old. He was sent to an aunt's house for two weeks, was never given any explanation for his father's death, and never saw his mother cry. After his two-week banishment, life went on as though nothing had happened. In the course of his adult life, John realized what a traumatic experience his father's death had been, but there was always a sense of inner frustration and stress because he had never mourned, and it always seemed too late. He told me, "It was as if that word *Odessa* kicked something off inside of me; that ship slowly moving away seemed like a symbolic good-bye—and all the unshed tears of a lifetime welled up in me."

One of the most dramatic insights to emerge from this century of research in psychology is that unfinished emotional business never goes away. It just gets buried and may influence our behavior for the rest of our lives unless we learn to deal with it, unless we find some meaningful and satisfying way to come to terms with it.

Grace was puzzled by her animosity toward her younger sister; Jenny was really a loving, happy person, but as far back as Grace could remember, she had always felt impatient, angry, and ready for a fight when she was with her sister. Grace was fifteen months older than Jenny. Soon after Jenny was born it was discovered that she had a serious intestinal blockage, and during the first year or two of her life she had to have a series of operations. Grace told me, "Now, looking back, from an adult's point of view, I can see that I must have been put on the back burner when Jenny was born. She needed constant attention. I guess my babyhood was over very abruptly, and I suppose I was pretty unhappy."

Three years ago, at the age of 40, Grace had to have a serious operation. Both her mother and her sister came to take care of her during her recuperation. Grace told me, "It was so *weird!* I never expected such attention—it was heaven! I just lay there and let them fuss over me. It suddenly occurred to me that even though I was still weak and in pain, I had never been so happy and I had never loved Jenny so much before. After they'd both gone home, I had this funny feeling that some debt had been paid to me—all my resentment against Jenny seemed to have evaporated. Is it possible that one episode like that can make up for something that happened forty years ago?"

It not only is possible but seems to happen more often than we know, perhaps not in such dramatic and isolated episodes as I have just described but in many of the events of our lives. A man marries a motherly woman to get the attention and affection he missed as a young child; a woman becomes a nursery school teacher to give other children the attention and affection she may have missed; a father glows over a son's athletic prowess, hardly conscious of the pain he once felt himself when the kids on the team called him "Fatso." Each of us has had painful experiences in the course of growing up, and it is a natural and instinctive impulse to either undo or redo what has made us suffer.

The problem is that some "unfinished business" is so serious that unless we learn to deal with it directly it may haunt us and make us behave in ways that disturb us for far too long a time. Rachel was the oldest of seven children. All she can remember about her childhood is "slave labor." She told me, "I was always dressing somebody, giving somebody a bath, feeding somebody, finding somebody's socks, helping somebody with homework. I didn't really have any childhood at all. You would think that such an experience would have made me a very responsible person, but it had exactly the opposite effect. By the time I was twenty-five, I couldn't deal with anything; I was anxious and depressed all the time. I didn't want to go to work; I didn't want to get married or have children—I just retreated from life until finally I had a complete breakdown. I spent two years in a hospital where the doctors encouraged me to act childishly! *I didn't know how to be a child!* But after a while, I began having temper tantrums and insisted on a light on in my room all night; I refused to eat things I didn't like and made a mess of my room. That lasted for about a year, then gradually I became bored with it and told my doctor I wanted to begin to talk about getting out of there. It was a slow process, but actually, two years to make up for a whole childhood isn't really such a long time."

There is a dialogue in *The Chalk Garden*, a play by Enid Bagnold, in which a middle-aged mother tries to understand why her son had gone to see a psychiatrist. She comments, "When I was young we let sleeping dogs lie." Her son answers, "But sometimes those dogs bark in the night and wake up your children." There are two ways in which an understanding of unfinished emotional business can be helpful to us. First of all, in our lives as adults we can be on the alert for behavior in ourselves that seems irrational, or personality characteristics that bother us. If we are really uncomfortable, if our feelings or behavior bother us enough, we may want to try to explore it with a psychotherapist. Or we may want to do some personal reflecting on what we remember or what others can tell us about our early life experiences. What we seem to have figured out about the human psyche is that a first step in understanding ourselves better probably has to do with insight and information, but that is never enough; we have to take the next step and take care of old business. If Jane realizes that an overly compulsive mother is probably partly responsible for her being a slob, she probably can't do much about this tendency until she allows herself to give in to it for a little while in an appropriate way. If she feels, "My mother was right to insist upon my being so neat all the time, and I was just a rotten kid," chances are Jane will continue to throw her clothes on the floor and never clean her closets and leave the dishes in the sink. If, instead, she says to herself, "All that fussing drove me nearly crazy when I was a child and needed a chance to play rough and get dirty and be messy. I'm going to give myself a gift; I'm going to spend my vacation camping out in the woods and wear the same dirty jeans for two weeks, and use paper plates and never curl my hair or manicure my nails!" she may find the realistic chores of daily living less objectionable.

The second way in which an awareness of the importance of unfinished business can be helpful is in the raising of children. There is not the slightest doubt in my mind that within a broad spectrum of individual variation, there is a normal and necessary developmental sequence in growing up, and if we push children to move too quickly from one sequence to another, we end up with a whole lot of unfinished business. For example, in my generation, babies were usually toilet trained by the age of 6 months, with great emphasis on regular bowel movements every day at the same time of day. When I went to camp at the age of 8, we got a gold star every day after we'd gone to the bathroom; if we didn't, we got castor oil. As a result of being trained too early, with too much fuss about the whole subject, a great many people now in their fifties, sixties, and seventies are entirely too preoccupied with the workings of the lower colon; or have spent too much of their lives worrying about being too clean; or have been obsessed with unimportant details; or have been compulsive collectors of things they don't need. My daughter's generation (toilet trained by Spockian good sense when they were ready) is far less focused on such aspects of life. However, they have a different peculiarity—a great many of them would rather die than read a book. When *they* were young we gave up demanding early toilet training; by then we were into the nonsense of trying to develop their brains faster than nature had in mind. We were talking and writing about teaching 2-year-olds to read, and *Sesame Street* was designed to accelerate pre-school learning of numbers and letters. The unfinished business of today's young people is the necessary time to experience life without being pushed into premature academic performance. Most of them go to the bathroom without giving it a second thought; but many of them are exceedingly resistant to intellectual pursuits.

What I am suggesting is that a basic ingredient for responsible, sensitive parenting is the awareness that unfinished business never goes away (without special help) and that it is far better to allow a child to grow at his or her own rate, taking one step at a time, without any sense of pressure to perform at some higher or later level of maturation. In addition, we need to understand that every life experience has a profound and significant effect on a child's life and that when such events as divorce, death, or illness occur, it is no kindness to a child to exclude him or her from the grief and anxiety a family is encountering. If a child is not allowed to experience those painful feelings that are appropriate to the situation, the feelings just get buried and "bark in the night."

Terry called me early one Saturday morning. She said, "I really need you. Could you come here?" Terry and I have known each other since first grade. Ours is one of those rare and precious lifelong friendships, and because I know she respects my time and my work, I knew that such a request must be very important. I dressed and went to her apartment. When I arrived she was in tears.

That morning *The New York Times* had had an article ("Infant Death and Parental Grief," by Margot Slade, Sept. 13, 1980) reporting on a new field of research having to do with the psychological stresses on parents who lose a baby either through a miscarriage quite late in a pregnancy or shortly after birth. The theme of the article was that the medical profession (and just about everyone else) had greatly underestimated the kind of traumatic experience such a loss can be, and the enormous importance of allowing parents to experience their grief and mourning as fully and completely as after the death of any loved one.

Twenty-eight years ago, Terry and her husband had had such an experience. A baby son was born prematurely, could not breathe properly, and died within two days. Terry and her husband, Marc, had two older children at the time and the reaction of most people (as well as Terry's and Marc's) was that it was too bad this had happened, but after all, they had two healthy children and Terry could certainly become pregnant again. Because the baby lived such a short time, there was no funeral service; the event was minimized in every way. The baby had been named John, and Terry and Marc saw him from a distance in an incubator, but there were never any pictures of the baby and everyone tried to go on as if nothing of any great importance had happened.

The *New York Times* article described some of the reactions and feelings that were now coming under scrutiny. For many parents the lack of a genuine opportunity to mourn a real loss had left a residue of serious stress over a long period of time. The abrupt loss of a baby under such circumstances often left mothers feeling as if they had lost part of their own bodies—as if an arm or a leg had been amputated.

Shortly after John's death, Terry began having migraine headaches. Despite trying many kinds of treatment, the headaches continued to occur for many years. About ten years ago she decided to see a psychiatrist who helped her to recognize that she was suffering from the unfinished business of mourning the death of her baby; she had succeeded far too well in handling that episode in her life "sensibly." She had gone on with the business of living as if nothing of much importance had happened to her. After the therapy the headaches came less frequently, but still recurred once in a while.

On that Saturday morning, as Terry and I cried together, and talked about the new research that indicated how important it was to grieve for the loss of a child one hasn't even had a chance to know or touch or love, Terry said, "Maybe all these tears, twenty-eight years later, will help the headaches go away altogether."

Terry and Marc live in a house with a lovely backyard. I suggested that next spring my husband and I, Terry and Marc, plant a flowering bush or tree in their garden and have a little memorial service for that baby who died twenty-eight years ago. Perhaps we could finally bring closure to that unfinished business of grief and mourning; take part in the necessary shared ritual that will express our love and our pain—and finally, our acceptance of what we cannot change.

The important thing to remember about unfinished business is that it is never too late to try to finish it.

The Real Mother's Day

❋ My daughter, now 34, knows that were she to acknowledge
Mother's Day in any way, around me, she'd be in a lot of trouble.
I have always hated the designation of a day devoted to honoring
mothers. It seemed to me that many of the mothers who made the
most fuss about it enjoyed parenthood the least and were desperately searching for some compensation—too late and too cheap.
Although we all know that Congress decreed a Mother's Day to
please gift retailers, we still somehow get sucked into the dangerous
idea that our children should pay homage to us. I informed my
daughter very early in life that Mother's Day was against my
religion!

In spite of this negative beginning, I have had moments that
were "Mother's Day." Never on the right day of the right month,
but when it happens, it is SENSATIONAL! On one such occasion
Wendy was visiting us from her home in New Hampshire. I was
standing at the sink washing some fruit and she was sort of hanging
around, talking. She was telling me about the parents of some of
her friends, and in a perfectly ordinary, conversational tone I heard
her say, "You know, the truth is that with all the parents I've met,
you and Daddy are the only ones I *really* respect. You're really
great." And without a pause for breath, she was off on some new
subject.

Bells clanged in my head, sirens shrieked—a full symphonic orchestra reached a wild crescendo. By gripping the edge of the sink I managed not to dance or float through the roof. MOTHER'S DAY? I was having mine! It remains one of the most moving and thrilling moments of my life.

For me the essential difference between my personal Mother's Days and the traditional ritual is that mine seem to have something truthful to say about motherhood; that it can hurt like hell a lot of the time, but boy, were there ever *some* moments! I feel free to acknowledge this precious moment of personal joy because to me it does not suggest for one moment that I was an especially "good mother," or that Wendy owes me anything at all. I was often a rotten mother—impatient, ill tempered, confused, frightened, stupid, childish, insensitive—the full range of human fallibility. There were many times from the very beginning when I regretted having a child, when I felt overburdened and underappreciated; when I felt trapped. There were crises in her growing that scared me so much I felt I wanted to die on the spot.

And of course there were many lengthy periods of time when she surely regretted having been stuck with me for a mother and wished herself almost anywhere else instead. At one time when I was really on the receiving end of more hostility than I could cope with, I relieved my misery by writing an article entitled "The Year I Became a Monster Mother."

I recall with perfect clarity that being a mother was tough, hard, often very trying work, and that being a child is full of pain. But when there is a loving commitment to seeing it through, when a true meeting and growing takes place between a parent and a child, there can be an exultation, a testament to what is most beautiful about being human. That lovely moment of fulfillment has stayed in my mind for many reasons, both personal and professional. It brought into sharp focus my current painful awareness of the mood about motherhood afoot in our land. I may hate Mother's Day, but I certainly don't hate motherhood, and it sometimes seems to be taking an awful beating these days.

A friend told me some years ago that she and her 10-year-old daughter, Liz, were watching a talk show on which Ellen Peck, author of *The Baby Trap*, was being interviewed. Mrs. Peck was talking about the joys of non-parenthood—deciding to take a trip to Europe on the spur of the moment, listening to music all night if you felt like it without having to worry about getting up early to feed a baby. Liz listened to all of this very thoughtfully and finally commented, "That lady makes me feel guilty for being born."

We are living through strange and troubled times. And when I hear people denigrating parenthood, it seems to me a dangerous indication that we are afraid, that we do not believe in our future —which must, after all, be made up of our children. Many complex factors have played a part in bringing us to a time when rather than honoring motherhood we often seem to want to go completely to the other extreme and denounce it. Probably one of the first factors to play a significant part in this was the gradual shift from children being an economic necessity to becoming quite the reverse, an economic liability. When the family needed every child to help solve the basic problems of survival, pleasure in parenting was a remote consideration. It was there, for sure, but not a necessary requirement. A second major factor was the psychological revolution that opened up Pandora's box. We began telling parents that it was natural and normal to get angry, to even hate children at times. Such feelings, while they surely must always have existed, had been carefully hidden from consciousness; now we were saying, "Let's be honest and face our real feelings." At the very same time, we were also telling parents that the ways in which they behaved could have lasting influence on a child's life—a totally new concept that made parents culpable and responsible for how their children turned out. We have lived through an era in which the concept of training the perfect parent who could in turn raise the perfect child was considered a serious possibility.

As parents became increasingly anxious and guilty about not being able to live up to this "impossible dream," their anger and frustration increased; and since it was now all right to express such feelings, what we have seen happening is a wave of negative feelings that have tended to block out all the equally real and valid positive feelings that are part of being a parent. A mother says, "I feel embarrassed to tell anyone how much fun I'm having with

Emily; to enjoy being a mother seems to be a sign that you're a jerk, these days."

One book that addressed the negative feelings about motherhood was written by Shirley Radl; it was entitled *Mother's Day Is Over.* I thought it was a petulant and whining book until I happened to meet Mrs. Radl on a TV talk show. I found her a good and decent lady who seemed to be the typical victim of the times in which she became a mother—terrified of not measuring up, guilty about every fall from grace, and absolutely drowning in all the negative feelings that she had been taught it was all right to feel. With impossible standards for herself, and with the flood of frustration and anger she was experiencing, she was immobilized as a mother, unable to experience the potential joys and gratifications.

Some aspects of the women's liberation movement have also tended to focus attention on the negative aspects of motherhood. In redressing a necessary balance, we seem to be going to the opposite extreme. It is certainly true that many women had children they didn't want and lived lives of quiet despair, unfulfilled as human beings in their own right, but the lesson of that situation is *not* that motherhood is a terrible form of slavery. In the decent and just struggle for human rights, it seems to me we are going to new extremes of a fanatic nature. Because we should have day-care centers for all women who must or want to work, must we also say that mothers who want to stay at home with young children are second-class citizens? Or must we insist that institutional care is better for children?

The factor that has probably played the most significant part in changing attitudes about motherhood are easier, more successful and available forms of birth-control, making it possible for parenthood to become a genuine choice. We are going through the first throes of that decision-making. Nobody ought to have children unless it will give them great pleasure to do so, we say. That's a fine idea. It surely ought to be chosen, and we all need to think more responsibly about population problems—but what about this business of *pleasure?* It seems to me that what has happened is that we have forgotten what *real* pleasure is all about. We think it's having things easy, doing what we please when we please, not worrying or having to make any effort, never feeling angry, impatient, frustrated.

A friend of mine teaches at a graduate school of social work. One day her students asked for her theory about why there are so many more divorces today than there were when she was young. Her own husband has been an invalid for twenty-five years. She said she felt embarrassed by the question and finally told the students, "I'm afraid if I answer your question I'll have to introduce some very old-fashioned ideas into this discussion—words like 'loyalty,' 'responsibility,' and 'commitment.'" One of her students looked at her dreamily and said, "That sounds *wonderful!*"

So it is with parenthood. It is not flowers and sentimental cards on Mother's Day; it isn't sweet background Muzak and love, love, love. It's sweat and pain and work. It is, by God, "loyalty, responsibility, and commitment." But that is what real pleasure is all about. It is being angry and stupid and impatient; it is also being sensitive and courageous and full of compassion. It is endless nights of croup and days of yelling and unbearable racket, and it is also seeing one's child become a new person, shining and lovely and fully alive—a testament to one's love and hard work and belief in the future. It is standing at the kitchen sink, shaken by a shimmering moment of joy and thanksgiving that one's working at loving has ripened, despite all the terrors and trials of being a mother.